The Powers and Dangers

Of

TRANSITION

…Finding the Courage to Finish your Assignment
in Excellency!

By

Dr. Francis Myles

Dedication

This book is especially dedicated to four of the men I most admire.

To my natural father,

Daniel Mbepa whose undying commitment to our family has shown me that the most important things in life are found in the matrix of family relationships. His commitment to God was a shining example of true piety while I was growing up as a young man. I will never forget the day he released me to pursue all that God was revealing to me concerning my future destiny. I love you dad.

To my spiritual father,

Dr. Jonathan David
A friend whose touch has warmed me;
A mentor whose apostolic wisdom has guided me;
An Apostle whose words have lifted me up; His teachings on the dangers of transition radically altered my destiny and became an integral part of the revelation that God has been giving me on transition for the past ten years;

A leader I am honored to follow...

To my spiritual mentors,

Apostle Clifford E. Turner

For showing me the price it takes to have a bona fide apostolic ministry. For showing me how to survive difficult times of personal transition and how to outlive false accusations and slander. For being generous towards my wife and I when we really needed it.

Prophet Kevin Leal

My spiritual "big brother," Prophet Kevin Leal who helped me make my spiritual transition from the blessing model of doing ministry to a building model. Kevin, thank you for taking my wife and I under your wings; and for being patient with us while we made our many transitions.

FOREWORD

Francis Myles takes a *"no nonsense – lay it on the line"* approach to the challenges of transition in his teaching and in this book. It is a *"must read"* for every pastor or leader who is faced with the necessity of change. I received it at a divinely appointed time of transition in my own ministry and it has become such a blessing to me. I plan to keep this one in my library for further reference!

Dr. Warren Drake
Senior Pastor – Panama City Christian Center
President - Anchor Bay Evangelistic Association

Other Book Endorsements:

"I have known Francis Myles since 1998. His truly a man who loves God and has a real passion to see the Kingdom of God established here on earth. I have seen Francis Myles and his lovely wife Trina transition from the blessing model of doing ministry to the kingdom building model. Some of these transitions were quite painful for both of them as the fires of God's prophetic revelations began to challenge and dismantle some of their old paradigms concerning ministry in the Kingdom. I have had the privilege of counseling them through some of these painful transitions. As a building prophet to the local church for many years, I have seen Churches that were pulverized by transition and those who became great because of it. There is nothing as common to life as transition. At some time or another transition will come knocking on your door, without exception. It would be prudent of us to have in our spiritual arsenal the tools necessary to deal with transition. This is especially true for leaders of local churches who have the responsibility of leading their congregations through the different valleys of transition. Let my dear friend, Francis Myles who has tasted the victories and pains of transition show you a more excellent way of navigating seasons of transition. I highly recommend this book!"

Prophet Kevin Leal
Key Ministries,
Pensacola, FL

"I cannot say enough about the relevant and realistic content of 'The Powers and Dangers of Transition...' I must say that as a man under mentorship by Apostle Francis over the last five of so years, most of the content of this book has been imparted to me as solid advice and wise counsel. I quickly acknowledge that this advice has played a significant role in successfully moving me to a place of peace and victory through the midst of life's storms. There is NO other Christian author who has focused an entire work on this subject, yet change is the only constant in all of our lives. I have learned from Apostle Myles' teaching to embrace change and welcome its benefits- and when you really understand change, you will stop fighting it and begin to yield to it divine powers. Read closely and you will never be the same."

Larry Favalora
Maven Holding Company, LLC
JirehComm Marketing Solutions, Inc.
GatorPond Entertainment Group
www.MavenHoldings.com

When Francis Myles first preached his powerful message on the powers and dangers of transition at our Church on the beautiful island of the Bahamas, I knew that it hard struck a core in the hearts and minds of the people of our Church. I was personally moved by this powerful revelation; I started calling other pastors to tell them about this powerful word and the man whom God has crafted to proclaim it. Without a doubt there is nothing as common to the success journey as the subject of "transition". The world we live in is constantly changing consequently imposing many "transitions" upon us. Some of these transitions are spiritual, some are emotional, some require a mental migration, some are geographical and some are physical. How we handle these constants transitions while pursuing our God given destiny is the subject of this book. My dear friend, apostle Myles has addressed this critical subject with surgical precision. A must read for every pastor who has ever gone through transition or is currently transitioning. This is a book for every person who is struggling to make sense of whatever they are going through.

Dr Jay Simms
Senior Pastor
Christian Life Church
Nassau, Bahamas

God has released another weapon in His arsenal against the enemy!

A new dimension of understanding has just been revealed in this tremendous book. I believe that this writing will bring clarity, consistency and commitment to the Lord's purpose in the lives of believers who are fighting in the front lines of the battlefield. In order to escalate into new dimensions, we must understand "transition." Every new order requires this. Apostle Francis Myles has taken a fresh approach to this issue, and with Apostolic and Prophetic precision, he has executed this mandate with energy and skill.

This information is essential!

Apostle Dr. G.E. Bradshaw
Outpour Assemblies Network
Dolton, Illinois

"Pastor Myles has tackled a subject that up to now has been taboo in the ministerial realm—transition! We all have our cozy comfort zones, and would rather pretend change will not happen, but it does, and Pastor Francis Myles has delivered the subject with an in-your-face honesty but his tenderness to those who are going through transition is like a velvet touch. This book is a must read for everyone who knows that change is on the way in their lives and ministry "

Paul Price
Senior Pastor
Cornerstone Worship Center
Indiana, PA

What an exciting composition of prophetic insight and apostolic guidance. This book is relevant for all ages, backgrounds and vocations. Transition is an equal opportunity lender and intruder in all of our lives. What an exciting roadmap outlined throughout this book. Apostle Myles helps us to understand the journey of timing, testing and triumph during each transition. This book is a must read and we all need to not only read it — but allow ourselves to 'experience' what God is saying to us throughout our transitions of life!

Dr. Vanessa Weatherspoon
Gathering Of The Eagles Ministries & Gathering
Of The Eagles Worship Center
Dallas, TX
Founder and Senior Pastor

What a powerful revelation on transition from Apostle Francis Myles. All current truth believers are always in some stage of transition. This book is the manual for those that are moving from one place of glory to the next. This is a must have book in your library. It is like a set of binoculars to help you see the road ahead.

Apostle Joseph Prude
Justice Fellowship International Network of Churches
Cleveland, Ohio

Transition, transition! As a pastor for over 25 years this is one word that I have heard more times than I can remember. But the many times I have heard God's people speak of it, assures me that transition is a common human experience. As a pastor I am more interested in finding a way to have my people deal with transition more effectively. This book by my friend Francis Myles is filled with practical strategies to help people and Churches navigate the valley of transition more effectively.

Bishop Darrell Gooden
Rehoboth Christian Center
Tallapoosa, GA

Acknowledgements

I want to thank the Lord Jesus Christ for being my Lord and Savior. Your entrance into my life changed my life forever. Without you Lord this book would never have been possible.

I also want to acknowledge the invaluable companionship of my dear wife and co-pastor Trina. Honey I love you dearly, you are truly the unforgettable woman of Proverbs 31.

To my beloved editor, Lynda Wallen in Arkansas, who spent countless hours prayerfully editing this book so it can be presented with excellence to the Body of Christ at large. Lynda I do not know how to thank you, except commend you to God, who can truly bless you.

TABLE OF CONTENTS

Introduction

There is nothing as permanent and as consistent as change and yet many people in our world are unskilled at the task of grappling with change. This would explain why most people can never change without pain. I know that this statement may be too difficult for some people to accept, but the fact of the matter is that most people have positioned themselves as resistors of change instead of embracing the possibility for progress which is inherent in all periods of transition. If we were to plot many people's change graph, their graph would be filled with many serious downside curves representing their personal struggles with the winds of change. Their serious lack of skill in navigating seasons of transition would be quite evident. **"For most people transition is an abstract art and subjective experience instead of being an exact and user-friendly spiritual science, which can be studied and mastered."** My humble attempt through this book is to package transition into *"a user friendly and duplicatable spiritual technology"* for navigating the winds of change in our valley of transition, whether it is personal or corporate.

By repackaging transition into a spiritual and natural science which can be studied and mastered by anyone, we will lessen the vast numbers of those who have fallen to prey to transition. When the winds of change begin to blow into our lives, they will quickly usher us into our valley of transition. It can therefore be argued that transition is the *mother of change* and the *grandmother of progress*. Those who are interested in progress must prepare themselves to walk through the valley of transition. **Transition is the ancient bridge which stands between our present reality and what we can become. Transition separates our past and present from our future.** The difference between our present and future is found in the level of transition we are willing to go through to maximize our personal and corporate potential.

As a senior pastor it pains me to see the statistics of many good churches who became casualties of transition and fell by the wayside. When a church fails to successfully navigate the valley of transition, it usually loses its powerful Kingdom thrust and the necessary spiritual dynamics to effectively impact the community it was designed to serve. Many church splits have left brothers and sisters who once worshiped together, embittered and sometimes lifelong enemies. Some church splits have forced those who are spiritually weak to walk away from the Lord all together. I have talked to pastors who went through a church split because their churches went through a period of transition and the people in the church were not equipped to deal with the transition. These senior pastors, along with their wives and families are some of the greatest casualties of transition. It is no wonder so many children of senior pastors want nothing to do with the church. They have experienced the trauma and frustration first hand, which has left a bad taste for ministry in their mouth.

In addition to being the senior pastor of a thriving church, I also am an entrepreneur which has allowed me the experience of watching major corporations reduced to pulp by one failure to navigate a major transition within the company's business structure. Periods of transition within a corporation normally result in serious loss of revenue, staff lay offs and the loss of sizeable margins of market share, if the corporation was inadequately prepared for the transition.

The benefits of repackaging transition into an exact spiritual and natural science is very obvious. The mathematical equation $2 + 2 = 4$ is a universal and exact science. It remains the same whether the equation is written in Japanese or Chinese. If a million people from different nations were to calculate this equation, they would all be expected to arrive at the same answer. Imagine reducing transition to an exact spiritual and natural science. Spiritual leaders and leaders of corporations would be able to lead vast numbers of their people through the valley of transition without too much casualty. The possibilities are breath taking!

The purpose of this book is to give those who are interested in progress and maximizing their personal potential during periods of transition the necessary tools they need to do so. It is designed to be *a **supernatural compass*** that will help people to successfully walk through the valley of transition. This book will also endeavor to plot the dangers that we are most likely to face during periods of transition and how we can avoid becoming its victims.

Attempts will be made to analyze and define the secular and spiritual implications of transition. We will begin to discover how the great companies or ministries of today can easily become the dinosaurs of tomorrow if they do not know how to successfully navigate the valley of transition.

We will analyze why transition is the safest and most accurate method for transferring spiritual and govern-mental authority. We will look at how the Lord Jesus Christ used transition to prepare His disciples to become the founding apostles of the New Testament church.

One of the critical dangers of seasons of transition is the danger of aborting our prophetic destiny. God has a prophetic destiny for each of His dear children. *We were created by purpose for a purpose and the discovery of that purpose is the greatest discovering on earth!* However, we can never fulfill our purpose without understanding the impact that transition has on our corporate and personal potential.

God's family is like a beautiful rainbow consisting of precious children of God of all colors and races with differing spiritual views and persuasions but united by the common thread of belief in Christ for divine salvation. **It's my deepest prayer that this book will not become clouded in religious controversy or bigotry. It has been written for every person who desires to become skilled at navigating times of transition more successfully.** It's for Senior Pastors and business owners who are tired of seeing their organizations fall prey to transition. **I have lived long enough to know that transition affects every person on the planet regardless of their race or reli-gious beliefs.**

I feel the need at this point to clearly define the use of the term **"Prophetic"** in this writing and its contextual role in this teaching on transition. In his bestselling book *"The Purpose Driven Life,"* our brother Rick Warren has shown us that we were all created by God for a purpose. He has shown us that God had a very specific purpose and plan for our life before He created us. If we truly believe these truths so graciously shared by our brother Rick Warren, then we are *"Prophetic."* The belief that God has a sure plan for our life, business or church before we fully know what it is; is what I mean when I say that all of God's children are prophetic. In this regard, all of God's dear children, no matter their differing spiritual persuasions, are all prophetic as far as the Bible is concerned. I want to go on record as saying that I have used the terms *prophetic* or *prophetic anointing* in this light and context.

I want to humbly declare that this book will attempt to give the reader Kingdom strategies for navigating the valley of transition and how to successfully surf the waves of change.

God bless you,

Francis Myles
God's Servant, @ 2006

Chapter One

Defining Transition

I once heard a dear man of God say, *"You cannot govern what you have failed to define!"* I could not agree more. Before endeavoring to understand the powers and dangers of transition and how we can successfully navigate the valley of transition, we must first take on the surgical task of defining transition. Without establishing clear and concise definitions of transition, it will be difficult to accurately apply the principles outlined in this book to our lives and business endeavors. *The inaccurate application of truth is just as dangerous as the lack of application thereof.*

Man's Unique Design

The scriptures teach us that man is a spirit being who possesses a soul and resides in an earthly tabernacle, called the body. To say it in another way, **man is a spirit being having a bodily experience.** In the book of first Thessalonians the Bible tells us that man is a triune being who must be preserved or kept by the power of God in the three compartments of his divine being.

"And the very God of peace sanctify you wholly; and I pray God your whole spirit and soul and body be preserved blameless unto the coming of our Lord Jesus Christ."[1]

As a consequence of man's unique design, natural or spiritual transition will impact man's spirit, soul and body. Man's spiritual, psyche and physical state never remain the same after any given period of transition, regardless of the degree of personal deception or enlightenment. To deny the power and inevitability of transition is the greatest deception there is on this side of heaven.

> *"The inaccurate application of truth is just as dangerous as the lack of application thereof."*

We know for a fact that through his spirit, man can interact with the spirit world while simultaneously interacting with the intellectual and material worlds through his soul and body. To take into account man's unique state we will define transition on two levels. We will deal with both the secular and spiritual definitions and implications of transition.

The Hebrew Definition

The Hebrew word for *transition* `abar aw-bar' a primitive root, which carries the meaning *to cross over*; used very widely of any transition (literal or figurative; transitive, intransitive, intensive, causative). This Hebrew word is used several times in Scripture. It is used to describe the translation of Enoch into the heavens.

"By faith Enoch was translated (abar aw-bar) that he should not see death; and was not found, because God had translated him: for before his translation he had this testimony, that he pleased God."[2] (adapted by author)

This word *(abar aw-bar)* is again used to describe the crossing of the Jordan by the children of Israel under Joshua's prophetic leadership. Joshua became the spiritual leader of the nation of Israel immediately after the death of Moses, the servant of the Lord.

"Now after the death of Moses the servant of the LORD it came to pass, that the LORD spake unto Joshua the son of Nun, Moses' minister, saying, Moses my servant is dead; now therefore arise, go over this Jordan, thou, and all this people, unto the land which I do give to them, [even] to the children of Israel,"[3]

Secular Definitions of Transition

According to Merriam-Webster's Collegiate Thesaurus, these are some of the root meanings for the word "transition" that will shed light on this critical subject. **Transition means,** *passage from one state or condition to another, alteration, shift, metamorphosis, transformation, evolution, development, growth or progress.*

These words reveal the vast secular implications of transition. They reveal why certain promising corporations suddenly disappear from the frontlines of the corporate world and lose their huge market shares to seemingly new and unknown competitors. These words reveal why new technologies can cause great firms to fall, making them become echoes of what they once were in the same industry. These words reveal why girls become ladies and ladies become women. They reveal why and how boys become men. We will discuss the secular impact of transition in our present world more fully in the next chapter.

Transition is the *passage from one state or condition to another*. Transition therefore, is the ancient bridge that transports the boy into manhood. **Without transition it's impossible to embrace higher levels of the spirit of leadership.** Once a boy reaches manhood, his emotions, thoughts and outlook on life change dramatically. The childish things that were his way of life suddenly become repulsive behavior patterns. The boy, who has now become a man, rises to embrace a greater level of the spirit of leadership. **Unfortunately life is filled with boys who are trapped in the bodies of men. On the outside they look like men, but spiritually and emotionally they are boys who never became men, because they fought with the winds of transition instead of embracing them.**

It's tragic when a woman finds that she is married to a boy who is trapped in a man's body. Women married to such men suffer from a lack of visionary leadership in their homes, as their husbands, who are actually boys trapped in a man's body, do everything in their power to shy away from taking on responsibility and embracing higher levels of the spirit of leadership. **These emotionally undeveloped men are classic casualties of transition. Their physical bodies have grown, but their spirit, mind and emotions have remained largely undeveloped and unchallenged by time and the winds of change.**

"When I was a child, I spake as a child, I understood as a child, I thought as a child: but when I became a man, I put away childish things"[4]

28

Transition also means *to shift*. During periods of transition, corporations, people and nations shift. Some of these shifts are shifts in emphasis, direction or focus. **Some transitional shifts are so powerful and so radical that they give birth to serious paradigm shifts**. They change the way people think, interact and do business. Before the discovery of internet technology, nations were kept apart by natural borders and boundaries. Internet technology and the ensuing world of cyber space brought such a radical and widespread transitional shift that within a short time, distance and natural borders no longer separate nations from one another.

> *"It's tragic when a woman discovers*
> *that she is married to a boy*
> *who is trapped in a man's body."*

The distance between nations is no longer measured in miles or kilometers, but in the click of a mouse. For all practical purposes, the boundaries and borders between nations have disappeared into cyber space. Africans can visit the United States from the comfort of their own homes without acquiring a visa. Americans can visit Europe, Australia and Asia, without boarding a plane and without acquiring a passport. Money and real estate can change hands in seconds and trillions of dollars change hands daily in cyber space. Virtual banks are quickly replacing the traditional brick and mortar banks of yesterday. We will discuss these rapid changes in the globe in the next chapter.

The Different Types of Transitions

We have already underscored the fact that transition is the mother of change and the grandmother of progress. Absolutely nothing changes without transition and there is no progress without change. I want you to know that they are different types of transitions which you are likely to face while pursing God's purpose for your life. I also want you to know that there is a biblical solution for all of these transitions. I will quickly give you a quick overview of these different transitions.

Spiritual Transitions:

Spiritual transitions are transitions which are precipitated by spiritual discoveries which completely reconfigure how we perceive the person of God and the world we live in. For instance popular gothic writer Anne Rice a self proclaimed hardcore atheist surprised her publishers and millions of her fans when she appeared on CNN and Fox News proclaiming her new found faith in Christ and vowing that she would never write a gothic novel ever again. An article from the October 2007 issue of Charisma Magazine has this to say about this amazing transformation.

"The author of the Queen of the Damned is now worshipping the King of kings. Anne Rice, the acclaimed icon of modern Gothic fiction, who once rode in a coffin through her native New Orleans in the back of a blacked-out hearse flanked by a horde of personal undertakers, is writing Christian fiction and has vowed never to write anything else.

Books about vampires, witches and erotica by the Southern author have sold more than 100 million copies. They have made a household name of the vampire Lestat, who was the subject of a Tony-nominated Broadway musical in 2006 and who was played by Tom Cruise in the 1994 film adaptation of Rice's first novel, *Interview with the Vampire.*

It was therefore startling to her publisher and millions of readers when in 2003 Rice, then known as an avowed atheist, announced that her 26th book would be a fictional first person narrative given by Jesus at age 7, titled *Christ the Lord: Out of Egypt". (Charisma Magazine pg48, Oct 07)*

Anne Rice walked away from a very lucrative career writing gothic novels because she made a very startling spiritual discovery, that the God she had fought so hard to kill in herself and in those who read her books actually existed. Like the apostle Paul who had a personal encounter with Jesus on his way to Damascus; Anne Rice also came to know firsthand that Jesus is a very real Savior. As in Paul's case, this spiritual discovery turned Anne Rice's world upside down. This discovery placed her right in the center of a life altering spiritual transition.

2 Corinthians 5:17 "This means that anyone who belongs to Christ has become a new person. The old life is gone; a new life has begun!" NLT

Mental Transitions:

Mental transitions are transitions which are caused by a radical change in the way we think. One of the greatest mental transitions which I experienced happened to me at the airport. I was flying from Dallas to Chicago to speak at a conference. While at the Dallas airport I bought a book by Donald Trump and Bill Zanker, titled *"Thinking Big and Kicking Ass"*. Please forgive the last part of the title. But this book is filled with *"small thinking shattering"* think big ideas. By the time my flight landed in Chicago I had repented several times to God for being a small thinker and for placing God in the box of my own mental limitations. The bible is clear that a man's actions, as well as his future can never be separated from his thoughts. This would explain why in Romans 12:1-2 the Apostle Paul begged the believers in Rome to become transformed by the renewing of their minds. Some of these mental transitions can either be positive or negative in nature.

Romans 8:6 "So letting your sinful nature control your mind leads to death. But letting the Spirit control your mind leads to life and peace". NLT

The most powerful positive mental transitions are those which superimpose the mind of Christ upon our carnal minds. These mental transitions move us from death to life, because any movement towards Christ-likeness is a very positive mental transition. Some mental transitions are very toxic and degenerative. Negative mental transitions are caused by the entrance of evil thoughts in our daily thought processes. The bible calls these evil thoughts *"lofty thoughts which exalt themselves against the knowledge of God" (2 Cor 10:4-5)*. In some cases negative mental transitions can be caused by a mental disease or unchecked stress in a person's life which may lead to an emotional and mental breakdown.

Physical Transitions:
Physical transitions are transitions which are caused by changes in our mortal bodies as a result of age, unhealthy eating habits, sickness or accidents. Physical transitions are much more obvious than any other transition. In the

Modeling industry for example, men and women are under undue pressure to stay young, beautiful and energetic. This is the only way to ensure that they have a career in an industry that is overly competitive and has high staff turnover.

I am reminded of the story of a beautiful Swedish Model who died of anorexia because she was starving her body in order to stay thin and beautiful! What a tragedy! The fear of aging that many of today's celebrities have has resulted in the creation of a multibillion dollar industry for plastic surgeons. Never mind that plastic surgery is not a very safe science. The Music world was shocked and saddened by the sudden death of the mother of famous hip hop star Kanye West. In her understandable desire to delay physical transitions in her aging body she went to get a plastic surgery against the better judgment of one of her doctors.

In some cases physical transitions are caused by unhealthy eating habits which create excess fat in our bodies causing many people to become overweight. I have prayed over so many women who despise looking at themselves in the mirror because they hate the sight of their own reflection. In other cases physical transitions are caused by unexpected accidents which may leave someone paralyzed, maimed or handicap. The latter are some of the most difficult physical transitions to deal with.

The point I am trying to drive to is this, *"It does not matter what force is behind your physical transition, the quicker your accept God's scriptural solution in your transition the quicker you can walk in peace and harmony"*. No matter what physical transition we find ourselves in God's Word says....

Psalm 139:14 "Thank you for making me so wonderfully complex! Your workmanship is marvelous—how well I know it". NLT

Emotional Transitions:

Emotional Transitions are transitions which are caused by events which induce positive or negative emotional responses to whatever we are passing through. These emotional transitions are also caused by natural growth. When we move from childhood to adulthood our emotions go through a major transition. Spiritual maturity in the things of God can also cause us to go through positive emotional transitions.

1 Cor 13:11 "When I was a child, I spoke and thought and reasoned as a child. But when I grew up, I put away childish things". NLT

When a person begins to grow spiritually in their walk with Christ, their emotional responses to things and people around them begins to become much more stable. They do not jump from one emotional roller-coaster to the next; because their emotional responses are anchored in a God who never fails. Unfortunately I have met many adults who have the emotional makeup of a toddler. They are quick to throw emotional tantrums when they do not get their way. They leave churches or their jobs as easily as they join them.

Some emotional transitions can be emotionally devastating and harmful to the physical well being of a person. Negative emotions may force the body to release large amounts of stress hormones such as cortisol in the blood system. Too much of these stress hormones in the body is toxic to the body. Divorce for instance is a devastating emotional transition. They say that in most cases divorce is much more painful than the sudden death of a loved one. Some people who have gone through a messy divorce never survive the impact of such a negative emotional transition. Some become bitter and untrusting for the rest of their lives. Some cave-in and live in self pity the rest of their lives. Some are so emotionally devastated they simply let themselves *"go"*. They stop caring for their bodies or their appearance, until they look like some weird character from a gothic movie.

Geographical Transitions:

Geographical transitions are transitions which require a complete geographical relocation in a person's life before he or she can move forward. Geographical transitions can be caused by divine orchestration or by natural circumstances. One of the most important prophetic geographical transitions found in the bible is the divine relocation of Abram and Sarah from Haran to present day Palestine.

Genesis 12:1 "The Lord had said to Abram, "Leave your native country, your relatives, and your father's family, and go to the land that I will show you". NLT

Abram would never have become *"Abraham"* the father of many nations had he refused to make the geographical transition which God was requesting of him. I am sure leaving his aging father who was still mourning the death of his youngest brother, was no easy task. But Abram had enough sense to know that if he did not obey God in making the necessary geographical transition he would live to regret it for the rest of his life.

*Genesis 13:10-11 "Lot took a long look at the fertile plains of the Jordan Valley in the direction of Zoar. The whole area was well watered everywhere, like the garden of the L*ORD *or the beautiful land of Egypt. (This was before the L*ORD *destroyed Sodom and Gomorrah.) 11 Lot chose for himself the whole Jordan Valley to the east of them. He went there with his flocks and servants and parted company with his uncle Abram". NLT*

On the other hand some geographical transitions are demonic in nature and catastrophic in their outcome. For instance, when Abraham and Lot separated, Lot chose to live near the wicked Cities of Sodom and Gomorrah. At the time Lot made this horrible decision there was a well watered valley on the outskirts of Sodom. This geographical transition by Lot set him on the collision course with God's impending judgment against the wicked City of Sodom. When the angels of God came to check out this wicked City, Lot had backslidden to the point were he had become an elder in Sodom! The angels told him that God was going to burn the wicked City to the ground. The angels quickly ushered Lot and his family out of town. Lot came out of Sodom with nothing, except for the clothes on his back. This inaccurate geographical transition brought spiritual and financial bankruptcy in Lot's life! This is why I cannot over emphasize the importance of making geographical transitions prayerfully and strategically.

Leadership Transitions:
Leadership transitions are transitions which are precipitated by changes in leadership in church or business organizations. These transitions can have a positive or negative impact depending upon four main factors.

1. The nature of these leadership transitions
2. The timing of these leadership transitions
3. The quality and leadership skills of the leaders who are leading these organizations during these transitions
4. The scope of these leadership transitions

Joshua 24:29-31 "After this, Joshua son of Nun, the servant of the LORD, died at the age of 110. They buried him in the land he had been allocated, at Timnath-serah in the hill country of Ephraim, north of Mount Gaash. The people of Israel served the LORD throughout the lifetime of Joshua and of the elders who outlived him—those who had personally experienced all that the LORD had done for Israel". NLT

After the death of Joshua he was survived by a team of elders who had been with him when God called him to take over from where Moses left off. Even though the death of Joshua superimposed a leadership transition in the spiritual leadership structure of the nation of Israel, the people of Israel remained faithful to God because of the godly influence of the elders who had served under Joshua. When the last of the elders of the Joshua era died, the bible says that the children of Israel departed from the ways of God.

In some cases leadership transitions are caused by the moral failure of those in esteemed positions of leadership. These types of leadership transitions are particularly painful for the flock or staff members. This is especially true for the families of those who hold these esteemed positions of leadership in the Church. In the Church world spiritual leadership is intricately tied to moral purity, the loss of which results in quick and embarrassing demotions from positions of spiritual leadership. I know of people who walked away from a relationship with God and His church because of the moral of failure of a spiritual leader that they had trusted.

Political Transitions:

Political transitions are transitions which are engineered by changes within the political climates of nations. Most political transitions are caused by the following common factors, which signal a change in the political climate of the nation.

1. Changes in political leadership, such as changes in the presidency.
2. Changes in the Law
3. Changes in the political mood of a majority of the citizenry
5. War or Imminent threats to national security
6. Military overthrow of democratically elected governments
7. Deep reaching spiritual revival

Proverbs 29:2 "When the godly are in authority, the people rejoice. But when the wicked are in power, they groan". NLT

Political transitions are some of the most powerful and most difficult transitions to overturn because they usually involve changes in the law of the land or changes in a nation's political leadership. This is why it is very self defeating for God's people to stay out of the political process in their countries of natural residence. This is because whatever is enacted into law or adopted as national policy by politicians does affect the status and well being of the Church. When Politicians in the former Soviet Union decided to adopt Communist laws which abolished any allegiance to God except to mother Russia, God's people behind the Iron Curtains suffered greatly.

Luke 2:1-41 "At that time the Roman emperor, Augustus, decreed that a census should be taken throughout the Roman Empire. 2 (This was the first census taken when Quirinius was governor of Syria.) 3 All returned to their own ancestral towns to register for this census. 4 And because Joseph was a descendant of King David, he had to go to Bethlehem in Judea, David's ancient home. He traveled there from the village of Nazareth in Galilee." NLT

Sometimes political transitions are caused by divine intervention so that certain preordained prophetic events can be fulfilled. Hundreds of years before the birth of Jesus Christ Old Testament prophets prophesied the virgin birth of Christ in a town called Bethlehem. Notwithstanding when Mary was found to be with Child birthed by the Holy Spirit, Mary and her husband Joseph were living in a Galilean town called Nazareth. Had God not moved on the heart of the Roman Emperor Caesar Augustus to call for a census throughout the Roman Empire Mary would have given birth to Jesus in Nazareth. Had this happened the credibility and spiritual accuracy of every prophecy in the bible concerning Jesus as God's promised Messiah would have crumbled instantly! To reveal the validity of His Word and the immutability of His promise of redemption, God was working behind the political scene in the

Roman Empire. Giving birth to a political transition which resulted in creating the necessary geographical transition which Mary and Joseph needed to make in order to be at the right place at the right time!

Scientific and Technological Transitions:

Scientific and Technological transitions are transitions which are ignited by scientific and technological discoveries. Many of these transitions have had a positive impact on society as well as some unforeseen negative impact on the societies they were meant to serve. Take the discovery of the internet as a prime example. The discovery of internet technology has completely changed the way people communicate and do business. Billions of dollars change hands in seconds every day in Cyber space.

Matthew 5:27-28 "You have heard the commandment that says, 'You must not commit adultery.' But I say, anyone who even looks at a woman with lust has already committed adultery with her in his heart". NLT

On the other hand the discovery of internet technology has multiplied the proliferation of web based pornography which has destroyed countless marriages and weakened our nation's morality. These scientific and technological transitions require that God's people take a stand and monitor how these scientific and technological discoveries are used in the light of God's holy word.

One of the most prolific examples of spiritual transition which was initiated by new scientific discoveries is the spiritual conversion of atheist physicist Francis S. Collins. In his bestselling book, *"The Language of God"* Dr. Francis Collins, head of the Human Genome Project who has spent most of his life in the study of DNA was a hardcore atheist. Challenged by the question of one of his dying patients concerning the existence of God, Dr. Collins launched a ferocious study to prove that there is no God. The more he studied he began to discover that there was mounting scientific evidence which called for the existence of a very intelligent supernatural being behind the intricacies of human DNA, Cosmology and Quantum Mechanics. As his long held myth that science can disprove any existence of God dissipated Dr. Collins's atheism lost its initial appeal. He turned his life over to God.

Economic Transitions:

Economic transitions are transitions which are caused by positive and negative gains in national and global economies. Economic transitions have deep and far reaching impact because they affect the financial means of everybody. I have a friend in Chicago who has a mother in law who lived through the great American economic depression of 1929. From 1929 through 1939 the United States went through the worst economic transition it has ever faced as a nation. Within a short time of the markets clashing, many millionaires and billionaires were reduced to rubbles. This economic transition was so drastic many rich people committed suicide.

1 Kings 17: 1-2 "Now Elijah, who was from Tishbe in Gilead, told King Ahab, "As surely as the LORD, the God of Israel, lives—the God I serve—there will be no dew or rain during the next few years until I give the word!" Then the LORD said to Elijah, 3 "Go to the east and hide by Kerith Brook, near where it enters the Jordan River. 4 Drink from

*the brook and eat what the ravens bring you, for I have
commanded them to bring you food." NLT*

Sometimes economic transitions are caused by God's
intervention in the affairs of men. The above passage
uncovers a time of serious economic transition in the
nation of Israel as a result of God's judgment on Israel.
Even though this economic transition affected the lives
of every person in Israel, God provided a place of shelter
and provision for His servant, supernaturally. The moral
of the story is simply this, *"God always has a way out
of economic downturns for those who are serving Him
faithfully"*. God's power is ready to assist us during times
of economic transition. In most cases negative economic
transitions are caused by corrupt politicians, bad fiscal
policy, bad stewardship and unforeseen natural disasters.
This is true whether the economic transition is personal or
national.

Cultural Transitions:
Cultural transitions are transitions which are caused by
changes in the prevailing culture. By definition the word
"Culture" is, *"the sum total of ways of living built up by a
group of human beings and transmitted from one generation to another"*. Working from the above definition we
can see that *"Cultural Transitions"* are the most difficult
to birth and navigate. This is because Culture is hidden in
the internal motivation, attitude and unconscious behavior
of those who ascribe to it. This would explain why many
well supported and well intentioned missionaries in foreign
lands fail. Especially those who attempted to do apostolic
work without the power of the Holy Spirit. But when

Cultures change in God's favor they become the greatest allies to the Kingdom of God here on earth.

Matthew 15:3 "Jesus replied, "And why do you, by your traditions, violate the direct commandments of God?"
NLT

My dear friend Prophet Kevin Leal once asked me a question which really baffled me. Here is the question he posed to me! *"Francis what is more powerful, the anointing of God or Culture?"* I quickly told him that it was *"the anointing"*. He laughed and told me that *"culture was more powerful than the anointing"* because it is deeply imbedded in the conscious and subconscious behaviors of people. This would explain why the Pharisees could easily dismiss the miracles of Jesus which they saw with their naked eyes. They saw the miracles but did not really see them. This is why the primary task of the gospel of the Kingdom is not just to bless the people materially. God's primary mission is to shift the prevailing culture of the people in any given territory to a spiritual culture which is not hostile to the Kingdom of God.

Toxic Transitions:

1 Timothy 4:1 "Now the Spirit speaketh expressly, that in the latter times some shall depart from the faith, giving heed to seducing spirits and doctrines of demons".

Toxic transitions are transitions which move people, cultures and nations away from God's standard of divine morality. These transitions are completely demonic in nature and involve a high level of spiritual deception. The apostle Paul looked into the future by the Spirit of God and predicted that in the last days there would be several tragic toxic transitions.

1. Some believers in Christ shall depart from the faith by giving heed to seducing spirits and doctrine of devils.
2. Many people will migrate from a lifestyle of truth to a lifestyle of lies and hypocrisy.
3. Many people's conscience will become seared as a hot iron. This means that there will be beyond the reach of divine conviction.

The proliferation of the gospel of inclusion which teaches that everybody on earth is already saved they just don't know it yet is a prime example of toxic transitions. The gospel of inclusion is just another way of saying that all roads lead to heaven. The proponents of this doctrine of demons also teach that *"hell"* as the bible teaches does not even exist.

The purpose and emphasis of this book is not to discuss secular transition, but rather spiritual transition and its impact on the spiritual and prophetic destinies of God's people here on earth. God's people, for the most part, have been casualties of transition because they generally do not navigate the valley of transition well.

Some of these spiritual definitions of transition are borrowed from the *Dangers of Transition* CD series by Dr. Jonathan David.

In Between the Promise and the Manifestation

"Transition is the period of time between receiving the promise and seeing its actual fulfillment."

One of the most exciting and dangerous times in the life of a child of God is the period between the prophetic promise and the season of its actual fulfillment. *This transitional period is a very dangerous time in the spirit world because Satan and his demonic cohorts know that even though we are custodians of God's prophetic promise, we have not yet entered into the reality of what God has promised us.* Satan knows that during this period of transition, he can still stir up spiritual havoc, confusion and emotional turmoil, which can make us stagger at the promise of God. We must endure to the very end like our father Abraham. We cannot afford to stagger at the promise of God because we are faced with mountains of contradictions in the present. Abraham did not allow the deadness of Sarah's womb to stop him from pursuing God's promise. We need this same prevailing mentality in order to stay on course towards our destiny during our period of transition.

"For ye have need of patience, that, after ye have done the will of God, ye might receive the promise."[5]

The apostle Paul was very much aware of the spiritual dangers and attacks of the enemy which can exist between the realization of the prophetic promise and the time of its complete manifestation. This is why he personally admonished the Hebrew believers not to despair. He told them that they needed patience so that after they have done the will of God, they could inherit the promise. Paul was no stranger to the pain and feelings of fear, confusion and abandonment which sometimes accompany those who are going through any kind of transition. Some of his co-laborers turned their backs on the apostolic faith and went back to the ways of the world, leaving him to continue his apostolic mission by himself. ***Paul was no foreigner to the spiritual dangers which can arise during periods of transition.***

When the Lord Jesus was ascending into heaven on mount Olivet after His resurrection from the dead, there were about five hundred disciples who witnessed His glorious ascension into the third heaven. The Lord Jesus Christ admonished this group of disciples not to depart from Jerusalem until they had received the promise of the Father.

"And, being assembled together with them, commanded them that they should not depart from Jerusalem, but wait for the promise of the Father, which, saith he, ye have heard of me. For John truly baptized with water; but ye shall be baptized with the Holy Ghost not many days hence."[6]

Not withstanding, ten days later on the day of Pentecost, only one hundred and twenty of the original number of disciples were found waiting for the promise of the Father in the upper room. Over two thirds of the disciples that Christ had admonished to wait for the promise of the Holy Spirit had either fallen away or were encumbered with the cares of daily living. For whatever reason when the time of prophetic fulfillment came, two thirds of those who received the same prophetic promise were no where to be found. It's a travesty and tragedy of biblical proportions.

God wants us to become like our father Abraham who did not stagger at the promise of God during the period of transition, when he waited for the word of the Lord to catch up with his circumstances. Abraham knew that one day his prophetic promise from the mouth of God would eventually become a physical reality. He knew that God's word would eventually invade his material world with unstoppable power. You can imagine the looks of pity and mockery that must have traveled his way when he changed his wife's name from Sarai to Sarah, *which* means *princess or mother of nations!*

Women must have giggled in mockery when they heard Sarah call Abram, *Abraham*, which means *father of many nations*. Their neighbors must have reasoned that Abraham and Sarah's desperation to have a child of their own had driven them to insanity and hallucination. The spiritual among the bunch must have suggested employing the services of an exorcist to expel demons from the aging couple. In all of these things Abraham and Sarah did not stagger or doubt the promise of God. Abraham knew that in the fullness of time, the deadness of his body and that of his wife would not stand in the way of God honoring His word.

"As it is written, I have made thee a father of many nations, before him whom he believed, even God, who quickeneth the dead, and calleth those things which be not as though they were. Who against hope believed in hope, that he might become the father of many nations; according to that which was spoken, So shall thy seed be. And being not weak in faith, he considered not his own body now

47

dead, when he was about an hundred years old, neither yet the deadness of Sarah's womb: He staggered not at the promise of God through unbelief; but was strong in faith, giving glory to God;"[7]

The Scriptures declare that Abraham refused to be swayed by or manipulated by the deadness of Sarah's womb. He looked past it and kept confessing that, in the fullness of time God would quicken and give life to her mortal body so she could conceive the promised son, Isaac. When all natural hope of ever conceiving a child had vanished for Sarah, Abraham continued to hope against hope that God would still perform a miracle. ***This prevailing mentality, displayed through Abraham and Sarah's lives is the same spiritual mentality that God wants all of His children to have when they are living in between the promise and the manifestation of the promise.*** If we give up before we enter into the manifestation of our prophetic promise, we are relinquishing our prophetic future and destiny into the hands of the enemy. Satan will laugh us to scorn on his way to the bank.

During the time between our prophetic promise and its actual fulfillment, God will release the grace that we need to enter into His predetermined purpose for our lives. I really believe that the future and nature of many spiritual destinies of God's people are largely determined by remaining steadfast in faith despite the enemy's attacks during the time of transition. ***Those of us who allow God to work deeply in our lives, and remain in a spirit of total obedience, will receive the grace that we need to rise above the attacks of the enemy and cross into our spiritual inheritance.*** Some, on the other hand, will allow despair, worldliness, confusion, peer pressure and spiritual warfare to derail them from patiently waiting for the fulfillment of God's promise.

"If we give up before we enter into the manifestation of our prophetic promise, we are relinquishing our prophetic future and destiny into the hands of the enemy."

God Is Waiting To Cook It Just Right

"Transition is the time of waiting for all the right conditions to be fulfilled while remaining obedient until salvation is made manifest."

I vividly remember my days as a young man growing up in Africa. Like most young African boys of my age, I was a soccer fanatic. I could literally play soccer all day. After hours of chasing the ball all over the playing field, I would be physically exhausted and hungrier than a starving lion which had not eaten in days.

On one such day I stormed into our house to see if mom had prepared some food for me to eat. When I entered the kitchen, I was welcomed by the aroma of Mom's fried chicken. I screamed, *"Mom, please give me some food right away! I am very hungry!"* My mom's response was, *"Son, just wait a little while. I have got to cook it just right. If I give you the food now, it will make you sick!*

During periods of transition it's possible to feel like God has forgotten about us. In her teaching on "Transitioning" Dr. N. Cindy Trimm, says that *"the voice of the devil is loudest during periods of transition. This is why so many people abdicate their spiritual assignment during these times."* **King David (the man after God's own heart) also had periods in his life when he felt like God had forsaken him in his journey of faith.** Anybody who has ever walked with God for any considerable amount of time has experienced moments of desperation when their spirit went on a frantic search for Gods presence, only to find none. Even the Lord Jesus Christ in the hour of His passion felt like God had forsaken Him as He stood between the cross and the resurrection. During this transitional period, the Lord Jesus was surrounded by great spiritual darkness as the sin of the whole world was laid upon Him. His spirit reached out in desperation for the familiar presence of His Heavenly Father; but God, who could not look at sin, had turned His back on His only begotten son.

"And about the ninth hour Jesus cried with a loud voice, saying, Eli, Eli, lama sabachthani? that is to say, My God, my God, why hast thou forsaken me?"[8] .

One of the most powerful Bible stories which can help illustrate the work of the Holy Spirit during periods of transition is the story of the exaltation of Mordecai, by the King of Persia. Mordecai unveiled a conspiracy to assassinate the King of Persia. As a result of Mordecai's work, the assassination attempt on the king's life was foiled and the culprits were brought to swift justice. The established practice and protocol of the Kings of Persia was to host a public ceremony to honor any man or woman who had done a great service to the crown. When Mordecai unveiled the plot to assassinate the King, there was a serious break in both practice and protocol, because the king and the king's first chamberlain did nothing to honor him. The king immediately left for a lengthy war with another combatant nation just after the assignation attempt was foiled.

During this same period Mordecai's niece, Esther or Haddasah in Hebrew, had just been chosen to be the next Queen of Persia to replace the infamous Queen Vashti. During this same era, Haman the Agagite, a sworn enemy of the Jews, had risen to a position of great power and authority in the kingdom of Persia as the King's first chamberlain. Haman had one obsessive agenda on his mind - the total annihilation and extermination of the Jews. He particularly hated Mordecai who, on several occasions, failed to show him the respect which he thought he deserved. So Haman went on a vengeful campaign and put his diabolical plan to destroy the Jews in motion. He managed to secure the signature of the king to seal his diabolical agenda. After securing the unchangeable seal of the king, his evil decree to annihilate the Jews could not be revoked. The fate of the Jews was sealed, their extermination was now imminent.

"And when Haman saw that Mordecai bowed not, nor did him reverence, then was Haman full of wrath. And he thought scorn to lay hands on Mordecai alone; for they had shewed him the people of Mordecai: wherefore Haman sought to destroy all the Jews that were throughout the whole kingdom of Ahasuerus, even the people of Mordecai"[9]

Haman got the king's messengers to quickly circulate the letters containing this evil decree against the Jewish people all over the Persian Empire. Haman's diabolical plan was quickly becoming like a raging volcano. Haman's machinery of destruction and torture was gathering momentum. There was a great outcry among the Jewish people because of their impending doom. Mordecai sent a message through one of the king's guards to inform Esther about the conspiracy of Haman and his evil decree to exterminate the Jewish people. The news of the imminent destruction of her people hit Queen Esther like a small car colliding with an eighteen wheeler truck. Mordecai's letter included instructions for Esther to go before the king and intercede for her people.

Queen Esther was terrified at the prospect of entering the king's presence uninvited. The very attempt would be a sentence of death if the king refused to stretch out his scepter. She knew that the king's personal body guards were sworn to kill anybody who came close to the king uninvited. She knew that they would surround her within seconds. It was an odious and foreboding task at best. Esther sent a message back to Mordecai and reminded him about the proper protocol of approaching the king and the dangers involved in ignoring the set protocol and practice. Mordecai was not moved by Esther's excuses; on the contrary, Mordecai reminded Esther that Haman's evil decree had already placed the sentence of death upon her life and that her residence in the king's palace would not deliver her from the unchangeable decree of a Persian king.

"Then Mordecai commanded to answer Esther, Think not with thyself that thou shalt escape in the king's house, more than all the Jews. For if thou altogether holdest thy peace at this time, then shall there enlargement and deliverance arise to the Jews from another place; but thou and thy father's house shall be destroyed: and who knoweth

whether thou art come to the kingdom for such a time as this?"[10]

Queen Esther was very moved and convicted by Mordecai's words to such a degree that she chose to do the unthinkable. She decided to enter the king's presence uninvited and believe God for supernatural favor. She asked Mordecai to ask all the Jews who were in Shushan to go on a three day fast before she entered into the king's presence. After her days of fasting Esther put on her best clothes and approached the king's presence. When the king saw her, his heart warmed and he instinctively stretched out his scepter to her. The king told Esther that she could have whatever she wanted. She told the king that she wanted to host a special dinner for him and Haman and the king granted her request.

The night prior to the dinner, the Spirit of God came upon the king to such a degree that he could not go to sleep. In his restlessness the king called the keeper of records and told him to go through the chronicles of the kings of Persia. When the keeper of records got to Mordecai's story about how he had saved the king's life from sure assassination, the King's spirit leaped with unfeigned excitement. *He told the keeper of records to read no further. He wanted to know what had been done by the crown to honor Mordecai for his great service to the empire. The keeper of records told the King that nothing had been done for Mordecai. The King was embarrassed and appalled by the fact that nothing had been done to honor Mordecai.* When the morning sun broke through the sky, the king still had Mordecai on his mind.

When Haman reported for work that morning, the king asked him a profound question. *"What should be done for the man the king desires to honor?"* The Bible says that when Satan fell from heaven he lost his wisdom. Simply stated - *the devil is a fool*. He is always the last one to catch on when God is pulling a fast one on him. When Haman heard the king's question, his heart began to pump profusely with unfeigned excitement. Haman was convinced that he was the object of the king's affection. Little did he know that Mordecai, his archenemy, was the recipient of the king's affection.

> *"The Bible says that when Satan fell from heaven he lost his wisdom. Simply stated - the devil is a fool. He is always the last one to catch on when God is pulling a fast one on him."*

Haman put together an illustrious list of things that must be done for the man whom the king chose to honor. It's ironic how during transition, God may even use our worst enemies to promote us. When Haman finished putting together his generous list, the king told him that Mordecai, the Jew, was the man the king had in mind. Haman gasped for air and almost lost his balance. What had looked like the beginning of a great day for him had just turned into his worst nightmare! Can you imagine how embarrassing it was for Haman to have to drive Mordecai around the capital of Shushan while the people shouted shouts of adoration to Mordecai? Can you imagine what this event must have done to boost Mordecai's ego, faith and confidence in God? On his best day, Mordecai could not have planned a day like this. This was the doing of the Lord. Within forty-eight hours Haman's evil decree had so backfired on him that he and his family were executed before the day he had set for the extermination of the Jews. How ironic!

"Then the king said to Haman, Make haste, and take the apparel and the horse, as thou hast said, and do even so to Mordecai the Jew, that sitteth at the king's gate: let nothing fail of all that thou hast spoken.Then took Haman the apparel and the horse, and arrayed Mordecai, and brought him on horseback through the street of the city, and proclaimed before him, Thus shall it be done unto the man whom the king delighteth to honour. And Mordecai came again to the king's gate. But Haman hasted to his house mourning, and having his head covered. And Haman told Zeresh his wife and all his friends every thing that had befallen him. Then said his wise men and Zeresh his wife unto him, If Mordecai be of the seed of the Jews, before whom thou hast begun to fall, thou shalt not prevail against him, but shalt surely fall before him" [11]

The reason for telling you this story is to show you that during periods of *"transition"* God is simply waiting for the **right conditions to be fulfilled**. God is waiting on us to **obey all the right commands** so He can move on our behalf. Mordecai must have thought that God had forgotten him when the king failed to honor him immediately following his service to the crown. The truth of the matter was that God had never for a second, forgotten or abandoned His covenant people.

During the transition time, God was waiting for Mordecai and Esther to obey all the commands that He had given them. *For Queen Esther, obeying God's divine commands meant breaking established royal protocol by approaching the king uninvited.* The problem with many of God's people is that they want every instruction from the Lord to make sense and be absolutely safe and risk free before they obey. More often than not, God's commands will go against what we perceive to be normal and appropriate, but we are still called to be obedient. After Mordecai, Queen Esther and the rest of the Persian Jews had walked in obedience and the prevailing spiritual and natural conditions were conducive, God broke on the scene and gave His people an unforgettable deliverance.

I don't know what you are going through right now or what the Lord has told you to do. But here is what I do know, *if you will just continue obeying the Lord's divine commands, God will give you a mighty deliverance at the end of your transition period.* Your breakthrough will be so powerful you will totally forget the pain or suffering you may have experienced during your period of transition.

> *"The problem with many of God's people is that they want every instruction from the Lord to make sense and be absolutely safe and risk free before they obey."*

To borrow the words of my mother, God has not forgotten you. He is the great chef who takes pleasure in the food which He prepares for His loved ones. *He is simply waiting until it is cooked just right!* God knows that you may not be ready to walk into your breakthrough right at this moment. *A supernatural blessing received prematurely can either corrupt you or destroy you!* If you do not give up on your purpose you will soon find yourself eating at the King's table.

Don't Faint, It's Only a Test

"Transition time is the time of testing our faith and character to see if we believe God's word and trust Him fully in obedience, finding our true confidence in Him."

Teaching is the art of transferring knowledge. Knowledge is not an abstract, intangible asset. It's a tangible and verifiable asset. Since knowledge is a tangible and verifiable asset, there must be ways to ascertain that it has been transferred properly. To achieve this important objective, every institution of learning in the world has a grading system which can determine the degree to which knowledge has been transferred. This grading system is preceded by a *test or examination.* After the students have been taught by their teachers on certain subjects, the teachers call for a class test on those same subjects. The results of the test will reveal how much of the teacher's knowledge has been transferred accurately to the students and to what degree.

Institutions of learning have also formulated uniform and acceptable standards of grades that must be achieved before students can go on to the next level of their education. These grading standards become stiffer the higher you go on the ladder of learning. The rewards of graduating and getting higher education begin to show almost immediately, once we get into the corporate world and begin competing for jobs. Those who did not pursue their education are given menial and less paying jobs, while those with prestigious degrees of learning are treated like royalty and offered the jobs with higher pay and the best benefits. It's usually during this stage in life that many of those who had played the fool while in school regret their childish ways. They soon realize the folly of having cheated on the educational process as their new reality on the job market hits them like a ton of bricks.

Please be reminded that so far we are just talking about the secular world. Heaven's economy operates on a higher level of spiritual education which requires higher evaluation standards. *God is the greatest teacher. He has more knowledge than the most proficient college professors. He will not allow any of His children to cheat in their spiritual classes.* If earthly universities will not give unsubstantiated degrees to people who are not qualified to hold them, why should the God of the universe, who is the source of all wisdom and knowledge, give unsubstantiated spiritual degrees and diplomas to saints who are not qualified to hold them?

During periods of transition, God initiates the process of qualifying the called. God may allow things to happen in our lives that will both test and stretch our faith. God wants to see whether we really believe what we have confessed to believe. You will be surprised to see just how many believers in Christ renounce what they once believed about God in the face of a personal crisis or spiritual attack. This is the reason the Lord Jesus did not stop the devil from coming to sift Peter. He only prayed that Peter's faith would not fail him during this sifting process.

There were inaccurate behavior patterns inside Peter's life, that even Peter was unaware of, which needed to be corrected. *God knew that despite Peter's faith talk he had the potential to renounce the saving grace of Jesus Christ.* Peter did not know that in a moment of crisis he was capable of denying Jesus, until God allowed Satan to sift him during his personal time of transition. Satan's attack on Peter revealed just how much he trusted and loved his fleshly life.

During periods of transition, God will expose hidden sins and iniquities inside our lives that have the potential of snatching us from the hand of God if they are not dealt with. God knew the vast influence that Peter was going to have on the future of the church and He was not going to let him enter his prophetic future without testing his faith and character.

"And the Lord said, Simon, Simon, behold, Satan hath desired to have you, that he may sift you as wheat: But I have prayed for thee, that thy faith fail not: and when thou art converted, strengthen thy brethren. And he said unto him, Lord, I am ready to go with thee, both into prison, and to death. And he said, I tell thee, Peter, the cock shall not crow this day, before that thou shalt thrice deny that thou knowest me"[12]

Time and space would not allow me to narrate the detailed accounts of how God's word tested men like Joseph and David, while God was transitioning them into what He had called them to be. Joseph was known as the dreamer by his own family because of the prophetic dreams God was allowing him to see. His dreams of greatness stirred serious jealousy and envy in his brothers.

> ***"Peter did not know that in a moment of crisis
> he was capable of denying Jesus, until
> God allowed Satan to sift him during
> his personal time of transition."***

Joseph had no clue what he was going to go through in order to realize his prophetic destiny. He was sold to the Ishmaelites by his own brothers and was then sold to Potiphar, captain of the guard once he arrived in Egypt. Just when things were beginning to go well for him in the house of Potiphar, Joseph got in trouble with Potiphar's lusting wife. When he refused to sleep with her, she cried *"rape."* Innocent Joseph was then cast into a high security Egyptian prison. His life had just taken a turn for the worst. Nevertheless it was in prison that he met Pharaoh's butler who eventually told Pharaoh about Joseph's ability to interpret dreams. Joseph was then called to stand before the Pharaoh. *After interpreting Pharaoh's dream, Pharaoh promoted Joseph. Joseph became the second most powerful ruler of Egypt in a single day! Joseph went from jailbird to prime minister in a matter of seconds! God had tested his faith and character during the period of transition and found him to be a faithful servant.* Joseph had passed his final exam in the school of the Spirit and it was time to graduate.

"He sent a man before them, even Joseph, who was sold for a servant: Whose feet they hurt with fetters: he was laid in iron: Until the time that his word came: the word of the LORD tried him. The king sent and loosed him; even the ruler of the people, and let him go free. He made him lord of his house, and ruler of all his substance: To bind his princes at his pleasure; and teach his senators wisdom"[13]

King David spent thirteen years running from one cave to the next after he was anointed to become the second king of Israel by the prophet Samuel. King Saul had chased David like a rabbit for thirteen years. *David killed the giant Goliath in one day with a single shot, but the greatest giant of his life was a jealous and backslidden king called Saul.* King Saul was assigned to David by God to test David's faith and character and to teach David how to depend on God.

I Have a Feeling Everything Is Going To Be Alright

"Transition time is the time when God will cause all things to work together for the good of those that love Him and are called according to His purpose."

There is nothing more potent or life defining than the discovery of purpose. Purpose is the mother of creation and innovation and the grandmother of vision. Without it life has no meaning, success has no real value, and problems have no lasting solutions. God's purpose for man is revealed to us in the first account of the book of Genesis.

"And God said, Let us make man in our image, after our likeness: and let them have dominion over the fish of the sea, and over the fowl of the air, and over the cattle, and over all the earth, and over every creeping thing that creepeth upon the earth. So God created man in his own image, in the image of God created he him; male and female created he them. And God blessed them, and God said unto them, Be fruitful, and multiply, and replenish the earth, and subdue it: and have dominion over the fish of the sea, and over the fowl of the air, and over every living thing that moveth upon the earth" [14]

This Genesis account reveals God's kingdom purpose for the creation of the species called man. This is a five fold purpose.

1. To have Dominion
2. To be Fruitful
3. To Multiply
4. To Replenish the earth
5. To Subdue the earth

When God's children are not walking in these five Kingdom mandates, they are out of touch with God's original purpose for His creation. During periods of transition, the Spirit of God seeks to realign men with God's original mandate for the creation of man.

When men and women who have discovered God's original purpose for their life and are walking in it go through a spiritual setback during any period of transition, God will supernaturally cause all things (even the bad stuff) to work out for their benefit. Whatever the enemy meant for evil and destruction will become for them a stepping stone to greater things in God. During our personal and corporate time of transition God will begin to work with the good, the bad and the ugly things of our lives for the good of His Kingdom agenda.

The devil really thought that he was killing Jesus when he hung Him on the cross. Little did he know that the death of the Lord Jesus Christ would become his ultimate destruction. *What should have been a great victory for Satan by defeating the Son of God, turned out to be the opening of the prison doors of hell to set free all those who were held captive by Satan's chains!* Evil was not permitted to have the final say in Jesus' life because He was called according to God's purpose. God was able to turn everything Jesus suffered during His crucifixion into the healing of the nations.

"And we know that all things work together for good to them that love God, to them who are the called according to his purpose"[15]

God Wants To Drive the Bus

"Transition time is the time when God will inter-vene in the affairs of men and *realign* them to His ultimate plans, redirecting them into His predeter-mined will in total obedience."

God wants to drive the bus. He may enter our lives as a divine passenger but before all is said and done, God will be driving bus and we will be seated comfortably in the passenger's seat. Man was never created to control God. When a product migrates from its preset design and turns on its manufacturer, it's in serious malfunction and must be repaired or destroyed. This is what happened to the apostle Paul who was previously known as Saul of Tarsus. Based upon God's prophetic call upon his life, Saul of Tarsus was destined to be an apostle and a teacher of the Gentiles. Unfortunately, when the power of Christ threw Him off his horse on the way to Damascus, he was operating as a devout and zealous Pharisee who was deter-mined to destroy the church of the living God.

"For ye have heard of my conversation in time past in the Jews' religion, how that beyond measure I persecuted the church of God, and wasted it: And profited in the Jews' religion above many my equals in mine own nation, being more exceedingly zealous of the traditions of my fathers. But when it pleased God, who separated me from my mother's womb, and called me by his grace, To reveal his Son in me, that I might preach him among the heathen; immediately I conferred not with flesh and blood:"[16]

Saul of Tarsus was doing the exact opposite of everything that God had created him to be. God's call on his life was to be a fervent builder of the church, not its ardent destroyer and oppressor. He was called to preach Christ and Him crucified but he was busy and zealously preaching the Law of Moses and viciously denouncing the ways of Christ. ***He was called to walk with the "people of the Way" but he hated the believers in Christ with a blazing passion. Saul of Tarsus was certainly a classic case of an original product of God that had seriously malfunctioned.***

During his period of transition from being a religious zealot to becoming an apostle to the Gentiles, the Spirit was working on Saul of Tarsus to realign him to fit and flow in God's predetermined purpose for his life. On the day Paul left Jerusalem with a decree from the high priest to arrest and torture believers in Christ in the City of Damascus, little did he know that he was going to meet with his maker.

"God wants to drive the bus. He may enter our lives as a divine passenger but before all is said and done, God will be driving the bus."

When Saul of Tarsus woke up that fateful day, he gathered his army of fellow religious zealots and charged towards Damascus like a wounded Buffalo. Suddenly the lightening of God struck the invading horde and Paul was knocked off his horse. All he could see was a brilliant white light, shinier than the blazing mid eastern sun. As he beheld the glory of God, Paul instinctively asked a question and answered it himself. He asked, *"Who art thou, Lord?"* The Lord asked him why he was kicking against the pricks; put in today's language- *why are you biting the hand that feeds you?* The Lord proceeded to tell Paul who he was and what He had called him to do.

The Lord Jesus then instructed Paul to go into Damascus and seek out a brother by the name of Ananias, who would give him further instructions as to the pertinent details related to his prophetic destiny.

"And as he journeyed, he came near Damascus: and suddenly there shined round about him a light from heaven: And he fell to the earth, and heard a voice saying unto him, Saul, Saul, why persecutest thou me? And he said, Who art thou, Lord? And the Lord said, I am Jesus whom thou persecutest: it is hard for thee to kick against the pricks. And he trembling and astonished said, Lord, what wilt thou have me to do? And the Lord said unto him, Arise, and go into the city, and it shall be told thee what thou must do" [17]

When Ananias arrived where Paul was staying in Damascus, he found him stumbling in darkness because the encounter with God had left him physically blind. God wanted Paul to know just how spiritually blind he had been all his life by temporarily taking away the use of his physical eyes. Ananias prayed for him and God filled him with the Spirit and opened his blind eyes. ***During times of transition God will give us meaningful personal and corporate encounters with His presence in order to realign us to His predetermined will for our lives.*** During these periods of transition God may choose to use some of our brothers and sisters in Christ to shed more light on our destiny. This is why we should not allow ourselves to become too proud to the degree that we fail to receive from seemingly insignificant brothers and sisters in the Lord.

During times of transition, God will *"shake us up"* in order to give us the humility to receive from anybody who has been sent to minister to us. You may be going through serious spiritual realignment right at this moment. ***This spiritual realignment may be very painful for you right now, but I want you to know that God is not out to destroy you.*** God simply wants to realign your desires, motives and life agenda to fit His perfect plan for your life. When He is finished preparing you He will use you in a mighty way!

God has Quarantined the Enemy

"Transition is also the period in which God quarantines the enemy while He changes us into the people who can inherit His promises."

"Now Jericho was tightly shut up because of the Israelites. No one went out and no one came in. Then the LORD said to Joshua, "See, I have delivered Jericho into your hands, along with its king and its fighting men." [18]

This powerful passage of scripture from the book of Joshua uncovers some very important truths about periods of transition that we need to be aware of. According to this revealing passage, God told Joshua explicitly that even before he and the children of Israel made their first move to cross the Jordan, God had already delivered the City of Jericho into their hands. The great City of Jericho was already theirs; all they had to do was rise and take it.

According to this explosive passage from the book of Joshua, God had supernaturally quarantined the enemies of Israel inside their city walls. What is quite interesting is that the people of Jericho had built their great city walls for the purpose of protecting themselves from their enemies. From the vantage point supplied by their great walls, the people of Jericho easily defeated their enemies before Joshua and the children of Israel came knocking on their doorsteps. *To their great dismay, once Israel arrived with a promise from God to take the city of Jericho, their great walls became prison walls which shut them inside the city while God prepared Israel from the outside to take over.* This passage from the book of Joshua clearly underscores one of the underlying reasons God leads His people into periods of transition. In transition God is not waiting for the enemy to become weaker or more reconciliatory towards His kingdom. To the contrary, God knows that the enemy is already quarantined. God is waiting for us to allow His Spirit to change the spirit of our character so we can become the people who inherit what God has already promised us.

"Now when all the Amorite kings west of the Jordan and all the Canaanite kings along the coast heard how the LORD had dried up the Jordan before the Israelites until we had

crossed over, their hearts melted and they no longer had the courage to face the Israelites. At that time the LORD said to Joshua, "Make flint knives and circumcise the Israelites again." So Joshua made flint knives and circumcised the Israelites at Gibeath Haaraloth. Now this is why he did so: All those who came out of Egypt—all the men of military age—died in the desert on the way after leaving Egypt. All the people that came out had been circumcised, but all the people born in the desert during the journey from Egypt had not."[19]

The portion of scripture above is even more revealing concerning God's purpose for His people during periods of transition. This passage clearly shows us the spiritual, mental and emotional state of the enemies of Israel inside the walled city of Jericho. The Bible tells us that while the sons of Israel were mumbling, complaining and feeling sorry for themselves, on the other side of the Jordan their enemies were rehearsing just how powerful and awesome the God of Israel was. When news arrived inside the city gates that the children of Israel had just miraculously crossed the river Jordan in the same way that that they had crossed the mighty Red Sea, the men of war inside the city gates melted with fear. ***Some of them were even peeing in their pants.*** *How would you like to fight an enemy who is already peeing in his pants in fear of you?*

"While the sons of Israel were mumbling, complaining and feeling sorry for themselves, on the other side of the Jordan their enemies were rehearsing just how powerful and awesome the God of Israel was."

The million dollar question which arises out of our study of these two passages from the book of Joshua is simply this, *"If the enemies of Israel had already given up in fear, what was God waiting for?"* The answer to this question will not only astound you but it will also pull the covers off the bed of transition. In other words, *you will see that periods of transition have more to do with the work of God than the spiritual resistance of the enemy.* The reason God took so long to give the children of Israel the city of Jericho and the whole land of Palestine, is because they were spiritually not ready to come into their spiritual inheritance. The time it took for the children of Israel to inherit the city of Jericho and the land of Palestine had nothing to do with the devil's resistance to the purposes of God. God didn't have to summon every angel He had at His disposal because the devil and his demons were putting up such a strong fight in the realm of the spirit. We already know that the enemy was paralyzed and peeing in his pants with fear before the Israelites started their march around the City.

The real reason for the delay in God's plan of conquest hinged not on the devil's ability to resist God, but on the spiritual condition of God's covenant people. The Bible tells us that all the men who were part of Joshua's army, before they crossed the Jordan, had not yet been circumcised. God had given Abraham the covenant of circumcision as an everlasting covenant to be honored by all his descendants. God told Abraham that all the male children had to be circumcised in their foreskins on the eighth day from birth. Those who refused the covenant of circumcision were set to be destroyed. They could not be numbered with Abraham nor could they inherit any of God's prophetic promises which He had sworn to Abraham hundreds of years before Joshua and the children of Israel came knocking on the doorsteps of the city of Jericho.

Even though the enemy was already quarantined inside the city walls, God was not going to give Abraham's inheritance to a group of uncircumcised Jewish men. To do so would have been a major slap in the face for Abraham and God would have also broken His own word. Even though Joshua was circumcised, his men of war were not. *Joshua's men of war were religious but they had not yet come into a living covenant with the God of Abraham. This reminds me of so many of God's people in our churches who are deeply religious but they have not yet experienced spiritual circumcision to enter into a meaningful covenant relationship with God.* Their fleshly life is much more active than their spiritual life. They are busy running around with all these prophetic promises but they fail to come into their spiritual inheritance because they have not allowed God to place their flesh life under the knife of spiritual circumcision. *The enemy is already quarantined and paralyzed with fear but spiritual inheritance eludes them because they are still fighting with God. They haven't yet made a covenant commitment to live for the will of God for the rest of their lives. They have one foot in the Kingdom and the other in the world.*

Finally, had God not quarantined the enemy inside the city walls, the Israelite's lack of consecration to God would have opened too many spiritual doors for the devil to attack them. Please remember that every time we fight with God and refuse to obey His voice, we open a door for the enemy to attack us. *If God in His mercy does not supernaturally quarantine the powers of hell during this period of transition in our spiritual walk, the enemy would have too many opportunities through our disobe-*

dience to destroy us. It was the mercy of God that kept the enemies of Israel, who were locked up inside the city gates, from finding out that the people they were terrified of were constantly murmuring, complaining and talking of defeat. *Had the enemies of Israel known that the men of Israel were also afraid of them, they would have been emboldened to put up a strong fight.* For many of God's children, their fleshly life is so out of control that if God's mercy does not quarantine the enemy while He is trying to grow them up spiritually, many of them would be destroyed like flies by the demon powers.

> *"Please remember that every time we fight*
> *with God and refuse to obey His voice,*
> *we open a door for the enemy to attack us."*

Transition: The Law of God

"Transition is like gravity, it is a governing spiritual and natural law of God."

The corridors of human history are painted with the memories and stories of thousands of men and women who died because they found themselves on the wrong side of the law of gravity. They fought against this immutable law of God and lost the fight. Thousands more were crippled for life because they fought against the law of gravity.

The law of gravity can only be overcome by employing a higher law called the law of aerodynamics. The point of this illustration is to show you that *"transition like gravity or aerodynamics is a governing spiritual and natural law of God.''* All laws are impartial and are respecters of no person. The governing law of transition is impartial and does not respect any human being. The law of transition will bless believers and non-believers alike when it is obeyed. *On the other hand, hundreds of Kingdom citizens have been destroyed or left seriously handicapped by fighting against the law of transition. Some have suffered financial ruin because they ignored the demands of transition even though they chose to blame the devil for their loss.* In some cases the devil had nothing to do with their loss. They lost everything that they owned for the simple reason that they chose to fight and test the power of the immutable law of transition.

"But we all, with open face beholding as in a glass the glory of the Lord, are changed into the same image from glory to glory, even as by the Spirit of the Lord."[20]

According to the above scripture, the apostle Paul is letting us know that without embracing the law of transition, the spiritual state of the human race would never change. It is not good news for anyone to be trapped in the same spiritual condition. Through the law of transition, men can choose to seek a better and higher spiritual state for themselves. Through the governing law of transition, men and women can go from one degree of glory to another. Glory to God!!!

Notes on Chapter One

1. 1 Thessalonians 5:23, 2. Hebrews 11:5, 3. Joshua 1:
    1-2, 4. 1 Cor 13:11
5. Hebrews 10:36, 6. Acts 1:4-5, 7. Romans 4:17-20, 8.
    Matthew 27:46
9. Esther 3:5-6, 10. Esther 4:13-14, 11. Esther 6:10-13,
    13. Luke 22:31-34,
14. Psalm 105:17-22, 15. Genesis 1:26-28, 16. Romans
    8:28, 17. Galatians 1:13-16
19. Acts 9:3-6, 20. Joshua 6:1-2, 21. Joshua 5:1-5, 22.
    2 Corinthians 3:18

Chapter Two

A World of Changes

❦

The Apostle Paul knew the importance and inevitability of change in the life journey. Change is an integral part of life. Change is an integral part of progress.
There is no progress of any kind without change. Change
is happening all around us. Boys are becoming men and
girls are becoming women. Every second, somewhere in
the world a child is born. As the baby cries its way out
of its mother's womb, the recipient family is permanently
altered by the arrival of the new infant. The world we live
in is changing at a rapid pace.

*"When I was a child, I spake as a child, I understood as a
child, I thought as a child: but when I became a man, I put
away childish things"[1]*

Every day new scientific and technological discoveries are being reported and reconfiguring the way people,
corporations and even religious institutions communicate
and do business. ***On a spiritual tone, the closer we get to
the finish line or the end of this apostolic age, the more***

desperate Satan and his demonic kingdom are becoming.
These demonic spirits are rapidly descending into the
earth's spiritual atmosphere and driving men into great
spiritual wickedness.

Surfing the Waves of Change

I have always loved to watch men and women who surf
with great skill. They are a beautiful sight to behold. At
any given moment they are subject to being engulfed by
the waves of the restless sea. Suddenly you see their magic,
when the sea throws them its worst. They glide upon the
surging waves with the ease of a bird gliding in the air.
These professional surfers have mastered the power of
cooperating with the changing waves of the ocean. Instead
of fighting the waves of the sea, they yield themselves and
allow the power of the changing tides to take them to the
next wave.

Life is like a boiling pot of water that is bubbling with
relentless bubbles of change. There is nothing more permanent and relentless as change. If we can be assured of one
thing, it's simply this, things are going to change!

*"Therefore rejoice ye heavens, and ye that dwell in them.
Woe to the inhabitants of the earth and of the sea! for the
devil is come down unto you, having great wrath, because
he knoweth that he hath but a short time. And when the
dragon saw that he was cast unto the earth, he persecuted
the woman which brought forth the man child"*[2]

According to the apocalyptic revelation, there is going
to be a greater invasion of demonic spirits into the earth's
spiritual climate in the last days than at any period in world
history. **The spiritual climate of the world we live in is**

changing rapidly and these relentless changes are neces-
sitating the need for quick and sustainable transition. In
order to surf the waves or glide the winds of change, we
must become allies of transition and not enemies of it. As
people of the kingdom, we need to become very sensitive
to the voice of the Holy Spirit who is called to lead us to
the finish line. *Without this special and acquired sensi-*
tivity to the voice of the Holy Spirit, it will be impossible
to successfully navigate the valley of transition in this
decade of destiny.

The corridors of corporate America are littered with
tragic stories of great corporations that plummeted into
bankruptcy because they failed to successfully navigate
the winds of change and instead became casualties of transition. These corporations made the mistake most church
leaders make. They began to feel like their past successes
would insulate them from having to consistently cooperate
with the law of transition. *They failed to realize that tran-*
sition is a fact of life that will never change. If transition
ever ceases, the train of progress will screech to a halt.
We can never outgrow our need to cooperate with the law
of transition just as we can never outgrow being obedient
to the laws of our land. They say nobody is above the law,
may I submit to you that no one is above transition.

> *"There is nothing more permanent and relentless*
> *as change. If we can be assured of one thing,*
> *it's simply this, things are going to change!"*

I am reminded of the story of a pastor of a mega
church in Oklahoma, who arrived at his church on a
Sunday morning only to discover that two thousand of
his members had walked out. How could two thousand

people walk out on a leader in one single service without any prior warning? The truth of the matter is that this great pastor ignored warning signs of a change and loss of confidence in his leadership by a majority of his flock. *He was too intoxicated with yesterday's success to give heed to the signs of an imminent church split. He found himself on the wrong side of the law of the transition and it crippled his ministry.*

Casualties of Transition

The Scriptures are full of memoirs of men and women who became casualties of transition. The history of the world is full of examples of rogue nations, democracies, political leaders and ideologies that found themselves on the wrong side of transition and were exterminated by it.

"But as the days of Noe were, so shall also the coming of the Son of man be. For as in the days that were before the flood they were eating and drinking, marrying and giving in marriage, until the day that Noe entered into the ark, And knew not until the flood came, and took them all away; so shall also the coming of the Son of man be"[3]

Let's take the people of Noah's day as an example. When Noah received a prophetic message from God to build the largest boat in the history of the ancient world, the people of the day laughed him to scorn. They concluded that Noah had lost his mind. When he started dragging the animals of the wild into his big boat, the people of his day could hardly believe their eyes. They laughed at him and ignored his prophetic warning about the coming of a devastating flood. They could not see how any amount of rainfall could completely disrupt the predictable flow of their lives, let alone flood their walled cities. *During this period of transition, God gave them time to heed Noah's message and save their lives, yet they chose to continue their partying, drinking, eating and having sexual orgies!*

When the flood of water swept through their city, destroying everything in its path, they could hardly believe their eyes. They realized that a death sentence was upon them, and driven by panic, they frantically sought for shelter in Noah's cruise liner. To their dismay, God had already closed the doors of the huge ship and they couldn't get in. Noah watched as hundreds of hopeless souls made a desperate attempt to swim their way to safety, but to no avail. After the relentless rain subsided and the waters of the flood receded, there were multitudes of dead bodies left in the wake of the disaster. *Had they been gathered up and put into one mass grave their obituary would have simply read, "Here in lies the bodies of those who thought they could prevail against the inevitable tide of transition."*

Unfortunately history has a way of repeating itself. Countless generations since Noah's era have died for failure to properly navigate the valley of transition. It's my personal observation that God's people, or religious people in general, have tremendous difficulty embracing transition. *Religious institutions are some of the most difficult organizations to navigate during periods of transition. This is largely due to an elite group in the congregation who refuse to accept change.* The zealous fight for authenticity of faith blinds many spiritual leaders to the need for present day innovation which can enhance the aspects of how people of faith share their faith. *I really believe that there is a place, where the authenticity of an ancient faith and present day innovation can co-exist successfully.* Unfortunately they're spiritual leaders and churches who are terrified of technological innovation.

In recent years there has been a major bridging between religion and science. For the longest time, religious leaders ascribed scientific aspirations to the work of the devil. The history of the Catholic Church inquisitions is filled with horror stories of men and women of science who were tortured and burned at the stake as heretics for pursuing the sciences. This was truly a grave travesty. The Catholic Church has since apologized for these crimes of ignorance and religious bigotry.

> *"I really believe that there is a place, where*
> *the authenticity of an ancient faith and present*
> *day innovation can co-exist successfully."*

What truly amazes me is the fact that many church-going folk can successfully handle transition at their places of work, but resist it at their home church. Companies are constantly changing staff, their products and their marketing strategies in order to remain strong and profitable. Unfortunately, I have met too many pastors who are terrified of making changes in their ministry, especially if the changes would result in a radical shift from previously established practices. They are afraid that making the necessary leadership changes will cost them a portion of their members. As a result, many churches become spiritual dinosaurs and echoes of a past but lost glory. It would be wonderful if we could capture the zeal and commitment found in the corporate world and infuse it into the church world as an anointing to carry them through the times of transition. Just imagine the impact God's people would have on the world with this type of unity and enthusiasm!

My warning to senior pastors and apostolic leaders of churches and networks or denominations is simply this *we must retrain our people to become champions of change and not resistors of change!* We are living in spiritually desperate times. We cannot afford to be found guilty, as the Apostle Paul was, kicking against the *"pricks"* of transition.

Pioneers of the Future

"Moses my servant is dead; now therefore arise, go over this Jordan, thou, and all this people, unto the land which I do give to them, even to the children of Israel. Every place that the sole of your foot shall tread upon, that have I given unto you, as I said unto Moses"[4]

The world in which we live has two classes of people. These two classes are *pioneers* and *settlers*. The vast majority is comprised of *settlers*. *Pioneers* are a major minority in our world but without them we would still be living in the dark ages. Without pioneers, many of us would still be living outside our spiritual inheritance. We would be watching the promise land from distant shores instead of crossing our Jordan to inhabit our land of promise.

The New World, now known as the United States of America, would never have been discovered had there not been pioneers who braved menacing ocean storms in search of new and uncharted frontiers. From the safety of the shoreline the settlers watched the pioneers board exploration ships to distant and unknown lands. Undaunted, the pioneers braced themselves for yet another adventure. Once the pioneers discovered new lands they quickly staked their claim and, in most cases, were rewarded with great riches and became the new landlords of the discovered territory. As soon as the news spread to the settlers back home that the pioneers had discovered a new territory, there was a mad gold rush by the settlers towards the new territory. When the settlers arrived at the shores of the new territory, they started staking their claim and building their homes. Within months the settlers had established a settlement or colony around what the pioneers had discovered.

"Yet there shall be a space between you and it, about two thousand cubits by measure: come not near unto it that ye may know the way by which ye must go: for ye have not passed this way heretofore"[5]

Pioneers are champions of change. They are knights of transition. Without their efforts, societies would regress back to the dark ages. The train of progress screeches to a halt. ***Pioneers live for the changing of the times. They have an in-built intuition that lets them know that, beyond the menacing storms of life lies undiscovered lands laden with treasures for the adventurous soul.*** Settlers on the other hand are obsessed with the need to preserve the status quo. The need to preserve present comforts is far more important to them than the pursuit of discovery. On the other hand without *settlers,* the lands discovered by the pioneers would remain uninhabited and untamed terrain. We need both classes of people. ***During times of transition, pioneers must pray for special grace from God to help them to have patience with their brothers and sisters who have the settler's spiritual DNA and mentality.*** On the other hand, settlers must be taught how to honor the pioneers and how to embrace the winds of change under the leadership of the pioneers.

> *"Pioneers are champions of change.*
> *They are knights of transition.*
> *Without their efforts, societies would*
> *regress back to the dark ages."*

Change is an integral part of progress. You cannot have progress without change. Many Christians love the idea of change, but do not like the process of change itself. I am convinced that the greatest mockery of truth is believing that one can have meaningful progress without change. In life, things change. They don't stay the same. This is why we cannot allow ourselves to be emotionally manipulated by people who refuse to do better. I have heard people make comments like this, *"Ever since she got a doctorate degree she's changed!"* **The truth of the matter is that people are supposed to change as they climb the ladder of success or spiritual growth. Change is an integral part of progress.** You will walk differently the day you go to the podium to pick up your doctorate degree as opposed to the way you walked up to receive your high school diploma. A person who has just bought a Royce Rolls will drive with a sense of prestige and power that they didn't have when they were driving their old beaten up Honda. This is because changes in attitude, rank or class are an integral part of progress. I am not suggesting that people should become mean and snobbish when they become more successful but rather, embrace the change with a thankful heart.

If we cannot handle transition we will become victims of our future instead of becoming the leaders of our future. As Kingdom citizens, God has called us to be pioneers of our future rather than victims of our past. We have the greatest Navigator living inside our regenerated spirit. Jesus told us that one of the primary assignments of the Holy Spirit is to reveal to us things to come. In other words, the Holy Spirit will give us supernatural *"insider information"* about how to position ourselves to have a greater stake in our future. ***The Holy Spirit already has been where He is taking us. He knows all the roads and shortcuts to get us there in the least amount of time.*** We will discuss the role of the Holy Spirit during periods of transition more fully in a later chapter.

"Howbeit when he, the Spirit of truth, is come, he will guide you into all truth: for he shall not speak of himself; but whatsoever he shall hear, that shall he speak: and he will shew you things to come. He shall glorify me: for he shall receive of mine, and shall shew it unto you"[6]

God knew that Egypt was going to be a very powerful economic bloc and began to move Joseph towards Egypt through a series of divine orchestrated transitions. Even though Joseph left Canaan as a slave, he later thanked God for moving him to Egypt years before the entire world economy shifted to Egypt. ***As a result of allowing God to make him a pioneer of the future by putting him through the valley of transition, Joseph had a greater stake in the economy of Egypt and the world.*** When the greatest famine that the world has ever known struck and Egypt was the only nation that had food, Joseph was able to save his entire family and preserve God's eternal purposes for the nation of Israel.

> *"As Kingdom citizens, God has called us to be pioneers of our future rather than victims of our past."*

The Impact of Disruptive Technologies

"My investigation into why leading firms found it so difficult to stay atop the disk drive industry led me to develop the "technology mudslide hypothesis": Coping with the relentless onslaught of technology change was akin to trying to climb a mudslide raging down a hill. You have to scramble with everything you've got to stay on top of it, and if you ever once stop to catch your breath, you get buried."

"In assessing blame for the failure of good companies, the distinction is sometimes made between innovations requiring very different technological capabilities, that is, so called radical change, and those that build upon well-practiced technological capabilities, often called incremental innovations. The notion is that the magnitude of the technological change relative to the companies' capabilities will determine which firms triumph after a technology invades an industry..

(The Innovators Dilemma, by Clayton M. Christensen)

I already have mentioned the fact that transition is a governing spiritual and natural law of God which seriously impacts our spiritual and material worlds. In this section, I want to draw a parallel between the impact that disruptive natural technology and disruptive spiritual technology have on life and business during periods of transition.

In the corporate world of commerce there are two types of technologies that consistently force themselves upon industries, creating waves of change. The first class is called *sustainable technology or incremental technology*. This class of technology is so named because it builds upon existing technology. Most industries are better prepared to deal with transition that is imposed by this first class of technology. The second class of technology is called *disruptive technology*. This class of technology has destroyed more companies than any other type of technology. *This technology is called disruptive technology because it does not build upon current technology; it completely rewrites the science books.*

When this technology invades the industry, leaders of corporations run back to the drawing boards, knowing that the day of doing business as usual is over! Disruptive technologies bring about radical transitions in the industry they choose to invade. *Companies that built their entire business on the basis of the system that has now become obsolete either collapse or regroup quickly around the new disruptive technologies.* The corporations that refuse or fail to transition, quickly lose their market shares to new and unknown corporations who have an operating system around the new disruptive technology.

You may be wondering what parallel exists between disruptive technology and the things of the Spirit. There are a great number of parallels and we do well to understand them. Please remember that all natural things were built from the *"raw material of spiritual things."*

"Through faith we understand that the worlds were framed by the word of God, so that things which are seen were not made of things which do appear"[7]

The natural world is a shadow of the spirit world. All natural things originate from the realm of the invisible world, which leads us to conclude that *if there is natural technology then there must be a higher spiritual technology upon which all natural technologies are based.* We will now look at disruptive spiritual technologies and how they superimpose radical spiritual transitions in the way we do business in the Kingdom of God.

For over four thousand years, the Jewish people had an established religious system of offerings and sacrifices. This was their spiritual technology for approaching the presence of God. For thousands of years they sacrificed bulls and lambs to atone for their sins and everything worked just fine. They had a history of success with their system of worship. Their forefathers Abraham, Isaac, Jacob and Moses had all used the same system of worship and it had worked for them as well.

Four thousand years later, a young Jewish Rabbi who called Himself the "Messiah" was walking with a great company of His disciples while the general public followed Him sheepishly. As they were walking, this Jesus of Nazareth made a sudden announcement that shocked his disciples and made the Pharisees go nuts.

"I am the living bread which came down from heaven: if any man eat of this bread, he shall live for ever: and the bread that I will give is my flesh, which I will give for the life of the world. The Jews therefore strove among themselves, saying, How can this man give us his flesh to eat? Then Jesus said unto them, Verily, verily, I say unto you, Except ye eat the flesh of the Son of man, and drink his blood, ye have no life in you. Whoso eateth my flesh, and drinketh my blood, hath eternal life; and I will raise him

up at the last day. For my flesh is meat indeed, and my blood is drink indeed. He that eateth my flesh, and drinketh my blood, dwelleth in me, and I in him"[8]

The disciples and those in the crowd could not believe what Jesus had just said. How could eating a man's flesh and drinking His blood bring divine salvation and release them from sin which could not be found in the daily sacrifices of bulls and goats? *They were visibly offended with him and judged him insane. In one statement Jesus had disrupted over four thousand years of standard Jewish protocol and practice for obtaining divine salvation.*

Not far from where Jesus was delivering His highly offensive sermon to a very shocked audience, the high priest had just entered the temple to prepare the evening sacrifice in accordance with the Mosaic Law. The faithful Jewish high priest did not realize that the *"door of favor"* on his daily preparation of animal sacrifices to obtain divine salvation was rapidly closing on him. Jesus, who was on the other side of the street, had just released a very important press statement on behalf of the Kingdom of God concerning the future of using animal sacrifices to obtain divine salvation. The *day of transitioning from "the daily sacrifices" to the "one perfect sacrifice chosen by the Father from before the foundation of the world" had come.* With one unwavering and unapologetic prophetic decree, the Lord Jesus Christ had just introduced a world of change. *Jesus' statement had just introduced one of the most disruptive spiritual technologies concerning approaching the presence of God and obtaining divine salvation that has ever been issued by a man of God.*

This new disruptive spiritual technology that Jesus was introducing was going to center divine salvation and remission of sins around a rugged cross on Calvary and the blood that was shed on it. ***The cross is God's greatest disruptive spiritual technology which forces every one who encounters it to go through a radical spiritual transition.*** This transition takes some to everlasting life and some to eternal damnation!

"For the preaching of the cross is to them that perish foolishness; but unto us which are saved it is the power of God. For the Jews require a sign, and the Greeks seek after wisdom: But we preach Christ crucified, unto the Jews a stumbling block, and unto the Greeks foolishness; But unto them which are called, both Jews and Greeks, Christ the power of God, and the wisdom of God. Because the foolishness of God is wiser than men; and the weakness of God is stronger than men. For ye see your calling, brethren, how that not many wise men after the flesh, not many mighty, not many noble, are called:"[9]

Security and Operational Updates

I am quite impressed with the consistency of the Microsoft Corporation in its perpetual endeavor to remain the leading software company in the world. Every morning when I start up my computer, there is a message from Microsoft about an important update. Sometimes these updates are important security and operational updates. I remember ignoring many of these updates in the past until the day my computer crashed. I lost valuable personal and financial information that I have never been able to recover.

In our high tech world, new scientific and technological discoveries will inevitably force corporations to reconfigure their old operating systems. The

reconfiguration of old operating systems is very important in keeping a company in sync with the latest technologies in the corporate industry. If it's critical for secular corporations to reconfigure their old operating systems, it's far more important that the church allows God to reconfigure its old operating systems so the church can operate on a higher spiritual level. *The Lord Jesus called one of these spiritual reconfigurations "being born again."*

"Jesus answered and said unto him, Verily, verily, I say unto thee, except a man be born again, he cannot see the kingdom of God. Nicodemus saith unto him, how can a man be born when he is old? Can he enter the second time into his mother's womb, and be born? Jesus answered, Verily, verily, I say unto thee, except a man be born of water and of the Spirit, he cannot enter into the kingdom of God."[10]

Transition and the Law of Morality

In our endeavor to master transition, we must not forget that *"Transition does not negate or violate the laws of divine morality but rather enhances them."* This is a very important truth for us to understand because we live in a world where we see our political leaders constantly violate the laws of morality in order to appease public opinion. Changing times may bring us under tremendous personal pressure, where the temptation to sell out to the winds of secular conformity could become quite overwhelming.

During periods of transition we may find ourselves tempted to lower our personal standards regarding moral values and personal integrity. *Globally, the fight for moral values is taking centre stage in the affairs of nations with standards of morality becoming more and more unclear. The winds of secular and liberal thinking are quickly reintroducing inaccurate patterns of behavior that past generations have considered moral taboos, into popular patterns of behavior.* The propagators of liberal heresy champion their cause by pointing to the fact that times have changed and old ways of thinking must be redefined to accommodate the popular cultures and scientific achievements of the day.

While it's true that nations must be flexible enough to rethink old paradigms of thinking as they relate to our understanding of science and technology, *God never ever gave man the power to alter the unchangeable standards of divine morality. The reason is obvious. No nation can ever outgrow their need for divine morality.* In his classic book *"Mere Christianity"*, bestselling author C.S Lewis calls this inherent divine morality, the *"Moral Law or the Law of Decent Behavior"*. For instance, lying is simply wrong whether you are living in the dark ages or in the highly modernized societies of today. When the leaders of Enron, in collaboration with their auditing firm Arthur Andersen, decided to cook the books and project false profits on their balance sheets when the company was actually losing money faster than a sweating pig, the company collapsed. As a result of that collapse, thousands of hard working employees lost all their life savings.

"During periods of transition we may find ourselves tempted to lower our personal standards regarding moral values and personal integrity."

As we approach the millennial reign of the Kingdom of God, we are going to see the structure and moral fiber of nations collapse under the constant barrage of liberalist thinking. We will see the birth of righteous and evil nations within the structure of nations. We will see the phenomenon of nations within nations, which will culminate in an end-time showdown between the adherents of conservative biblical values and the propagators of liberal agendas and thinking.

On July 18th, 2006 President George W. Bush held a press conference on the very sensitive subject of *"stem cell research."* The senate had just passed a bill that was designed to increase federal funding for stem cell research and legalize the use of more human embryos in the search of cures for perplexing disorders such as Parkinson's Disease. Proponents of the bill say that we must do whatever is necessary to find a cure, even if we have to use human embryos to do it. On the surface this seems to be a very straight forward issue, if you ignore all the moral issues involved to achieve its objective. *(Incidentally there are more potent stem cells that can be harvested from a new born baby's umbilical cord, which would not involve the destruction of human embryos. Most proponents of stem cell research will not tell you this because the devil has an agenda to continue killing the unborn).*

Stem cell research, as it stands in its current approach, raises very serious moral questions which we do well to answer before we cross a restricted moral boundary which may bring us more tragedy than the promise of a cure that it stands on. To use an old adage of Jesus Christ, *"what shall it profit a man to gain the whole world and lose his eternal soul forever?"* There is tremendous wisdom contained in this statement made by our Savior. So what are these moral questions that deserve our deepest and thoughtful consideration?

Stem cell research raises these three powerful questions....

1. When does life really begin?
2. Who has the authority to tell us when life really begins?
3. Does the end justify means?

The present version of stem cell research challenges an ancient moral issue, *when does life begin,* to the proponents of the 07/2006 stem cell research senate bill who state that life does not begin until the formation of the fetus in the womb. If this were true, stem cell research under the 07/2006 stem cell research senate bill poses no moral threat. But the real question is, ***"What does God say about the beginning of life?"*** Let the book speak for itself.

"Before I formed thee in the belly I knew thee; and before thou camest forth out of the womb I sanctified thee, [and] I ordained thee a prophet unto the nations."[11]

According to this powerful passage of scripture, written by the prophet Jeremiah over three thousand years before the current stem cell debate, God answered the question that has been the subject of hostile political, religious and scientific debate. ***According to God, who is the source and creator of life, life begins in the mind of God before it ever appears in the form of a human embryo or as a fetus in the mother's womb.***
Jeremiah was as real and as alive in the mind of God as he was when his mother gave birth to him. The fact of the matter is that the life of any product really begins in the mind of the manufacturer and man is the product of

God's mind. This is why there are laws in every nation which protect intellectual property from being stolen from its originator. The reason they are called intellectual property laws is because these laws protect the full rights and privileges of the manufacturer or inventor who originated the *original thought.*

If we can simply see this simple fact, *the right to abortion* movement across the nations of the earth would capsize. We will quickly realize that mothers have no rights and privileges to end the life of a product (child) that was conceived in the mind of God (except when their physical life is threatened by the birth of the child). When pregnant women flippantly abort their unborn babies, they are stealing God's intellectual property and the day of reckoning is coming if they do not repent. Perhaps this would explain why many women who have had an abortion remain traumatized after the fact. They find themselves wondering about how their precious baby would have looked had it lived. I have prayed for women who were traumatized by the guilt of having taken the life of their child through an abortion. Most of these women only found freedom after mourning the loss of their child as a human being instead of trying to pacify the inner pain and guilt by telling themselves that it was just a fetus. This is called the testimony of the conscience.

"The fact of the matter is that the life of any product really begins in the mind of the manufacturer and man is the product of God's mind".

The 07/2006 stem cell research senate bill, as it stands, also raises another question, *"Who has the authority to tell us when life really begins?"* This question must be answered with clarity because it's a matter of life and death. If man is his own authority on deciding when life begins or ends, then the 07/2006 stem cell research senate bill would never have overturned the divine laws of morality. Once again let's let the book speak for itself.

"The Spirit of God hath made me, and the breath of the Almighty hath given me life." [12]

According to the book of Job, which was written over five thousand years before Roe versus Wade, God is both the creator of man and the source of all human life. This means that God is the only One who has the right to begin or end a life. Our biggest problem is that we are living in a world where the liberal agenda is gaining momentum faster than a charging torpedo. Here is a statement from a well known liberal scholar ***"the mind is a terrible thing to waste on the idea that there is such a thing as a God who holds final authority in the arena of life."*** *(author unkown)*

The 07/2006 stem cell research senate bill finally leads us to the question, ***"Does the end justify the means?"*** I call this the ***"Adolf Hitler Doctrine."*** Adolf Hitler was determined to prove to the world that the Germans were the most superior race on earth. In a demonic quest, Hitler had no qualms about killing millions of innocent people to prove his point. Over fifty million people were killed in the first and second world wars before the Hitler doctrine was defeated by the Commonwealth of Nations.

The *"Adolf Hitler Doctrine"* has re-emerged in the form of wide spread terrorism against sovereign nations by terrorists who believe that the end justifies the means. This Hitler doctrine is empowering terrorists groups to raise companies of *willing and fanatical suicide bombers* who have no qualms about walking into a bus or a plane filled with innocent people and blowing themselves up to make a political statement. Welcome to the new world of terror!

The 07/2006 stem cell research senate bill, in its original version has made itself *"an involuntary ally of the Hitler doctrine."* The summation being, ***"if killing the embryo of an unborn child can save the lives of others then the end justifies the mad science."*** I do not agree with all the policies of the George W. Bush administration, but I was very proud of our President when he boldly vetoed the 07/2006 stem cell research senate bill, while advocating a moral approach to stem cell research.

For the Bush bashers, his veto of this bill just added more fuel to the fire. This was one more reason why George W. Bush should never have been President as far as they are concerned. But the President knew that even in times of transition in scientific research, ***"scientific research must never be allowed to destroy the sacred borders of divine morality."*** The President showcased beautiful babies who were born from frozen embryos that the advocates of this movement wanted to destroy in order to cure other diseases.

Even Bible believing Christians are torn over this issue. But we must never forget that demon powers can also hijack scientific and technological discovery that was designed by God to better human life and transform them into dark sciences. I really believe that there is a divine alternative to stem cell research that will allow scientists to create a cure for many diseases while maintaining the sacred borders of divine morality.

The Limitations of Transition

Another important aspect of transition that I must point out is simply this,

"Transition does not override absolute truths, principles and concepts that God has declared unchangeable in His word." There are certain truths, principles and concepts that God almighty in His infinite wisdom has declared unchangeable.

From the beginnings of time, the institution of marriage has always been between male and female. Even in the animal kingdom which is the lowest form of life, the marriage of male and female remains an unchangeable truth. The global liberal agenda has popularized the alternative lifestyles of homosexuality and lesbianism, while looking at the institution of marriage with unfeigned contempt.

Conservatives who ascribe to the ancient Judaic-biblical view of marriage as being between a man and a woman are being called *"Small minded religious bigots."* These secular prophets would have us believe that the definition of marriage must be altered to include the marriage between *"Adam and Steve." The only problem with this proposal is that God never intended to allow periods of transition, even in the growth of the cultures of nations to violate truths, principles and concepts that God has declared unchangeable in His word.*

Even though transition is God's brain child which He uses to bring about important changes in the spiritual direction of individuals and nations, transition does have its limitations. Transition can change governments, science, technology and cultures but it cannot change truths, principles and concepts which God has declared unchangeable in His word.

> *"Transition does not override absolute truths,*
> *principles and concepts that God has*
> *declared unchangeable in His word."*

In closing here is a summary of some of the important truths on transition that we have discussed in this chapter.

Principles of Transition

1. *Transition is the ancient bridge that divides the past from the future*
2. *Transition is both a spiritual and natural law*
3. *Transition is no respecter of persons*
4. *Transition will bless or empower anybody who yields to its power*
5. *Transition will destroy or handicap anyone who resists its power*
6. *Transition is the safest way to transfer governmental power and spiritual authority*
7. *Transition is the surest and safest way to end one season and begin another*
8. *Transition is the mother of change and the grandmother of progress*
9. *Transition does not negate or violate the laws of divine morality but rather enhances them.*
10. *Transition does not override absolute truths, principles and concepts that God has declared unchangeable in His word.*

Notes on Chapter Two

1. 1 Corinthians 13:11
2. Revelation 12:12
3. Matthew 24:37-38
4. Joshua 1:1-5
5. Joshua ?
6. John 16:13-14
7. Hebrews 11:3
8. John 6:51-55
9. 1 Corinthians 1:18-26
10. *John 3:3-5*
11. *Jeremiah 1:5*
12. *Job 33:4-5*

Chapter Three

The Powers of Transition

Before proceeding to analyze the spiritual dangers we are likely to face during periods of transition, I will dedicate this entire chapter to impressing upon you the vast powers of transition. In this chapter you will see the importance, the inevitability and blessings of transition. *It's impossible to respect anything whose power we are unsure of.* It's my prayer that this chapter will persuade you to become an ally and a champion of transition.

Transferring Power and Authority

I was born in Central Africa in a country called Zambia, before migrating to South Africa and then settling a couple years later in the United States. Having been born in Africa I know that the history of many African nations is a history tempered by horrific civil wars, hostile military takeovers and blatant financial corruption by top government and corporate leaders. Famed writer and leadership expert Dr. John C. Maxwell in his bestselling book, *"Developing The Leader Within You"* says that *"Everything rises and falls on leadership." Having lived in Africa I can attest to the truth of this statement.*

The United States of America definitely has its own share of moral and spiritual problems. But with all its faults, the United States has the best system of government in the history of the world. The system of government which the United States is founded upon places no one above the law of the land, including the President. One of the clearest marks of a mature democratic government is revealed in how it handles transition in government.

In the United States of America, every four years Americans go to the polling stations to vote for the next president of the free world. After winning the Electoral College vote, the President-elect has about two months to prepare to take the reigns of power. During those two months the President-elect has to choose his cabinet for his new administration. During those two months the President-elect has no functional political power to issue any Presidential veto or sign any bill into law. His powers are more Constitutional than Executorial because he or she has not yet been sworn into the office of the President of the United States by the Chief Justice of the Supreme Court. The two months before the President-elect is sworn into office is known as the period of the interim or transitional government.

During this transitional period, the outgoing President immediately turns into a transitional President. He becomes the President of a transitional or interim government. He or she is essentially a President who belongs to the past. *The task of the transitional President is to make sure that the transfer of power and authority between his outgoing administration and the incoming administration goes*

smoothly so that there are no unnecessary disruptions to the economy or politics of the nation.

In a volatile economy were the prices of currencies, stocks, securities and bonds can rise or drop significantly, based on how investors view the changes in government, its critical to navigate the valley of transition in government in the safest and smoothest way possible.

The transition between the Presidency of William Jefferson Clinton and that of George W. Bush was a very taxing and highly contested transition. George W. Bush and former Vice President Al Gore were both fighting over the results of the elections in some parts of Florida. Al Gore had won the popular vote but he needed to win the Electoral College votes for the State of Florida before he could claim the Presidency. After weeks of legal battles between the lawyers of the *"Bush Camp"* and the *"Gore Camp"* before the Supreme Court, the Supreme Court made a ruling that gave the Electoral College votes of the State of Florida to George W. Bush.

George W. Bush became the President Elect by the decision of the courts. Al Gore grudgingly conceded and gave his concession speech and in the spirit of true democracy, rallied the nation behind its new President. From that point on, the transition was relatively smooth. I watched the American political process unfold on television from the comfort of my house in Chicago.

I was very impressed that even though the elections were very contested and stirred bitter emotions among the electorate, there was no talk of civil war by either political party. I had just observed how mature democracies handled and navigated the valley of transition. ***I realized then that transition is the safest way to transfer power and authority***

between two governments. I had experienced the power of transition in the American political process.

On the other hand times of transition can also be very dangerous if the peoples involved do not respect the power of transition, as our case study will show.

CASE STUDY:
THE STORY OF THE RWANDAN GENOCIDE
(APRIL 6-JULY 2000)

Rwandan President Habyarimana and the Burundian President are killed when Habyarimana's plane is shot down near Kigali Airport. Hutu extremists, suspecting that the Rwandan president is finally about to implement the Arusha Peace Accords, are believed to be behind the attack. The killings begin that night.

The Rwandan Armed Forces (FAR) and Hutu militia (the interahamwe) set up roadblocks and go from house to house killing Tutsis and moderate Hutu politicians. Thousands die on the first day. Some U.N. camps shelter civilians, but most of the U.N. peacekeeping forces (UNAMIR—United Nations Assistance Mission in Rwanda) stand by while the slaughter goes on. They are forbidden to intervene, as this would breach their "monitoring" mandate.

On this day, ten Belgian soldiers with UNAMIR, assigned to guard the moderate Hutu Prime Minister, are tricked into giving up their weapons. They are tortured and murdered. France and Belgium send troops to rescue their citizens. American civilians are also airlifted out. No Rwandans are rescued, not even Rwandans employed by Western governments in their embassies, consulates, etc.

The International Red Cross estimates that tens of thousands of Rwandans have been murdered. At the Don

Bosco school, protected by Belgian UNAMIR soldiers, the number of civilians seeking refuge reaches 2,000. That afternoon, the U.N. soldiers are ordered to withdraw to the airport. Most of the civilians they abandon are killed. The U.N. Security Council votes unanimously to withdraw most of the UNAMIR troops, cutting the force from 2,500 to 270.

State Department spokeswoman Christine Shelley is asked whether what is happening in Rwanda is a genocide. She responds, **"...the use of the term 'genocide' has a very precise legal meaning, although it's not strictly a legal determination. There are other factors in there as well."**

However, a secret intelligence report by the State Department issued as early as the end of April calls the killings a genocide. Although disease and more killings claim additional lives in the refugee camps, the genocide is over. An estimated 800,000 Rwandans have been killed in 100 days. (http://www.pbs.org/wgbh/pages/frontline/shows/evil/etc/slaughter.html)

The Rwanda genocide raises critical questions about times of transition that must be answered with the accuracy of a brain surgeon. What went wrong? How could one million people be slaughtered like cows within100 days while the international community stood by? Why did political leaders argue about whether to call the massacre of thousands of innocent people a *"genocide or a riot?"*

Whatever your final analysis of this situation, you will have to admit that there is nothing as important as decisive leadership during periods of transition. You will have to admit that **in times of serious transition, political rhetoric or correctness is not even worth the paper it's written on if the leaders that be have no moral compass**

in the spirit of their character. President Bill Clinton and the United Nations Secretary General in their address to the parliament of Rwanda apologized for allowing themselves to be caught up in political rhetoric while Hutu extremists slaughtered innocent lives. For the million people whose bodies were now decomposing in the soil of the earth, the apologies of these two great world leaders had come 100 days too late!

Even though our previous case study shows us just how dangerous inaccurate transition can be, it does not in anyway negate the serious importance of transition in the life journey. *We must never forget that transition did not originate with man; it's always been God's idea. Transition is God's brainchild.* You see, transition is the safest and most effective way of transferring spiritual power and authority. Transferring natural power and authority incorrectly can have disastrous consequences. Transferring spiritual power and authority incorrectly is even more dangerous!

"The former treatise have I made, O Theophilus, of all that Jesus began both to do and teach, Until the day in which he was taken up, after that he through the Holy Ghost had given commandments unto the apostles whom he had chosen: To whom also he shewed himself alive after his passion by many infallible proofs, being seen of them forty days, and speaking of the things pertaining to the kingdom of God: And, being assembled together with them, commanded them that they should not depart from Jerusalem, but wait for the promise of the Father, which, saith he, ye have heard of me. But ye shall receive power, after that the Holy Ghost is come upon you: and ye shall be witnesses unto me both in Jerusalem, and in all

Judaea, and in Samaria, and unto the uttermost part of the earth" [1]

For over three years Jesus mentored a band of fishermen and tax collectors that he called the twelve disciples. This group made up mostly of unlearned men was destined to become the group of the founding apostles of the New Testament Church. They were going to be given the almost impossible task of convincing a nation of stiff-necked religious Jews that the era of the Mosaic Law had come to an end to give way to the day of grace.

These men were destined to become the authors of the entire New Testament and their writings would affect the spiritual destinies of millions and millions of people on the planet throughout eternity. They were going to be given the spiritual authority to exercise the power of the Kingdom of God. They would have power to heal and cast out devils. They were going to be given the apostolic commission to take the gospel of the Kingdom to every nation on earth. They would have the power to reshape the spiritual landscape of entire nations. *The spiritual task ahead of them was no child's play and Jesus, being the greatest leader on earth was not going to hand such power and authority to a group of men who had no clue as to how to handle this level of spiritual power and authority.*

For over three years, Jesus patiently took his disciples through a transitional period of fathering and mentoring. He destroyed the worldly notion that a leader is a replica of pharaohs from the past, pampered by a group of "yes men." He told them that in His Kingdom, the greatest of them all must become the greatest servant of all. He showed them how greed can corrupt a man of God and taught them to be aware of the leaven of the Pharisees. He taught them how to love each other and walk in integrity. He taught them about the heavenly Father and the governmental order of the Kingdom of God. He taught them how to cast out demons, heal the sick and carry out the Great Commission.

He prepared them for the persecutions that they were going to go through for His name's sake. He taught them about the importance and power of forgiveness. He taught them how to work with women in a culture that pretty much excluded women from spiritual ministry. The Lord Jesus left no stone unturned. After His resurrection from the dead, the Lord Jesus spent his final forty days on earth teaching and demonstrating the awesome power of the Kingdom that was about to come upon their lives. Jesus knew what every great leader knows; *"You cannot safely and effectively transfer power and authority without transition."*

"A Coup De tat is the bloodiest way to transfer power and authority."

When the day of Pentecost was fully come, the apostles received the promise of the Spirit in the upper room. The transitional period for their spiritual training had come to an end. The time for them to take the reigns of power in the church had begun. In the four gospels, all the miracles that took place were centered around the Lord Jesus. But after the end of the transitional period in the book of Acts, the miracles of God were now centered around the lives of the apostles. The extraordinary miracles of God were now flowing through the hands of these ordinary men.

"And by the hands of the apostles were many signs and wonders wrought among the people; (and they were all with one accord in Solomon's porch)"[2]

Coup De tat

Whenever political power and authority changes hands without transition in the political arena, it's called a *"Coup De tat." A Coup De tat is the violent overthrow of a legitimate government elected by the people, by power hungry insurgents. I have also seen this "Coup De tat" spirit manifest itself in most church splits or hostile corporate takeovers.* In most cases Coup De tats are carried out by the military. A Coup De tat is the bloodiest way to transfer power and authority. Wherever there has been a Coup De tat, the new government has been formed on the blood of innocent people and the new regime rules by the gun and not by the consensus of the general public. Having been raised in Africa, I am no stranger to the emotional turmoil, economic disruption and fear that the violent overthrow of a legitimate government brings to an entire nation.

The world was stunned when civil war broke out over the transfer of power in the African nation of Rwanda. While the world watched, over five hundred thousand people were killed through a machinery of meticulous ethnic cleansing. The streets of Rwanda were painted dark red with the blood of people killed during the civil unrest. By the time the civil war was over, close to a million people had been killed and the stench of death filled the air. By the time the United Nations and the rest of the international community intervened, there were mass graves every where. It was one of the worst cases of genocide and ethnic cleansing in the history of the world. The block-buster movie *"Hotel Rwanda"* starring Don Cheadle was very moving indeed. I cried as I watched the movie and contemplated the senseless loss of lives which took place because people refused to respect the immutable law of transition.

The Bible is filled with men and women who tried to seize the reigns of power without respecting the law of transition and the end results were spiritually disastrous. Most of these unhealthy transitions resulted in the loss of many lives. The one that quickly comes to mind is the story of Absalom, the spoiled son of King David.

"And Absalom rose up early, and stood beside the way of the gate: and it was so, that when any man that had a controversy came to the king for judgment, then Absalom called unto him, and said, Of what city art thou? And he said, Thy servant is of one of the tribes of Israel. And Absalom said unto him, See, thy matters are good and right; but there is no man deputed of the king to hear thee. Absalom said moreover, Oh that I were made judge in the land, that every man which hath any suit or cause might come unto me, and I would do him justice! And it was so, that when any man came nigh to him to do him obeisance, he put forth his hand, and took him, and kissed him. And on this manner did Absalom to all Israel that came to the king for judgment: so Absalom stole the hearts of the men of Israel."[3]

It took about thirteen years of transition for King David to assume the throne of Israel after the Prophet Samuel anointed him to be the king. (1 Sam 16:1-10). Several of those years were spent in the house of King Saul and the remaining years were spent running from King Saul. During those formative years, God built into David all the spiritual leadership traits that he was going to need when he assumed the throne. But when his son Absalom decided he wanted to ascend to the throne of power, he completely sidestepped the process of ascending into power or prominence God's way.

Instead of waiting on God, Absalom chose to seize the reigns of power through manipulation and deceit. He would sit by the gates to the City of David to intercept anyone who had a matter to bring before the King. Absalom would hear their cases and give them his own version of how he would rule on their behalf if he were made King of Israel. ***What Absalom did not understand is that men do not make kings; kings are crafted by the hand of God.***

When Absalom saw that he had turned the hearts of a majority of Israelites towards himself, he went to Hebron and declared himself king. He then marched on to the City of David with his own military, determined to kill and overthrow his own father. When David heard of it, he and his household along with his mighty men of war fled the city before Absalom besieged it.

Absalom, emboldened by what he perceived was King David's retreat, pursued after him. Absalom made all the mistakes and miscalculations of a novice in the field of battle. David's mighty men of war began to slaughter Absalom's unseasoned warriors like house flies. When Absalom realized that the war had turned against him, he fled for his life on his horse. While fleeing for his life, his hair was caught in the branches of a tree as his horse galloped on. Absalom was left hanging from a tree by his hair. When Joab found him, he struck three spears through him and killed him. Joab, then buried him under a heap of stones.

"For the battle was there scattered over the face of all the country: and the wood devoured more people that day than the sword devoured. And Absalom met the servants of David. And Absalom rode upon a mule, and the mule went under the thick boughs of a great oak, and his head caught hold of the oak, and he was taken up between the heaven and the earth; and the mule that was under him went away. Then said Joab, I may not tarry thus with thee. And he took three darts in his hand, and thrust them through the heart of Absalom, while he was yet alive in the midst of the oak. And they took Absalom, and cast him into a great pit in the wood, and laid a very great heap of stones upon him: and all Israel fled every one to his tent"⁴

It's ironic that Absalom the son of a King who violated the law of transition was buried under a heap of stones when it was all over. I really believe that God was using Absalom's story to warn those who desire to come into power to respect the law of transition, unless they want to end up under a pile of stones. Unfortunately, Absalom did not die alone. Thousands of innocent Israelites who had followed his short-lived reign died like flies in the woodlands. The woodlands were covered with streams of blood because they followed a leader who had violated the law of transition.

Over the years I have seen great churches split in half because of ambitious elders or deacons who wanted to become senior pastors overnight without going through proper transition in their leadership development. I have also heard of major corporations that have been destroyed by hostile takeover bids by ambitious board members who wanted to become overnight CEOs without going through the proper channels. Senior pastors and business owners must be very careful that they do not hand over spiritual authority and power prematurely to men and women in their churches or business organizations whose competency and loyalty have not been proven. Leaders must establish a transitional period to test and see if the people they are trying to promote are really ready to handle the reigns of power. *In our hurry to fill certain positions in the church or business organization, we may place people in power who don't have our spirit and our best interest at heart.* When our ministry or company hits a bump in the road, these same people we put in power could be the first ones to rise against us.

When I planted my church in Texas, I brought an associate pastor to work by my side whom I had not really proven. He was a very nice man, but we had never worked together under pressure. *Anyone who has ever been in church planting will be quick to tell you that the first two years of a new church plant are painted with pressure.* As the pressure of pioneering a new work mounted, I quickly realized that we had very different views about how to build the ministry. Needless to say, our time together was filled with constant strife and unnecessary misunderstandings. It wasn't long before we both were emotionally tired and spiritually disillusioned.

"Leaders must establish a transitional period to test and see if the people they are trying to promote are really ready to handle the reigns of power."

While I was praying, the Lord showed me that I had violated the law of transition and I was paying dearly for it. I finally told this man that either the dynamics of our relationship must change or he and his family must leave.

He chose to resign and I was happy to let him go. After he and his family left, the sense of relief I felt was amazing and the church began to grow almost immediately. God began to bring new people to the church. I must point out that my associate and his family were not bad people at all. They are a good and God fearing family, but I had violated the law of transition when I put too much spiritual authority and power upon them before they had been proven ready for the task.

Ending One Season to Begin Another

"To every thing there is a season, and a time to every purpose under the heaven: A time to be born, and a time to die; a time to plant, and a time to pluck up that which is planted; A time to kill, and a time to heal; a time to break down, and a time to build up; A time to weep, and a time to laugh; a time to mourn, and a time to dance;"[5]

Transition is not only the safest way to transfer power and authority, it's also the surest and most effective way to close one spiritual season and open up another. There are two classes of people that we are going to have relationships with in our spiritual pilgrimage here on earth, those who are *"called to us"* and those who are *"called through us."* Those who are called to us are people whose very calling in life is to work and walk with us to the finish line. They have our same type of spiritual DNA. They are just as passionate about the things we care about. They gladly share in our vision for the future.

An example of this type of relationship is our spouses. People may come and go, but our spouses are bound by the covenant of marriage to stay with us to the finish line.

On the other hand, people who are *"called through us"* are in the majority. These are people who will work and walk with us in our spiritual journey towards our prophetic destiny for a certain period of time. Some of these people will start out with us and then move on at some point in our prophetic journey. Some will join us when we are half way to our destiny and so forth. Some will join us at the tail end of our spiritual journey. *We must allow everybody to be a blessing to our ministry during their allotted time of destiny and then send them with a blessing when their spiritual season expires.*

God is a God of purpose. Everything He does is done by purpose for a purpose. *God only brings people into our lives in the spirit of purpose. Once the people have fulfilled God's purpose for being in our life, God will instigate a time of transition to move them out of our lives.* In most cases, these people will suddenly lose the spiritual passion they once had for our vision and become more and more distracted. The problem we have is that instead of recognizing this period as a divinely orchestrated time of transition, we begin to do everything humanly possible to hold on to the relationship. At this point, we find ourselves on the wrong side of the law of transition and when this happens things can get real messy.

We quickly discover that the people who had been such a blessing to us in the past now become a pain in the neck because we have forced them to overstay their season of purpose. By the time we finally decide to let them go, what was left of the relationship is now in ruins. This normally happens because the flesh loves to hold on to things, even when it is getting nothing in return. Once we become allies of transition we are not going to lose relationships with people whose season to move on has come. *We must spiritually mature to the point where we can celebrate people's entry into our lives as well us their exit, especially when we know that the Lord's hand is in it.* Why should we demonize people once they exit our lives when they had given us many years of fruitful service in the past? This is very immature and inaccurate behavior.

Every relationship on the planet has an expiratory date on it, even the ones with our wives and family. The day finally came when Solomon had to let go of his father, King David, as he passed into eternity. David's wife, Bathsheba, also had to let him go. This is life. It's no big mystery and yet thousands of people in our world fail to successfully handle transition in relationships. Jesus himself rebuked his disciples for grieving because He had just told them that He was going to leave them in order to allow the Holy Spirit to take His place.

"But now I go my way to him that sent me; and none of you asketh me, Whither goest thou? But because I have said these things unto you, sorrow hath filled your heart. Nevertheless I tell you the truth; It is expedient for you that I go away: for if I go not away, the Comforter will not come unto you; but if I depart, I will send him unto you. And when he is come, he will reprove the world of sin, and of righteousness, and of judgment:"[6]

Jesus knew that His season of ministry with the disciples here on earth was coming to an abrupt end. He began to talk to His disciples about the Holy Spirit much more often than He spoke of Himself. He knew that their next level of ministry was not with Him but with the Holy Spirit. Jesus told them that it was more important and beneficial for them if He left than for Him to remain. This is a very serious statement for us to consider because it reveals the powers of transition in a very striking way. ***What Jesus was saying to the disciples was simply this, "I have to obey the law of transition or the Holy Spirit will never come to the earth!"*** *Even for Jesus, transition was the surest and most effective way of closing one spiritual season to enter another!*

> ***"We must spiritually mature to the point where we can celebrate people's entry into our lives as well us their exit"***

Transferring the Inheritance

In the story of the of the prodigal son, Jesus showed His listening audience the dangers of demanding our spiritual inheritance when there has not been a transitional period to prepare for it. The younger son came to his father and demanded that the father give him his inheritance. His father gave him his inheritance and the prodigal son went to a far country and wasted it on riotous living. He had the inheritance but he had not allowed God to prepare him to handle the inheritance. (Luke 15:22-30).

"Now I say, That the heir, as long as he is a child, differeth nothing from a servant, though he be lord of all; But is under tutors and governors until the time appointed of the father. Even so we, when we were children, were in bondage under the elements of the world:"[7]

According to the Semitic tradition that the apostle Paul describes in this passage of scripture, a future heir during the transitional period was no different from a common slave. While one remains a child, they have no meaningful rights to the inheritance. During the transitional period, the father would place the child under tutors and governors whose meticulous task was to teach the future heir how to behave and manage their father's estate.

These tutors and governors would teach the future heir the sciences, mathematics, accounting, social protocol, politics and religion in order for them to be well vested in all matters of business and take their place in society. Once the father was convinced that his son had matured and become a man, he would call for a huge celebration. He would invite his friends and neighbors and then publicly adopt or beget his own son. At that point, the son has as much authority as the father does in deciding how to use the inheritance or the father's estate.

Transition: A Governing Law of God

Transition finds its greatest power in the fact that it is not just an event, it's an immutable spiritual and natural law of God. Fighting against it is futile and dangerous. Like any real law, transition will bless those who yield to its power and destroy or maim those who dare resist its power.

Since transition is a spiritual and natural law, it is no respecter of persons. It affects kings and queens in exquisite castles as much as it affects the common man on the streets. Without the law of transition, people and things would remain in the same spiritual state and natural condition forever. Imagine a two-year-old baby trapped in the body of a six-foot man because there has never been any transitional intellectual growth over the years. It would be pathetic. God uses the law of transition whenever He wants to bring those to the forefront whom He has found faithful on the backside of the desert like Moses (Exodus 3). Through the law of spiritual transition, Moses went from a fugitive to a mighty deliverer of Israel. Through the law of transition, David went from being a forgotten shepherd boy to the most beloved King and warrior of Israel.

Transition is the birth canal of every prophetic word and promise that comes out of the mouth of God. In the Garden of Eden, God prophesied Satan's doom through the coming of a violent seed (Christ) of the Kingdom through the loins of a woman.

"And the LORD God said unto the serpent, Because thou hast done this, thou art cursed above all cattle, and above every beast of the field; upon thy belly shalt thou go, and dust shalt thou eat all the days of thy life: And I will put enmity between thee and the woman, and between thy seed and her seed; it shall bruise thy head, and thou shalt bruise his heel"[8]

There was a transitional period of about four thousand years from the time that God prophesied Satan's doom until the time it actually happened. During this period, God began to prepare the world for a coming Messiah. Through a system of burnt offerings and sacrifices, God was preparing the world for a Savior who would sacrifice Himself for the sins of the entire world.

> *"Like any real law, transition will bless those who yield to its power and destroy or maim those who dare resist its power."*

God showed pieces of the redemptive puzzle to different prophets in each dispensation, like an accomplished builder laying brick upon brick. The transitional period was not God's way of delaying His prophetic promise; it was the unveiling of His perfect plan of redemption. The transitional period was the baking oven for what God intended to do in the future destiny. ***When the transitional period came to an end, Jesus was born in Bethlehem in a manger.*** The fullness of time had come and the transitional period for the Genesis three prophecies came to an abrupt end.

"Even so we, when we were children, were in bondage under the elements of the world: But when the fullness of the time was come, God sent forth his Son, made of a woman, made under the law, to redeem them that were under the law, that we might receive the adoption of sons."[9]

Notes on Chapter Three

1. Acts 1:1-8, 2. Acts 5:12, 3. 2 Sam 15:2-6, 4. 2 Sam 18:8-9,14-17, 5. Eccl 3:1-4
6. John 16:5-8, 7. Gal 4:1-3, 8. Gen 3:14-15, 9. Gal 4:3-5

Chapter Four

Demonic Abortion
of the Holy Seed

ॐ

*F*rom *this chapter forward, we will explore the spiritual and social dangers of transition more fully. These are the dangers that we are likely to face during periods of transition.* When professional mountain climbers embark on climbing a dangerous and notorious mountain, they first take time to thoroughly examine the mountain terrain and the surrounding natural landscape. They study weather patterns that are unique to that particular mountain in order to prepare them for what might be lying ahead as they ascend to higher altitudes.

They measure the height of the mountain to determine how long it will take for them to get to the top. This thorough examination of the mountain terrain helps these seasoned mountain climbers to become fully aware of the potential dangers that awaits them in order to reach their designation successfully.

Immature and unseasoned climbers on the other hand, refuse to take the time to deal with all of these seemingly wasteful details. They fail to appreciate the importance of preparing themselves more thoroughly because they believe that their passion will compensate for their apparent lack of training in mountain climbing. They fail to realize just how dangerous and strenuous mountain climbing really is. Sadly, many become victims of the unforgiving mountain terrain and the inclement weather it entertains. Some mountains are smeared with the blood of these presumptuous climbers as a warning to all those who have no respect for the mountain. In the following chapters we will thoroughly examine the spiritual and social dangers that we will face during periods of transition.

I feel the need at this point to clearly define my use of the term *"Prophetic"* in this writing and its contextual role in this teaching on transition. I am very much aware that God's family is like a beautiful rainbow consisting of precious children of God with differing spiritual views and persuasions but united by their common belief in Christ as the Savior of the world. It's my deepest prayer to the Lord that Satan will not cloud this book in religious controversy or bigotry. This book was written for every person, church and business organization who desires to become skilled at navigating times of transition more successfully. I have lived long enough to know that transition affects every person on the planet regardless of their religious beliefs.

In his bestselling book *"The Purpose Driven Life"* our brother Rick Warren has shown us that we were all created by God for a purpose. He has shown us that God had a very specific purpose and plan for our life before He created us. If we truly believe these truths so graciously shared with us by our brother Rick Warren, then we are *"Prophetic"*. If we believe that God has a sure plan for our life, business or church before we fully know what it is, then we are prophetic in this sense. In this regard, all of God's dear children no matter their differing spiritual persuasions are all prophetic as far as the Bible is concerned. I want to go on record that I have used the terms *"prophetic or prophetic anointing"* within this light and context.

One of the most critical dangers we are most likely to face during times of spiritual transition is "The danger of aborting our prophetic destiny and calling."

You Have a Prophetic Destiny and Calling.

"Unless you assume a God, the question of life's purpose is meaningless."

(Bertrand Russell, atheist)

"You were made by God and for God— and until you understand that, life will never make sense."
(Excerpt from The Purpose Driven Life, by Rick Warren)

Every walking, breathing and talking being on the planet has a specific prophetic destiny and calling that is hidden in Christ in God. God, through His foreknowledge, planned the course of our lives from before the foundation of the world. Whether we know this or not does not in any way negate the validity of this statement. *We were all made by God and for God. We were created to fulfill His purpose which is in accordance with the counsel of His own will.* Everything about us was deliberately designed by God and then integrated into the very fiber of our being to help us fulfill God's specific purpose for our life. If our purpose for living involves an active role in singing, we will find within ourselves certain unexplainable inward tendencies or inclinations towards music and all it entails.

Our vocal chords will, more often than not, carry a tune well without any such practice. I call this the *"inherent nature of purpose."*

"Then the word of the LORD came unto me, saying, Before I formed thee in the belly I knew thee; and before thou camest forth out of the womb I sanctified thee, and I ordained thee a prophet unto the nations. Then said I, Ah, Lord GOD! behold, I cannot speak: for I am a child. But the LORD said unto me, Say not, I am a child: for thou shalt go to all that I shall send thee, and whatsoever I command thee thou shalt speak"[1]

Every person born of a woman was born with a specific prophetic destiny, but few ever find the power and grace to become all that God intended. For a variety of reasons, many fall by the way side pulverized or sidetracked by the circumstances which they encountered in this world. Some people are like the young Jeremiah who discovered that there was a call of God upon his life, but felt inadequate to fulfill it.

> *"During periods of transition, bad things may happen to godly people but this is no reason to abort the call of God upon our lives."*

My assignment in this book is to shed some light on why many who are called by God to a specific purpose, never arrive at the finish line. We will examine how Satan manipulates circumstances to force God's people into a position of defeat. ***We will see how the devil drives God's people into making choices which leads to the demonic abortion of their prophetic purpose.*** The moral founda-

tion of American society is eroding because of an explo-
sion in the growth of the abortion culture. As serious as this
is, I am far more concerned about the thousands of God's
people who are aborting their purpose for living because
they cannot handle the periods of transition that may come
their way. During periods of transition, bad things may
happen to godly people but this is no reason to abort the
call of God upon our lives.

Demonic Alliances

*"But it came to pass, when Ahab was dead, that the king
of Moab rebelled against the king of Israel. And king
Jehoram went out of Samaria the same time, and numbered
all Israel. And he went and sent to Jehoshaphat the king of
Judah, saying, The king of Moab hath rebelled against me:
wilt thou go with me against Moab to battle? And he said,
I will go up: I am as thou art, my people as thy people, and
my horses as thy horses"²*

The tale of the three kings, Jeroboam, Jehoshaphat
and the King of Edom who formed an alliance to fight
against the King of the Moabites for rebelling against the
King of Israel, will be our guinea pig story to help us see
why many of God's people abort their prophetic destinies
during times of transition.

I once heard a ministry acquaintance of mine, Dr. Mike
Murdock, make the statement, *"Relationships are like the
currents of a river. They will either take you toward your
goals and dreams or away from them."* I wonder what
relational currents are flowing through your life this very
moment. I wonder what kind of influence they are having
on your life and on your ability to live out your prophetic

destiny. In my many years of apostolic service to the Lord, *I have come to the sobering conclusion that the social and spiritual alliances we have with certain people can place the sentence of death upon our lives or release us into the greatest spiritual breakthroughs of our lifetime.* We will fully explore the impact that relationships have upon our lives during periods of transition in a later chapter.

After the death of King Ahab, the passive and puppet husband of the wicked prophetess Jezebel, his son Jeroboam assumed the throne. The King of Moab who was the King of a tribute nation, rebelled against the authority of the king of Israel and stopped paying his annual tribute. King Jeroboam responded by numbering Israel so he could see how many men he had who could carry a sword or throw a spear. After the census, the king of Israel realized that he did not have enough manpower to secure a convincing victory. Out of political necessity he solicited the help of the kings of Judah and of Edom.

Jehoshaphat was the reigning king over the tribe of Judah when he received news that the king of Israel needed his help to bring the Moabites back into subjection. The Bible tells us that King Jehoshaphat loved God dearly and did his best to walk in righteousness. He was the descendant of the great King David.

Nevertheless, he made a tragic mistake when he formed a political and military alliance with the king of Israel because he failed to ask for God's guidance. The king of Israel was a practicing idol worshipper. This practice made him an easy prey for the devil. His idolatrous lifestyle had already conjured up demons from the underworld and these unclean spirits attached and aligned themselves with everything he did. Simply stated, the king of

Israel carried the sentence of death upon his life because of his very sinful lifestyle.

When King Jehoshaphat came into a spiritual alliance with the king of Israel, he got more than he bargained for. The same spirits of darkness that were operating freely in Jeroboam's life began to gain entrance to his life as well. This spiritual alliance with the king of Israel had exposed him to unnecessary attacks of the enemy. Had it not been for the intervention of the prophet Elisha, King Jehoshaphat would have died in a war that God had never called him to fight.

I have seen many God fearing and God loving believers in Christ lose their way and the pursuit of their destiny because of wrong earthly associations during periods of transition. They came into spiritual alliances with people who were not living for God. During periods of transition, the devil will do his best to force us to establish spiritual alliances with people who are not of the same spiritual persuasion or faith. These alliances are lethal in every sense of the word. They have the potential of seriously derailing us from pursuing our prophetic purpose. *In our loneliness or desire to succeed, we may enter into spiritual or business alliances with people God is not connecting us to, simply because we don't want to fail or be alone.*

Programmed For Defeat

"So the king of Israel went, and the king of Judah, and the king of Edom: and they fetched a compass of seven days' journey: and there was no water for the host, and for the cattle that followed them. And the king of Israel said, Alas! that the LORD hath called these three kings together, to deliver them into the hand of Moab! But Jehoshaphat

127

said, Is there not here a prophet of the LORD, that we may inquire of the LORD by him? And one of the king of Israel's servants answered and said, Here is Elisha the son of Shaphat, which poured water on the hands of Elijah"[3]

When the three kings led their forces into battle, they got lost in the desert of Edom and couldn't find their way. For seven days they wandered about in hostile and dry terrain. The land was very dry and virtually inhabitable. The lack of water quickly drove their thirsty men of war into physical exhaustion. These three kings had been in enough battles to know that thirsty and physically exhausted soldiers were, for all practical purposes, useless against an invading horde of well-rested enemy combatants.

To make matters worse, the lack of water was slowly killing their most important asset and arsenal - their horses were dying a slow death. This was further compounded by the emotional tension and the demonic attacks on their minds that they had to deal with. Ironically, the king of Israel who had initiated the war in the first place was the first one to crack under the ensuing pressure.

My good friend Dr. Bobby Johnson, has a saying, *"You will only know people when they are under pressure, because what people have under pressure is the best they have!"* My friend Bobby is a former basketball player who coined this core belief during his basketball days. I have come to the sobering conclusion that he is one hundred percent right, especially as I have observed how different people react under pressure.

"During periods of transition, the devil will do his best to force us to establish spiritual alliances with people who are not of the same spiritual persuasion."

Under the ensuing pressure the king of Israel began to reveal what was already a settled matter in his heart. He had not for one moment believed that they were going to defeat the Moabites. From the moment he discovered that he did not have enough manpower to destroy the king of Moab, his heart was set on failure.

Nevertheless, he conveniently put on a *"political face"* in front of the other two kings, which masked his true fears. How ironic that politicians have always known how to put up a false front. Only God and the devil knew the real truth. *God knew that the king of Israel was sweating profusely under his royal robes. He was terrified of the possibility of defeat and was very afraid of being captured.* He must have been asking himself, *"What will my enemies do to me if I am captured?"*

From a distance you would not have guessed just how terrified he was. But after seven days of wandering and searching for water ended in futility, the pressure and the thoughts of possible torture and execution at the hands of his enemies was simply too much to bear. The sounds of the tired groans of his men and the whining of the horses must have been more than he could bear. *Abandoning his cosmetic sense of confidence, the king of Israel stunned the kings of Judah and Edom when he confessed that he really did not believe that they were going to win the battle.*

The king of Israel had allowed the adverse circumstances to reprogram his mind for defeat and he was zealously selling his mentality of defeat to his already weary soldiers. How many soldiers do you think will put up a good fight once they hear their commander in chief blatantly confessing defeat? *During periods of transition, Satan will try to manipulate us into situations where he can force us to form spiritual alliances with people or business associates who are programmed for defeat.*

If the corridors of history could speak, they would tell us of the millions of spiritual destines that were annihilated or exterminated because of wrong alliances with people who were programmed for defeat. This is why I personally will not allow anybody, whether he or she is a brother or sister in Christ, to get too close to me if they are constantly confessing defeat.

I cannot listen to negative confession and still have the energy to pursue the great dreams which God has placed inside my heart. *A defeatist mentality can paralyze any move towards destiny. It's as lethal as pouring cyanide into ones blood stream and then wondering why the heart stopped beating.* A defeatist mentality, if not quickly arrested, can spread through the entire body (church, organization or family) like a malignant cancer, sucking the life out of every cell that it touches. It has to be stopped and amputated at the root or the demonic abortion of the prophetic destiny is inevitable. The confessions of the king of Israel were demoralizing the whole camp and sucking the spirit of victory out of the atmosphere.

Faulty Navigation Tools

If the creatures of the ocean could talk, they would tell us of the final hours of many exploration ships who lost their way on the vast seas and how the crew died. They would tell us of how quickly drunken sailors sobered up when they realized that they were lost at sea and that their food and water reserves were rapidly being extinguished. They would tell us of how angry sailors abandoned their stations and attacked their captains for failing to safely navigate them to safety. If only the oceans could talk...

History books tell us that during 1400-1850 AD, there was a mad rush by explorers and sailors from Europe who captained ships in search of distant shores for the purpose of colonization. As with any mad rush, the madness quickly caught on and the number of casualties began to rise steadily.

The deep seas held no prisoners and issued immediate death sentences to all who were swallowed by its fury. In the haste to find undiscovered lands, many explorers and sailors seriously underestimated the resources that they were going to need to successfully navigate the unforgiving ocean terrain. Little did they know that the moment they set sail and entered the ocean terrain, they were going to be in transition until they arrived at the distant shores. They forgot, or simply did not realize that proper navigational tools are the greatest allies anyone can have during times of transition.

After many ships had been lost and destroyed and thousands of sailors had died at sea, the mad rush waned down as the sailors and explorers gained a new respect for the unforgiving ocean terrain. They started giving serious attention to their navigational tools and their explorations became more and more successful.

"And he said, Which way shall we go up? And he answered, The way through the wilderness of Edom. So the king of Israel went, and the king of Judah, and the king of Edom: and they fetched a compass of seven days' journey: and there was no water for the host, and for the cattle that followed them. And the king of Israel said, Alas! that the LORD hath called these three kings together, to deliver them into the hand of Moab!"[4]

Not only did the king of Israel have a defeatist mentality, he also was a terrible navigator. When King Jehoshaphat asked the king of Israel from which direction they were going to attack the enemy, he simply took the direction that easily came to his mind with an obvious military strategy. He had never bothered to get the map of the wilderness of Edom or he would have known that it was mostly desert terrain. The king of Israel placed his trust in a simple compass and when it malfunctioned, he was stuck. The biggest problem with his navigational strategy was the fact that he was relying on something totally physical in nature and did not consider any spiritual aspects of his dilemma. The devil had him exactly were he wanted him. He was a sitting duck ready for the slaughter.

He chose the guidance of a compass above the supernatural guidance of God. It was customary for the kings of Israel to seek God's counsel before going to war. They understood that as God's covenant people, the battle was not theirs but the Lord's. In the history of the kings of Israel, *King David was the only king who never lost a battle till the day he died! He knew the importance of seeking God's counsel before entering into any battle.* God would give him specific prophetic strategies which David employed with stunning success. (1 Sam 30:1-12).

Nevertheless, when the king of Israel ventured into war, he was depending entirely on the counsel of his men of war and the compass which he held in his hands. *During periods of transition the devil will try to deceive us into thinking that we can navigate the valley of transition through the arm of the flesh. This is a very toxic pill to swallow.* We must trust God and not lean on our own understanding. Our well intentioned board meetings and comeback strategies will end in defeat if they are not sanctioned by God.

Nothing in the physical realm, from college degrees to vast amounts of money, will be sufficient enough to take us through the valley of spiritual transition. We need spiritual navigational tools in order to successfully navigate a spiritual transition. If we insist on trusting in the arm of the flesh, we may find ourselves seriously derailed from the path of fulfilling our prophetic destiny.

Navigating the valley of spiritual transition using faulty navigational tools can prove stressful and may have disastrous consequences. We may end up spending money on projects we were never called to finance, or find ourselves wasting time and energy praying and fasting for things that we were never called to have. All of these unnecessary things can weigh us down to such a degree that they seriously tax our spiritual energy, leaving us helpless to fight for our true purpose. Untold millions have abandoned the prophetic call upon their lives because they are spiritually burned out and physically exhausted.

> *"During periods of transition the devil will try to deceive us into thinking that we can navigate the valley of transition through the arm of the flesh."*

The Power of a Prophetic Word

"But Jehoshaphat said, Is there not here a prophet of the LORD, that we may inquire of the LORD by him? And one of the king of Israel's servants answered and said, Here is Elisha the son of Shaphat, which poured water on the hands of Elijah. And Jehoshaphat said, The word of the LORD is with him. So the king of Israel and Jehoshaphat

and the king of Edom went down to him. And Elisha said unto the king of Israel, What have I to do with thee? get thee to the prophets of thy father, and to the prophets of thy mother. And the king of Israel said unto him, Nay: for the LORD hath called these three kings together, to deliver them into the hand of Moab. And Elisha said, As the LORD of hosts liveth, before whom I stand, surely, were it not that I regard the presence of Jehoshaphat the king of Judah, I would not look toward thee, nor see thee"[5] "But Jehoshaphat said, Is there not here a prophet of the LORD, that we may inquire of the LORD by him? And one of the king of Israel's servants answered and said, Here is Elisha the son of Shaphat, which poured water on the hands of Elijah. And Jehoshaphat said, The word of the LORD is with him. So the king of Israel and Jehoshaphat and the king of Edom went down to him. And Elisha said unto the king of Israel, What have I to do with thee? get thee to the prophets of thy father, and to the prophets of thy mother. And the king of Israel said unto him, Nay: for the LORD hath called these three kings together, to deliver them into the hand of Moab. And Elisha said, As the LORD of hosts liveth, before whom I stand, surely, were it not that I regard the presence of Jehoshaphat the king of Judah, I would not look toward thee, nor see thee"[5]

When King Jehoshaphat could no longer stand the defeatist confessions of the king of Israel and the spiritual atmosphere of disaster that his words were beginning to precipitate, King Jehoshaphat began to shift their spiritual position. He asked to see if they could find a true prophet of God who could tell them what God was saying concerning their situation.

The king of Judah knew that the prophetic anointing could shed light on their predicament. He knew that the word of the Lord could turn their situation around and break the sentence of death which had come upon them! One of the servants of the king of Israel quickly mentioned the name of Elisha. He mockingly called Elisha *"Elijah's Water boy."* Little did he realize that in God's Kingdom, *the anointing you serve is the anointing that stays on your life!* Nevertheless, Jehoshaphat knew that if Elisha had served the prophet Elijah faithfully, the anointing and mantle of the prophet Elijah was surely upon him.

King Jehosphaphat led the other two kings to the door-steps of the aging prophet. When the prophet Elisha saw the king of Israel, he became furious. *Elisha could discern the presence of demons in the life of the king of Israel. Elisha knew that the king of Israel had a demonic alliance with spirits of darkness and that he had no connection with the God of Israel.* A spirit of heaviness was upon the king of Israel to such a degree that Elisha struggled to flow in his prophetic gift. He solicited the assistance of an anointed psalmist to come and play for him so he could connect with God and declare the word of the Lord. While the psalmist was playing before the Lord, God's presence descended upon Elisha and he began to prophesy.

"But now bring me a minstrel. And it came to pass, when the minstrel played, that the hand of the LORD came upon him. And he said, Thus saith the LORD, Make this valley full of ditches. For thus saith the LORD, Ye shall not see wind, neither shall ye see rain; yet that valley shall be filled with water, that ye may drink, both ye, and your cattle, and your beasts. And this is but a light thing in the sight of the LORD: he will deliver the Moabites also into your hand.

And ye shall smite every fenced city, and every choice city, and shall fell every good tree, and stop all wells of water, and mar every good piece of land with stones"[6]

The powerful prophetic word cancelled the negative words of the king of Israel and established a new position of victory for them in the spirit world. The prophet Elisha told them to go and dig ditches in the valley of Edom and God was going to supernaturally fill these ditches with fresh water. Their thirsty men of war and their horses would be refreshed.

The prophet of God proceeded to tell them, that the supernatural supply of water filling their ditches was the simplest part of the prophetic promise. The most significant aspect was the promise of total victory over the Moabites. *Elisha told them that the prophetic word of God was going to give them the grace to prevail over their enemies and a new spiritual position to take back the cities, which had previously belonged to their enemies.*

One prophetic word from the mouth of God had cancelled their past and put victory within their reach. This is why we need to strive to maintain the prophetic anointing upon our lives during times of transition. The prophetic anointing can help us reclaim our future when we cannot see our way forward. If we abandon or neglect the prophetic anointing, we will surely suffer shipwreck and abort our prophetic destiny. *We must never forget that the Holy Spirit is a prophetic spirit; He longs to give us eyes which can see through the present crisis to what awaits us on the other side of our transition.*

Once the prophetic word had reestablished their spiritual destiny, God proceeded to use the water which had been produced by the prophetic word as a supernatural optical illusion to lure the enemy into the battlefield. Early the following morning when the Moabites woke up and looked over the valley of Edom, they were astonished at what they saw. The water which had filled the ditches in the valley appeared like a sea of blood from where the Moabites were standing. It was an optical illusion of the God kind.

The Moabites started rejoicing and concluded that the three kings had argued and then turned on each and fought to the death. The Moabites rushed into the valley of Edom carelessly (most of them were unarmed) thinking that they were just going into the valley to pick up the spoils of war. They got the shock of their lives when they got into the camp of the Israelites and discovered to their great dismay that what they thought was blood was actually water. It was too late to retreat; they were surrounded immediately by the armies of the three kings who began to slaughter them like house flies.

"The prophetic anointing can help us reclaim our future when we cannot see our way forward."

Energized by the power of the prophetic word, the armies of the three kings began to overthrow the cities of Moab, uprooting every good tree just like the prophet of God had said would happen. In the heat of the moment, the armies of the three kings couldn't do anything wrong. Everything was going their way because God was on their side and it could have continued that way, except...

The Spirit of Abortion

"And when the king of Moab saw that the battle was too sore for him, he took with him seven hundred men that drew swords, to break through even unto the king of Edom: but they could not. Then he took his eldest son that should have reigned in his stead, and offered him for a burnt offering upon the wall. And there was great indignation against Israel: and they departed from him, and returned to their own land"[7]

The armies of the three kings could have taken the prophet Elisha's prophecy all the way to the finish line except for the fact that they quit too soon! They had the perfect opportunity to thoroughly annihilate their enemies on the day which was divinely appointed by God for their complete victory. They were in "God's Kairos," but they abandoned their mission just before they got to the finish line.

"Kairos" is a Greek word which refers to a "window of time in which all that God has foreordained must happen. It's a pocket of time that is bubbling with intense divine activity. It's a spot in time that is saturated with the favor of God!" In the story of the pool of Siloam (John 5) the Bible shows us the power of moments of Kairos. The Bible tells us that at a divinely appointed time, an angel sent by God, would step into the waters of the pool of Siloam. The first person to jump into the water afterwards was instantly healed of any disease that ailed them. God chose that specific Kairos moment and obligated Himself to heal all who recognized His appointed time.

Such is the power of Kairos. The day that the armies of the three kings were pursuing the retreating Moabites, they were in the Kairos of God. This special time of favor had been brought about by the prophetic word of the Lord which came out of Elisha's mouth. This was the day that the Israelites were supposed to win convincingly. They could have wiped the Moabites off the face of the earth for good. How tragic it is that they quit in the eleventh hour! What went wrong? Why did Israel stop pursuing its enemies and instead turned back?

The Bible says that when the king of Moab realized that the battle was against him and he was not going to win, he took seven hundred of his best warriors and tried to escape through the land of Edom, but he could not. Out of dire desperation the king of Moab, a devil worshipper, took his firstborn son who would have reigned in his stead, and sacrificed him to his demon gods on the walls of the city.

This human sacrifice was powerful enough to conjure up a great host of demon spirits who ferociously pushed the armies of Israel back! The Israelites had no clue what had hit them. All of a sudden they no longer felt like fighting. The transformation was amazing. Israel turned back from pursuing her enemies just a few steps away from the finish line! *I must say that one of the greatest dangers during times of transition is the danger of aborting our prophetic destiny because of misinterpreting the attacks of the enemy upon our lives.*

I sincerely hope that the following case study will help to strengthen our resolve to not abandon God's call upon our lives because of relentless persecution or contradictory circumstances.

CASE STUDY: THE JOHN ALEXANDER STORY

"On May25, 1847, in Edinburgh, Scotland a boy was born to Christian parents Mr. and Mrs. John Dowie, who they named John Alexander. Little did they know that there little baby boy was destined to become one of the most influential apostolic voices of the post Pentecostal era. After a ministry stunt in the nation of Australia, John Alexander Dowie arrived on the shores of California in 1888 and then later established the headquarters of his phenomenal healing ministry in the City of Chicago. In the City of Chicago that was run by organized crime bosses like Alcaponi, Dowie found great resistant to his ministry.

Church historian, Roberts Liardon has this to say about the reception this great apostle received in Chicago and how he overcame it.. "The Newspapers, mainly the Chicago Dispatch, were merciless, calling the homes [John Alexander Dowie's Healing Homes] "Lunatic Asylums" and continued to print every imaginable lie. Because of these healing homes, Dowie's enemies thought they had found a vulnerable spot. So early in 1895, they arrested him on the charge of "practicing medicine without a license." Obviously untrue, Dowie would have been the last person to allow medicine into his homes. He hired a brilliant attorney, but he only kept Dowie advised of the legal matters. So Dowie chose to represent himself in court, because no one else could articulate his call as accurately as himself.

Dowie's superior intellect was not enough to overrule the evil jurisdiction of the court. Despite his profound arguments, the court fined him. The city hoped Dowie would get discouraged if they continued to arrest and fine him. So before the year was over, he was arrested one hundred

times. Although severely persecuted, he was never discour-
aged. Persecution brought out great resiliency in his char-
acter. He actually thrived on his persecutor's affliction and
interrogation.

Evil will always try to persecute the power of God. But
Dowie was supernaturally secure and anchored in his godly
authority. The supernatural never bows to the natural. By
the end of 1896, Dowie had gained great influence over
the City of Chicago. His enemies were either dead, in
prison, or silent. The local police, who once arrested him
a hundred times, were now his friends and protected him
at a moment's notice. The political officials, including the
mayor had all been voted in by Dowie's people".
(God's Generals pg 32-34, by Roberts Liardon)

The story of the supernatural triumph of John Alexander
Dowie over the relentless persecution and spiritual resistance that he suffered at the hands of the Chicago press,
police and other political forces underscores the importance of not abandoning our prophetic call during periods
of transition. Had John Alexander Dowie lost his spiritual
focus or poise, his powerful ministry would never have
survived the first several years of relentless opposition that
he received in Chicago. The world would have lost one
of the greatest healing ministries of the twentieth century.
Dowie's life stands as testimony to the power of not aborting
our prophetic mission during periods of transition.

More often than not, the attacks of the enemy upon our
lives should be an indication that we are closer to seizing
our breakthrough than we have ever been. ***This is why***
people of faith must learn the benefits of suffering for
the cause of Christ while doing the will of God, rather

than thinking that every bump in the road is an indication that they have missed God!

Some believers in Christ who have been raised in *"word of faith churches"* sometimes suffer from this type of spiritual delusion. Please do not misunderstand me! I am not against word of faith churches or any other church. I am just against the spiritual practice of focusing on prosperity scriptures while ignoring those which say that we are also called to suffer even as Christ suffered. I believe that we must take the Bible in its entirety and not pick and choose the scriptures that say what we want to hear. ***There is a tendency by some proponents of the prosperity message to use a man's material possessions as evidence of God's divine approval, while any form of spiritual turbulence in one's life is frowned upon as a sign of divine disapproval! This is a great deception which can force us into a compromise during times of difficult transition.***

This type of mentality is foreign to the spiritual experiences and writings of the apostles of the Bible. If Paul and Silas had been like some *"Prosperity"* preachers I have met during my travels, they would have looked at their beatings and imprisonment in Philippi, (Acts 16) as a sure sign that they were not in the will of God. They would have left at the first sign of persecution. But Paul and Silas burst into a celebration of praise because they knew that both the beatings and imprisonment were part of God's perfect will for their lives at that particular time. I believe that God wants His people to be spiritually and physically prosperous in every way possible. But I also believe that God's people are called to share in the fellowship of His sufferings whenever the Lord so chooses.

"I believe that we must take the Bible in its entirety and not pick and choose the scriptures that say what we want to hear."

If Paul and Silas had not been imprisoned they would never have met the Philippian jailer and his household who became the founding members of the church in Philippi. Paul had seen a vision of a man from Macedonia bidding them to come and help them. Paul and Silas were both so convinced that God had called them to Macedonia that they gladly accepted both the beatings and imprisonment rather than abort their prophetic mission to Macedonia. My dear friend, during periods of transition it's so easy to mistake the attacks of the enemy as a sure sign from God that we need to quit! But our God is not a quitter; He is a finisher and He has called us to finish!

"Jesus saith unto them, My meat is to do the will of him that sent me, and to finish his work"[8]

Why some things that are born out of the spirit realm die

For a long time I have wondered why certain things that are born of the Spirit die. Why are miracles lost in translation? Why do people lose their healing? Why do people lose their spiritual breakthroughs? Why do people lose the spiritual ground that they had once taken from the hands of the enemy? Why do prophecies fail? If you are like me and have been in the church as long as I have, these questions may have crossed your mind too. While I was listening to Dr. Jonathan David's *"Dangers of Transition"* CD series, the answer suddenly became clear in my spirit and I want to share it with you!

*"And he said unto his father, My head, my head. And he said
to a lad, Carry him to his mother. And when he had taken
him, and brought him to his mother, he sat on her knees till
noon, and then died. And she went up, and laid him on the
bed of the man of God, and shut the door upon him, and
went out. And she called unto her husband, and said, Send
me, I pray thee, one of the young men, and one of the asses,
that I may run to the man of God, and come again"*[9]

The Shunamite woman could not bear children for
many years, but when she persuaded the prophet Elisha to
become a part of her life, the prophetic anointing upon him
caused her womb to open. She conceived and gave birth
to a son. After twelve years the boy had a serious migraine
headache and died. The Shunamite woman immediately
realized the mistake that she had made. She had neglected
nurturing her relationship with the prophet (pastor) whom
God had used to bring her miracle.

Because her child was a by-product of Elisha's relationship with the Lord, he needed the same prophetic or
spiritual atmosphere to continue living. When the child
failed to get the spiritual atmosphere he needed in order to
grow properly, he died. This is why I advise people not to
leave their home church in a dishonorable manner. I have
advised people not to trash the character of the pastor they
are leaving because much of their spiritual growth can be
attributed to his anointing and ministry (messages).

If believers continue to dishonor their former pastors
with their mouth, a sentence of death will come upon every
good, life giving word that they received when they were
attending that particular church! If you are transitioning
from a church or a denomination, just be honorable in your
attitude of departure. Do not burn bridges. Like my good

friend Tim Storey would say, *"I may not be what I want to be, but thank God I am not what I used to be!" When we do not honor our past spiritual leaders, we are placing a self inflicted curse on our future!* During periods of transition we may be tempted to trash or speak evil of the church, job or denomination we used to be part of; but we must resist this temptation. Such unbecoming behavior can simply abort the prophetic destiny that God has for us!

Notes on Chapter Four

1. Jer 1:4-7
2. II Ki 3:5-7
3. II Ki 3:9-11
4. II Ki 3:8-10
5. II Ki 3:11-14
6. II Ki 3:15-19
7. II Ki 3:26-27
8. John 4:34
9. II Ki 4:19-22

Chapter Five

Lord, My Soul Is Messed Up

❧

One of the greatest dangers that we have to face or contend with during times of transition is....

#2. The Dangers Of A Contaminated and
Unhealed Soul Condition

Man is God's greatest design. When God created man He used all of His creative genius and the result was the creation of a product that transcends the creative genius of any product in the history of the world. *The world's most complex computers do not come close to the creative genius of man's brain and the intricacies of the millions of neural pathways that meander through it.* This product of God called *"man"* has, according to scripture, three distinctive compartments to his being. Man is a spirit being who possesses a soul and lives inside a physical body.

"And the very God of peace sanctify you wholly; and I pray God your whole spirit and soul and body be preserved blameless unto the coming of our Lord Jesus Christ"[1]

The spirit faculty connects man with the spirit world, while his body helps him to relate to the material world. So what is the function of the soul? The two main functions of the soul are to act as a communication medium between his spirit and his body. ***The soul is the conduit between the spirit world of God and the material world of man. This function of the soul is very critical in and of itself, because if it's impaired in anyway, serious ramifications can result from the decisions we make during periods of transition.*** Nothing is as important as the role of the soul in navigating the valley of transition.

"Among all of God's creation, the human body, especially the brain, is the most intricate, complex and marvelous design, allowing "mind-body communications" to be constantly adapting to a changing environment and personal experiences. One such marvel is the function of memory, storage, retrieval and man's ability to develop an internal model of the "reality" of the external world. By using such a "model" or internal representation, we interpret sensory inputs and device "meaning" out of what's happening to us and around us.

We are constantly "evaluating" multitudes of incoming information, "comparing" with what is "already stored in the memories". Depending on the nature of such evaluation and interpretation (along with the chemical contents in the body), we may experience great joy and exuberance, confidence, motivation, etc, or we may experience fear, anger, sorrow, suspicion, etc. Memories influence every action, pattern of reaction and choices we make. Memories can sabotage our chances for success and effectiveness, or memories can serve us great rewards.

(Overcomers Teachers Manual,
by Dr. Aiko Hormann, Brain Scientist)

The soul has three main components- the will, mind and emotions which determine or control how people respond during periods of transition.

The Will is the **decision making faculty** of man. Where all decisions whether spiritual or natural are **decided.** Every man's life follows in the path of his decisions, causing the **will** to yield tremendous power over the spiritual destinies of God's people. When the Lord Jesus was transitioning between the Garden of Gethsemane and the resurrection, His greatest battle was when **His will collided with the will of His heavenly Father.** The Lord Jesus faced his greatest temptation when He had to choose between His will and that of His heavenly Father. Knowing he faced drinking the cup of sin for the redemption of mankind made the decision so difficult and stressful that He began to sweat blood. Imagine where we'd be had He not prevailed and made the right decision. **When our soul is not contaminated by spirits of darkness and past negative experiences, our decisions, even in moments of painful transition, will always choose God's will.**

The Mind is the **thought processing center** of man. Every thought, whether good or bad, holy or evil, has to be processed through the faculty of the mind. The mind is the reasoning or logic center of the soul. Once the mind has finished processing a particular thought or collection of thoughts, it then presents its conclusions or findings to be acted upon by the **will.** It's easy to see how an impaired mind can have a dangerous impact on us during times of transition.

Periods of transition will require that we make good decisions in order to move us in the direction of our God given destiny. This is only possible if our will and mind have not been contaminated. *If our mind is filled with garbage (deception, lies, false imagery or confusion) its ability to arrive at sound biblical conclusions will be seriously impaired during periods of spiritual transition.* If the mind is impaired, its findings will be false and as such the conclusions that it presents to the *will* also will be false. This is why the great Apostle Paul implored the saints in Rome to be transformed through the renewing of their minds.

"And be not conformed to this world: but be ye transformed by the renewing of your mind, that ye may prove what is that good, and acceptable, and perfect, will of God"[2]

The Emotions are the **expressive or animation center of the soul.** This part of the soul is responsible for creating the emotional sense of **feeling,** based upon information supplied to it by the conclusions of the mind, whether real or imagined. Scientific data has shown that the heart is about seventy percent neurons. Many of these heart neurons are responsible for controlling the phenomenon called human emotion.

Scientific Facts: *When a person is angry or fearful the amygdala in the limbic system of the brain gets activated. This signals the hypothalamus and pituitary gland, releasing "stress hormones" and neurotransmitters. An excessive amount of stress hormones (e.g cortisol) can cause "allostatic* *overload" meaning "beyond the stable variability range." This toxic stage can be neutralized by the lymphatic system and the liver but usually takes three days.*

Just think, if you get angry or fearful today, and before three days are up, you get angry again, your body accumulates toxic chemicals over time. These toxic chemicals may circulate through your body and affect certain organs that are already vulnerable through other stresses or genetic predisposition. The neurotransmitters and stress hormones can affect the autonomic nervous system (heart, lungs, and digestive/elimination), endocrine system and the immune system. They in turn make us susceptible to invading germs and viruses, even cancer.

Scientific tests of muscle growth were conducted using the Cybex Dynamometer which records strength of arm muscles and thigh muscles. They found that an angry state of a person drains his or her energy from 50% to 90%, depending upon the severity of it. Worrying also saps our energy, and is even worse – because it's more prolonged and may become chronic. Emotional upheavals produce stress that in turn produces more free radicals than the "normal" amount produced through digestion, respiration, and immune system activities.

Free radicals are highly reactive, unstable molecules that hunt other molecules to stabilize themselves, thus causing hundreds and thousands of chain reactions. These chain reactions can damage cell membranes, connective tissue, blood vessel walls and create mutant cells by changing the DNA molecules. These mutant cells are precursors to cancerous cells and can lead to premature aging and diseases!

(The Overcomers Teachers Manual by Dr. Aiko Hormann, Brain Scientist)

It's clear from both the teachings of scripture and from scientific data that negative emotions can seriously affect and impair our **will and mind** by triggering the wrong chemical reactions and mental perceptions which are not based on the teachings of scripture. Many of God's people have made terrible decisions during periods of transition because of **bad health and high stress**, causing our mind to lose its usual alertness and the will loses its usual stamina. Our ability to make sound godly decisions goes down the toilet at this point, leaving us vulnerable to Satan's attacks.

The Log Jam Condition of the Soul

"And they said unto me, The remnant that are left of the captivity there in the province are in great affliction and reproach: the wall of Jerusalem also is broken down, and the gates thereof are burned with fire"[3]

If you have ever lived in high traffic cities like New York or Los Angeles, you might be familiar with the nightmare of being caught in rush hour traffic. A drive that would normally take a couple of minutes suddenly drags on for hours in the ensuing traffic jam. It's a very frustrating feeling indeed as traffic comes to a near standstill and cars move bumper to bumper at a snails pace. This is one of the most graphic natural examples I can give you to illustrate the logjam condition of the soul.

God designed the soul to be the divine highway for the Spirit of God who resides inside every child of God. In the perfect scenario, man's human spirit was designed to receive from God who is a spirit and then channel what it has received from the spirit world to the body (our material world) through the highway of the soul. Unfortunately the Holy Spirit gets caught in the traffic and clutter that has clogged up the souls of so many of God's people with things like unforgiveness, bitterness, envy, jealousy, hate, anger, malice, lies, deceit, manipulation, false imageries, low self esteem, depression, wrath, adultery, lust, and perversion.

These things clog up the soul and hinder the flow of the power of the Holy Spirit. Spiritual contamination will cause God's people to feel as though He has forsaken them during periods of transition. *We need the unhindered flow of the power of the Holy Spirit to successfully navigate the valley of spiritual transition.*

"But those things which proceed out of the mouth come forth from the heart; and they defile the man. For out of the heart proceed evil thoughts, murders, adulteries, fornications, thefts, false witness, blasphemies:"[4]

Science has always taught us that the heart's main purpose is for pumping blood and our brain's primary purpose is processing thoughts. Until recently scientists and medical doctors generally believed that the main function of the heart was to pump blood through the human body. There was also a general belief that a human being has only one brain found in the head. Recent scientific discoveries have blown these past theories out of the water, as scientists have discovered to their dismay that *human beings actually have "3 brains" instead of one. They now have discovered that the heart and the gut consist of about 65% to 75% neurons the same neurons and neural transmitters that are found in the head brain are also found in both the heart and the gut.*

Scientists also discovered that *the heart brain has the largest concentration of neurons which are responsible for controlling the emotions!* It took scientists thousands of years to figure out what Jesus had already revealed in his teachings. The physical part of the heart belongs to the body while the *neurological part of the heart belongs to the soul!* Whatever we allow into our heart will eventually find its way into our soul and hinder our spiritual destiny (especially during periods of transition).

Terah: The Toxic Power of a Sorrowful Spirit

"And Terah lived seventy years, and begat Abram, Nahor, and Haran. Now these are the generations of Terah: Terah begat Abram, Nahor, and Haran; and Haran begat Lot. And Haran died before his father Terah in the land of his nativity, in Ur of the Chaldees. And Terah took Abram his son, and Lot the son of Haran his son's son, and Sarai his daughter in law, his son Abram's wife; and they went forth with them from Ur of the Chaldees, to go into the land of Canaan; and they came unto Haran, and dwelt there. And the days of Terah were two hundred and five years: and Terah died in Haran."[5]

The story of Terah, Abraham's father, is the best case study in how a *contaminated soul can rise to hinder us from pursuing our spiritual destiny during times of transition.* According to Semitic tradition, the call to go to Canaan initially did not come to Abraham. God first spoke to his father, Terah, about this important prophetic journey and destiny. Unfortunately, a terrible tragedy occurred which changed Terah's life drastically. His youngest son, Haran, died suddenly.

"If we don't allow the Holy Spirit to heal the wounded conditions in our soul, Satan will one day force us to settle at our weakest point."

The sudden death of his dear son vexed his heart and soul. Physically, Terah's son was buried in the earth beneath, but emotionally, ***Haran's coffin was buried in his father's heart!*** When the last mourner filed out, the funeral in Terah's heart had just begun. Instead of allowing God to heal him from the emotional devastation he had just suffered, Terah built a shrine to his son in his own heart. He was a man with a prophetic call who suddenly found himself carrying the weight of the world on his shoulders. The emotional weight proved to be too much for him to carry and stopped him from fulfilling his prophetic destiny. His soul became ***contaminated with a spirit of sorrow and heaviness.*** This is one of the critical dangers of transition that we must all be aware of. When sin entered the world, it changed it from one of divine perfection to a *"less than perfect place"* where bad things happen to very godly people. Sometimes life is not fair but we still can find victory through the power of God's word.

In spite of his grief, Terah attempted to move toward his God appointed destiny. He took his remaining sons, Abram and Nahor and the orphaned child Lot, and headed toward Canaan. Along their journey, they came across a town that had the same name as Terah's dead son, which quickly became his undoing. When Terah heard the name of the town, the ***ongoing funeral inside his soul*** suddenly erupted into a volcano of unstoppable sorrowful emotions. The emotional sense of loss was more than he could bear. Terah made a drastic decision to abandon his prophetic call and destiny. He chose to ***settle at the place of his***

greatest emotional weakness. The unhealed soul conditions in his heart rose to challenge his prophetic advancement during this period of spiritual transition in his life. *If we don't allow the Holy Spirit to heal the wounded conditions in our soul, Satan will one day force us to settle at our weakest point and stop us from moving into our purpose!*

I remember teaching on the dangers of transition at a church in Oklahoma City. When I started telling the story of Terah not letting it go of his dead son and sacrificing his prophetic destiny at the altar of his troubled emotions, a woman in the meeting started weeping profusely. I later discovered that her only son had been killed in a car crash a couple years earlier, leaving her in a serious state of mourning.

The Spirit of God instructed me to tell her to take off the necklace she was wearing. The woman's hands were shaking uncontrollably as she reached for the necklace, containing a picture of her dead son. When she finally got it removed, there was an instant supernatural emotional release. The veil of death she was wearing disappeared almost immediately and her face began to shine with a radiance her husband had not seen since before their son died. This woman had been in mourning for years, placing her prophetic destiny on hold. But that day I watched as she picked up her purpose for living during that service and ran with it! Glory to God in the Highest!

Emotional Conflicts in the Family

These unhealed soul conditions and bondages can translate into serious family conflicts when they are left unchecked. After Adam and Eve were expelled from the Garden of Eden, they gave birth to two sons, Cain and Abel. The Bible tells us that Cain was a tiller of the ground (farmer), while his younger brother Abel was a keeper of sheep. In the process of time, both of them brought a sacrificial offering to the Lord. Abel offered a lamb, while Cain's offering consisted of the fruits of the ground. God rejected Cain's offering but poured His divine favor upon Abel's offering. Cain became very jealous and angry with his brother when he saw that God was showering him with favor.

"And Abel, he also brought of the firstlings of his flock and of the fat thereof. And the LORD had respect unto Abel and to his offering: But unto Cain and to his offering he had not respect. And Cain was very wroth, and his countenance fell. And the LORD said unto Cain, Why art thou wroth? and why is thy countenance fallen? If thou doest well, shalt thou not be accepted? and if thou doest not well, sin lieth at the door. And unto thee shall be his desire, and thou shalt rule over him. And Cain talked with Abel his brother: and it came to pass, when they were in the field, that Cain rose up against Abel his brother, and slew him"[6]

The story of Cain and Abel is a special case study on how the contamination of the soul can destroy families, churches and business relationships during times of natural and spiritual transition. These unhealed soul conditions will rise to cause strife in relationships and jealousies in human behavior patterns.

One of the clearest indications that our soul is spiritually contaminated is when **we get angry with God and become enraged at those His hand is blessing.** We must never forget that during periods of our spiritual transition, there will be those who may be experiencing a greater level of success because they are further along in their prophetic journey than we are. Getting angry with God and becoming jealous of those His hand is blessing is futile. This only proves that our soul is defiled and wounded. Such a soul is in dire need of spiritual cleansing and healing before these negative emotions stop us from transitioning into a higher level of our destiny.

God warned Cain that if he did not deal with the spirit of offense inside his soul, sin was going to have dominion over him. Instead of listening to God, the spiritual contamination of Cain's soul was so serious that he walked out of his meeting with God with a malicious determination to kill his brother. He deceived his young brother into taking a walk with him into the woods where he killed him. Cain thought that if he killed his brother, who seemed to be the favored one of God, he would feel better about himself. Unfortunately, this *inaccurate pattern of behavior* in Cain is still displaying itself today through many members of the body of Christ.

> *"One of the clearest indications that our soul is spiritually contaminated is when we get angry with God and become enraged at those His hand is blessing."*

Without a doubt, Cain's inaccurate behavior must have brought tremendous sorrow and grief to this parents (Adam and Eve), when they discovered that he had killed his brother and then ran into exile. I cannot over emphasize the spiritual dangers posed by a contaminated soul and how this contamination can rise to destroy our prophetic call and destiny. God wants to transition us into the fullness of the calling He has placed upon our lives, but these unhealed soul conditions can hinder us and prolong our journey.

King Saul: The rise and fall

The story of King Saul, the first king of Israel, is one of the most tragic stories in the Bible. It's clear from what has been revealed to us in the Scriptures that God had every intention of establishing the lineage of King Saul, but Saul failed to make the transition into the place of total obedience to God. He failed to graduate to his highest calling in God. From the onset, Saul's **unhealed soul conditions** began to reveal themselves by the manner in which he responded to the prophet Samuel when the prophet proclaimed that God had chosen him to be the first king over the nation of Israel.

"And as for thine asses that were lost three days ago, set not thy mind on them; for they are found. And on whom is all the desire of Israel? Is it not on thee, and on all thy father's house? And Saul answered and said, Am not I a Benjamite, of the smallest of the tribes of Israel? and my family the least of all the families of the tribe of Benjamin? wherefore then speakest thou so to me? And Samuel took Saul and his servant, and brought them into the parlour, and made them sit in the chiefest place among them that were bidden, which were about thirty persons. "[7]

When Samuel told Saul that he was the chosen one, the emotional insecurities of his contaminated soul rose to challenge the prophetic decree. Saul had a serious case of false humility which hid a more sinister and serious issue of personal insecurity and low self esteem. The second time

Saul's contaminated soul rose to challenge his prophetic destiny was during his public inauguration.

"When he had caused the tribe of Benjamin to come near by their families, the family of Matri was taken, and Saul the son of Kish was taken: and when they sought him, he could not be found. Therefore they inquired of the LORD further, if the man should yet come thither. And the LORD answered, Behold, he hath hid himself among the stuff. "[8]

There are those who would give Saul a perfect score for manifesting true humility in his ascension to the throne of Israel. This is because most people have the wrong concept of what it means to be humble before God. ***True humility has nothing to do with living in denial and self-abasement; these are by products of a contaminated soul. There is nothing humble about denying the testimony of God concerning our lives.*** God's testimony is always true. If God says that we are winners, to say we are not is NOT humility.

The denial of God's testimony concerning our lives is rooted in the wounded and unhealed condition of the soul. Jesus never once denied the fact that He was the Son of God. This my dear friend is true humility, anything else is the product of a contaminated soul, which if not dealt with will one day rise to destroy us in our season of spiritual transition.

The unhealed soul conditions in King Saul's life became progressively worse throughout his tenure as the king of Israel. He began disobeying direct commands of God upon his life in order to secure the favor of the people. Saul's emotional insecurities caused him to live in fear of being rejected by the people he was leading. He was more concerned with being accepted by the masses than being rejected by the God who put him in power. ***God eventually rejected Saul, because he failed to allow God to heal the emotional insecurities that were deeply rooted in his soul and led him on the pathway of disobedience.*** As a consequence, God gave the Prophet Samuel a fresh instruction to go and anoint David to become the next king of Israel.

After the young shepherd boy killed the Philistine giant Goliath, he became a national celebrity overnight. Everybody in the nation of Israel was talking about this young man who had killed a formidable giant with a slingshot and won the war. Women composed songs of adoration about the valiant acts of David and when Saul heard them singing, he became enraged with unfeigned jealousy. The emotional insecurities in his soul would not allow him to share the spotlight with anybody! There are many spiritual leaders in the body of Christ who manifest this same type of spirit. Instead of allowing the law of transition to carry him into a higher level of spiritual maturity, King Saul allowed the spiritual contamination in his own soul to dictate his behavior, keeping him bound to his weakest emotions.

"And it came to pass as they came, when David was returned from the slaughter of the Philistine, that the women came out of all cities of Israel, singing and dancing, to meet king Saul, with tabrets, with joy, and with instruments of musick. And the women answered one another as they played, and said, Saul hath slain his thousands, and David his ten thousands. And Saul was very wroth, and the saying displeased him; and he said, They have ascribed unto David ten thousands, and to me they have ascribed but thousands: and what can he have more but the kingdom? And Saul eyed David from that day and forward."[9]

After God rejected King Saul, his downward spiral toward complete destruction was inevitable. He became progressively worse, as his mission to destroy David became desperately obsessive. He eventually died, a victim of an apparent suicide, in the field of battle. He died as a disgraced king who lost his divine mission on earth because of *unhealed soul conditions, which sabotaged and destroyed his prophetic destiny in God!* King Saul, like many others in history, found himself on the wrong side of the law of transition because of a contaminated soul and he lost the fight.

Judas Iscariot: The Toxic Power of Greed

The tale of Judas Iscariot is the very tragic story of a man who became a disciple, who became an apostle, who betrayed the Son of God and then killed himself. This is the most tragic biography of any man in the history of the world. What is shocking and regrettable is that the series of events in Judas's life, which led him to betray the Lord Jesus Christ, could have been avoided had he allowed God to heal him of the greed which was contaminating his apostolic soul.

"Men and brethren, this scripture must needs have been fulfilled, which the Holy Ghost by the mouth of David spake before concerning Judas, which was guide to them that took Jesus. For he was numbered with us, and had obtained part of this ministry. Now this man purchased a field with the reward of iniquity; and falling headlong, he burst asunder in the midst, and all his bowels gushed out. And it was known unto all the dwellers at Jerusalem; insomuch as that field is called in their proper tongue, Aceldama, that is to say, The field of blood. For it is written

in the book of Psalms, Let his habitation be desolate, and let no man dwell therein: and his bishoprick let another take."[10]

It's clear from Peter's discourse the day before Pentecost, that Judas Iscariot was called to the same apostolic and prophetic destiny as all the other apostles. He was called into the ministry by a personal invitation from the lips of Jesus Christ. His call to the apostolic ministry could never have been more legitimate than it was. Nevertheless Judas had serious unhealed soul conditions.

The Lord Jesus gave Judas Iscariot many opportunities to turn his life around, but he failed to seize the moment. The spiritual contamination of greed inside his soul became progressively worse. ***His unhealed soul became a major expressway to hell, freely traveled by Satan himself!*** Once Satan entered his heart, there was no turning back for Judas Iscariot. He failed to conquer the greed inside his soul, allowing it conquer him and stop him from entering into his spiritual destiny. He had been chosen as one of the first apostles of the New Testament church, but he tragically died before the transitional period was over. ***When the day of Pentecost came, Judas was history. He died on the wrong side of the law of transition.***

This is why the Scriptures are filled with stories of men and women who serve as examples of the serious dangers posed by a contaminated soul. If we are serious about fulfilling our prophetic purpose, we must make soul restoration one of our highest and most urgent spiritual tasks. We must bring our soul under the Lordship of Jesus Christ so that He can restore our soul through the power of the Holy Spirit.

Notes on Chapter Five

1. 1Thes 5:23, 2. Rom 12:2, 3. Neh 1:3, 4. Matt 15:18-19, 5. Gen 11:26-32
6. Gen 4:4-8, 7. 1 Sam 9:20-22, 8. 1 Sam 10:21-22, 9. 1 Sam 18:6-9,
10. Acts 1:16-20

Chapter Six

When Commitment Hurts

I am sure that we all have been in a place where we felt like canceling our previous commitments, especially when times became rough. There will always be periods in our life journey when *commitment hurts*. Nevertheless, it is those very moments that define who we really are. They reveal the characteristics that make up our being. In this chapter we will discuss the third danger we are likely to encounter during periods of spiritual transition.

#3. The Danger Of Breaking Covenant With God Because The Enemy is Attacking Our Lives.

A Covenant Keeping God

God has no other way of dealing with His own creation outside of a covenant. Outside the perimeters of covenant, God can only approach sinful man in wrath. All the dealings of God with the human race from Adam to Jesus to this present age, can best be viewed through the light of

His immutable covenants with mankind. We truly serve a covenant keeping God.

Before the flood of Noah destroyed the ancient world, God had not yet established a covenant with the environment that could limit the extent of His wrath. After the flood, God made a new covenant with Noah that included a divine guarantee that God would never again allow water to flood the entire world. In the Noahic Covenant, God also promised never to allow a single natural disaster to wipe out the entire planet. The rainbow was to be the heavenly sign attesting to the Noahic covenant, of which God has honored.

"And God said, This is the token of the covenant which I make between me and you and every living creature that is with you, for perpetual generations: I do set my bow in the cloud, and it shall be for a token of a covenant between me and the earth. And it shall come to pass, when I bring a cloud over the earth, that the bow shall be seen in the cloud: And I will remember my covenant, which is between me and you and every living creature of all flesh; and the waters shall no more become a flood to destroy all flesh." [1]

One of the greatest displays of the covenantal nature of God is found in how the Lord Jesus Christ dealt with the Canaanite woman. She came to him looking for deliverance for her daughter who was grievously vexed by demonic spirits. This story is a daring display of the fact that **God is not moved by need, He is moved only by His Covenant through the vehicle of believing faith!** This Canaanite woman came with a great need. She was very vocal about what she desired Jesus to do for her. She called Him by his covenantal name, *"Jesus thou son of David!"* Jesus totally ignored her. He acted like He had not even heard her.

Many people would have been instantly offended with Jesus. They would have immediately stopped pursuing Him. We need to remember that during periods of spiritual transition, God will sometimes remain silent, as though He is not listening to our prayers to see if we are becoming a covenant minded people or whether we are just spiritual flukes. God will not entrust the priceless treasures of His Kingdom to men and women who are not covenant minded. ***People who are not covenant minded are perpetual quitters!*** They will give up on God at the slightest sign of trouble.

"And, behold, a woman of Canaan came out of the same coasts, and cried unto him, saying, Have mercy on me, O Lord, thou Son of David; my daughter is grievously vexed with a devil. But he answered her not a word. And his disciples came and besought him, saying, Send her away; for she crieth after us. But he answered and said, I am not sent but unto the lost sheep of the house of Israel. Then came she and worshipped him, saying, Lord, help me. But he answered and said, It is not meet to take the children's bread, and to cast it to dogs. And she said, Truth, Lord: yet the dogs eat of the crumbs which fall from their masters' table. Then Jesus answered and said unto her, O woman, great is thy faith: be it unto thee even as thou wilt. And her daughter was made whole from that very hour."[2]

The Canaanite woman fell at Jesus' feet and worshipped Him, while simultaneously reminding Him of her desperate need. He finally spoke to her, but what He told her was not what she wanted to hear. He told her that He was only called to minister to the Jewish people and not to the Gentiles. He had just rejected her in public. For many of us this would have been the excuse we needed to write off Jesus as a racist religious leader.

When she pressed Him one more time, Jesus told her without mincing any words, *"It's not right for me to give the children's bread to the dogs!"* To the outside observer it may seem like Jesus was being deliberately rude, but this was not the case. To the Jewish mind, anybody who did not have a covenant with God was no different than a common dog. I know that this comparison may be quite offensive to some people, but during periods of spiritual transition, God will move us away from living like dogs (covenant breakers) to living like true sons of the Kingdom who live in the power of true covenant. The Lord Jesus Christ was not insulting this desperate mother; He was telling her that His reluctance in healing her daughter had nothing to do with race.

Most people do not understand that when the Lord Jesus was fulfilling His earthly ministry, He was operating strictly under the Mosaic Covenant. The Mosaic covenant was exclusively a covenant for the Jewish people and any foreigner who abandoned his nation's idols to serve the God of Israel. Jesus had to limit His ministry to people who were found within this covenant circle. Any operation outside this covenant circle would have turned Jesus into a covenant breaker and He was not going to break the Mosaic covenant just to meet a woman's need.

Jesus couldn't cross the boundaries placed upon him by the Mosaic covenant. He had cunningly showed her how she could cross the dividing line and become a *partaker* of the covenant of Israel. When she crossed over, Jesus immediately healed her daughter.

He was living between two covenants. The Mosaic covenant was still in effect and the New Testament covenant of grace was yet to be enacted by His sacrificial death on the cross. The Lord Jesus had to overcome one of the spiritual dangers of transition - the ***danger of breaking covenant in order to satisfy a personal need.*** The Lord Jesus was using the Canaanite woman to teach His people never to break covenant during periods of transition in order to meet pressing personal needs. ***Nothing can test our level of commitment to personal integrity in life and business matters like periods of transition which require tremendous personal sacrifice as our case study will show.***

CASE STUDY:
THE MICHELANGELO STORY

Michelangelo lived an incredible life. Possibly the greatest artist of Western civilization-and certainly the most influential-he was born to sculpt. He once said that when he drank his wet nurse's milk as a baby, along with it came a love for the stonecutter's tools. He sculpted his first mature masterpiece at age twenty-one. He completed his Pieta and David before age thirty.

In his early thirties, Michelangelo was summoned to Rome by Pope Julius II to sculpt a magnificent papal tomb, but was then asked to work on a painting project instead. At first Michelangelo wanted to refuse, having no desire to paint a dozen figures on the ceiling of a small chapel in the Vatican. Though as a boy he had been trained to paint, his passion was sculpture. But when the pope pressed him, he reluctantly accepted the assignment.

Scholars believe Michelangelo's rivals pushed for him to get the job, hoping he would refuse it and lose favor with the pope, or take it and discredit himself. But once Michelangelo accepted the assignment, he thoroughly committed himself to it, expanding the project from a simple depiction of the twelve apostles to include more than four hundred figures and nine scenes from the book of Genesis.

Four grueling years, the artist lay on his back painting the ceiling of the Sistine Chapel. And he paid a great price. The work permanently damaged his eyesight and wore him down. Michelangelo said, "After four tortured years, more than four hundred over-life-sized figures, I felt as old and as weary as Jeremiah. I was only thirty-seven, yet friends did not recognize the old man I had become."

The impact of Michelangelo's commitment was far-reaching. He pleased his benefactor, the pope, and received other commissions from the Vatican. But more important, he made a huge impact in the artistic community. His Sistine Chapel frescoes were so boldly painted, so original, so exquisitely executed that they caused many fellow artists to alter their style. Art historians maintain that Michelangelo'a masterpiece forever changed the course of painting in Europe. And it laid a foundation for his equally important impact on sculpture and architecture.

Undoubtedly Michelangelo's talent created the potential for greatness, but without commitment, his influence would have been minimal. When asked why he was working so diligently on a dark corner of the Sistine Chapel that no one would ever see, Michelangelo'a simple reply was, "God will see".

(Quote from The 21 Indispensable Qualities of a Leader, by John C. Maxwell, pg 16-18).

Satan, A Covenant Breaking Spirit

The world we live in is in dire need of men and women with the integrity and commitment of Michelangelo, especially during periods of painful transition.

How many CEOs in corporate America have sold their personal stocks in the companies that they are leading at the least sign of trouble, never giving a second thought as to how their actions will impact their many employees whose very lives depend on the survival of these corporations?

Consider the case of Martha Stewart who was recently convicted of insider trading when she dumped her personal stock in ImClone Systems. Martha discovered that she stood to lose several millions of dollars if the stock of ImClone Systems continued to fall because the company was going through a tough time. She chose to break the law and compromise her personal integrity rather than lose money. Martha chose to break the covenant of trust that she had with the hundreds of ImClone Systems shareholders who believed in her and followed her leading.

It's as easy to trace Satan's footprints and predict with surgical precision were he has been, as it is to track the tire marks of a car on a wet dusty road. Wherever Satan has been, there is visible evidence of broken covenants and shattered lives. Nothing ever remains in an innocent state once Satan has paid a visit. Even Heaven bears the eternal mark of a broken covenant between God and Satan (then called Lucifer) which resulted in the loss of over one third of His original angelic order.

"How art thou fallen from heaven, O Lucifer, son of the morning! how art thou cut down to the ground, which didst weaken the nations! For thou hast said in thine heart, I will ascend into heaven, I will exalt my throne above the stars

of God: I will sit also upon the mount of the congregation, in the sides of the north: I will ascend above the heights of the clouds; I will be like the most High. Yet thou shalt be brought down to hell, to the sides of the pit."[3]

One of the spiritual dangers of going through transition is the danger of breaking covenant because of the enemy's attacks upon our lives. The Bible tells us that we **do not wrestle against flesh and blood but against spiritual wickedness in heavenly places** (Ephesians 6:12). This means that there are demonic spirits that are bent on destroying our lives and derailing us from the pathway of destiny.

The devil's strategy is to wear down the saints of the Most High through constant and relentless attacks upon their lives. We all get tired of continuous fighting and waiting for God's salvation to be made manifest. When we get tired of fighting the good fight of faith, it is so easy to let our guards down and break our covenant with God and with those that God has connected us to. The Bible tells us that there came a time when the kings were supposed to go to war, but King David did not go as expected. He stayed home while his men fought at the frontlines of the battlefield.

He was fatigued from many years of fighting and opted to stay behind at the royal palace and rest. It was during this period that he noticed Bathsheba taking a bath as he walked idly by. One of my favorite preachers is Mike Murdock. I once heard Mike Murdock say, *"When fatigue walks in faith walks out!"* King David was very tired; his spiritual defenses were down, so when he saw the beautiful naked body of Bathsheba, the lust of the flesh overcame his better judgment.

He called her into his house, where he had sexual intercourse with her. In one act, King David broke his covenant with God and with his faithful servant, Uriah, Bathsheba's husband. This one act of sexual sin brought untold sorrow into the life of King David for the rest of his life. He ended up killing Uriah in order to cover up his act of adultery. God sent the prophet Nathan to pronounce God's judgment on David's sin. The sword would never leave his family, the prophet declared. What a tragedy! Satan had accomplished his mission; he had tempted King David to break covenant in order to meet a personal need. This period of spiritual transition changed David's life forever.

> *"This one act of sexual sin brought*
> *untold sorrow into the life of*
> *King David for the rest of his life."*

Abraham Where is Your Wife?

The call of Abraham and Sarah is one of the most important prophetic callings in the entire Bible. This is because Abraham was called by God to become the father of all those who walk by faith. Abraham was called to be the patriarch of a new race of people on the planet. He was a man way ahead of his time, living under a New Testament pattern long before the Lord Jesus died on the cross. God made a covenant with Abraham, commanding a blessing to the entire world through his seed, whom we know as Jesus Christ. In order to accomplish this task, God promised Abraham that He was going to give him a *"prophetic child named Isaac. This child was going to be the prophetic prototype of Jesus, the true son of promise!"*

Please remember that in the Garden of Eden, just before the Lord expelled Adam and Eve, He pronounced his divine judgment upon the serpent (Genesis 3). God told the serpent that he was going to crush its head through the seed of the woman. From that day forward, Satan has been terrified of any child born through the womb of the woman.

God did not specify the name of the chosen woman who was going to give birth to the *Messiah child.* When God made a covenant with Abraham, the devil went into panic mode and has been devising diabolical plans to try to pollute or sabotage the seed of the woman. When the devil overheard God's promise to Abraham and Sarah, he assumed that Isaac was the promised messiah child and devised a plan to plant his own seed in Sarah's womb. There was a sudden and unexplainable famine, which forced Abraham and Sarah to migrate toward the land of Egypt.

"And there was a famine in the land: and Abram went down into Egypt to sojourn there; for the famine was grievous in the land. And it came to pass, when he was come near to enter into Egypt, that he said unto Sarai his wife, Behold now, I know that thou art a fair woman to look upon: Therefore it shall come to pass, when the Egyptians shall see thee, that they shall say, This is his wife: and they will kill me, but they will save thee alive. Say, I pray thee, thou art my sister: that it may be well with me for thy sake; and my soul shall live because of thee. And it came to pass, that, when Abram was come into Egypt, the Egyptians beheld the woman that she was very fair. The princes also of Pharaoh saw her, and commended her before Pharaoh: and the woman was taken into Pharaoh's house."[4]

We must remember that from the moment the Lord gives us a prophetic promise until the time of its actual manifestation, we are in the valley of transition. This transitional period is one of the most important times in our lives as well as one of the most dangerous. During this period of spiritual transition, the devil will do his best to try and contest our prophetic promise.

The sudden famine created serious financial and practical problems for Abraham who was a keeper of livestock. The prevailing economic and weather conditions forced Abraham to move toward the pagan land of Egypt. When they got near the border of Egypt, Abraham had an unnerving talk with his wife, Sarah, which was clearly inspired by the devil. Abraham was playing right into the devil's hands. He told his wife that he was afraid the Egyptians might kill him in order to have her to themselves. He instructed her to lie and say that he (Abraham) was her brother instead of her husband.

Covenants are made and broken by words. With his own words Abraham, the custodian of the covenants of promise, broke covenant with the wife of his youth. From that moment on, the spiritual doors into Abraham's marriage had swung wide open and the devil rushed in for the kill. One of pharaoh's princes saw Sarah and immediately recommended her to the pharaoh. Pharaoh quickly took her to his house while Abraham nervously watched.

Horrified, Sarah found herself in the bedroom of one of the most powerful kings of the ancient world. Satan was determined to deposit his seed into the womb of the woman he assumed would give birth to the Messiah Child. Sarah knew that Pharaoh intended to have sexual intercourse with her and that she couldn't refuse him in her own power. She was like a lamb that had fallen into a lion's den. The poor thing! To her great relief God came busting through Pharaoh's bedroom doors and scared the daylights out of him.

God plagued the house of Pharaoh until he returned Sarah back to Abraham, but not before Pharaoh called Abraham a liar! Satan had managed to force Abraham to break covenant with his wife during this period of economic transition, but God's enduring faithfulness saved the day. We need to be careful not to break covenant during times of spiritual transition.

Will You Sell Me Your Birthright?

When you have a name like *Jacob*, it's very difficult to find the power to prevail and live a life of victory. *"Jacob"* literally means *"supplanter, deceiver or manipulator."* Whenever his parents or friends called him by his name, they simply solidified the solemn fact that he was born to live a life of lies and deceit.

While Rebekah, Isaac's wife, was pregnant, she inquired of the Lord as to why the babies in her womb were fighting so intensely. The Lord told her that she was going to have twins who would represent two nations of people. The youngest was going to be greater than his older brother. Before they were born, the spiritual destinies of the boys already had been set. When the time came for the twins to be born, Rebekah was anxious to see the *"chosen child"* who came out last. Esau was born first, then Jacob came, tightly grasping his brother's heel.

Esau quickly established himself as a prolific hunter and was dearly loved by his father Isaac, who enjoyed eating the venison (choice meat) of his son's bounty. Rebekah on the other hand, spent more time with Jacob and nurtured the prophetic word that God had given her concerning him. The older Jacob grew, the hungrier he got for the things of

God. He devised a plan to coerce his brother into selling his first-born birthright.

Esau came back from hunting one day and asked Jacob to give him some of the pottage that he was cooking because he was very hungry. Jacob told his brother that he could have all the pottage he needed if he could simply sign off his birthright. Esau quickly accepted Jacob's offer. A few weeks later, his mother overheard her husband Isaac instructing Esau to go into the field and get some venison (meat) and bring it back to him so he could bless him. With the help of his mother, Jacob dressed himself up like Esau and then went into his father's tent and pretended to be Esau. Conniving Jacob easily deceived Isaac, whose eyes were very dim at this stage. Isaac pronounced the irrevocable blessing of the firstborn upon Jacob, thinking he was blessing Esau.

"And he discerned him not, because his hands were hairy, as his brother Esau's hands: so he blessed him. And he said, Art thou my very son Esau? And he said, I am. And he said, Bring it near to me, and I will eat of my son's venison, that my soul may bless thee. And he brought it near to him, and he did eat: and he brought him wine, and he drank. And his father Isaac said unto him, Come near now, and kiss me, my son. And he came near, and kissed him: and he smelled the smell of his raiment, and blessed him, and said, See, the smell of my son is as the smell of a field which the LORD hath blessed:"[5]

After Isaac finished blessing him, Jacob ran out of his father's tent just before Esau entered it. When Isaac heard Esau's voice, he realized what had just transpired. Jacob had deceived both him and Esau and ran away with the blessing of the firstborn. Esau wept bitterly and Isaac also mourned his mistake, but the blessing that had gone forth couldn't be undone. Esau was so upset with Jacob he began to contemplate killing him. Jacob got wind of it through his mother and escaped to Syria to stay with his uncle Laban.

The point that I am trying to make using Jacob's life is simply this, *"During periods of transition, we must be careful not to break covenant with the higher virtues of honesty and integrity in order to get what we want!"* Breaking covenant is surely one of the most critical dangers that we will ever face during periods of spiritual transition.

Jonathan: A Victim of Tradition

The story of Jonathan and David is one of the most powerful scriptural displays of pure covenant love between two men. Jonathan was the son of an emotionally insecure king named Saul. King Saul was a pathetic people pleaser, who lost the favor of God over his life because he kept disobeying God in order to please men. God rejected him and cut off his ensuing dynasty. His eldest son Jonathan, who was the immediate heir to the throne, was consequently cut off from his inheritance by divine decree. The spirit of God left King Saul and instead rested on David. As soon as the Spirit of God left King Saul, a demonic spirit came to fill the ensuing spiritual vacuum.

"And the LORD said unto Samuel, How long wilt thou mourn for Saul, seeing I have rejected him from reigning over Israel? fill thine horn with oil, and go, I will send thee to Jesse the Bethlehemite: for I have provided me a king among his sons. Then Samuel took the horn of oil, and

anointed him in the midst of his brethren: and the Spirit of the LORD came upon David from that day forward. So Samuel rose up, and went to Ramah. But the Spirit of the LORD departed from Saul, and an evil spirit from the LORD troubled him."[6]

It was during this time that King Saul asked David to become his armor bearer as well as play soothing music before him. It was during this period David met Jonathan. As soon as Jonathan heard David speak, his soul began to love David like he loved himself. This is nothing short of covenantal love - the strongest love that can exist between any two people. As a result of Jonathan's love for David, Jonathan made a covenant with David. During the enactment of the covenant, Jonathan stripped himself of his robe, his garments, his sword, his bow and his belt, but he never stripped himself of his shoes.

"Then Jonathan and David made a covenant, because he loved him as his own soul. And Jonathan stripped himself of the robe that was upon him, and gave it to David, and his garments, even to his sword, and to his bow, and to his girdle."[7]

Jonathan brought himself and everything he owned into a covenant with David, except his feet. Jonathan knew without a shadow of doubt that David was the one whom God had chosen to become the next king of Israel. Jonathan knew that his father represented the past, while David represented the future. I strongly believe that God's will for Jonathan was for him to link up with David and move into his prophetic future with David, but he chose to remain royal to the past. He chose to cling to what God had done in the past instead of pressing into what God was presently doing.

> *"As soon as the Spirit of God left King Saul,*
> *a demonic spirit came to fill the*
> *ensuing spiritual vacuum."*

If we are not careful, our spiritual traditions will nullify the power of God's word in our lives and stop us from moving into our prophetic destiny. There is nothing wrong with appreciating what God has done in the past, but to sacrifice our future at the altar of yesterday is not wisdom. When Jonathan refused to give his shoes to David, Jonathan was in essence telling David that his feet, (which represented the path of his destiny) was the only thing he was not willing to bring into covenant.

By this one symbolic act of refusing to give David his shoes, Jonathan inevitably broke covenant with the future destiny that God had intended for him to have with David. His decision that day, eventually culminated in his death on the field of battle as he fought to defend the throne of a king whom God Himself had rejected! Jonathan, whom God had called to assist David in his future kingdom, died before seeing David take the reigns of power. Jonathan had broken covenant with his future by not giving God his feet which eventually walked him into the pathway of death. We have to be very careful not to break covenant with our prophetic destiny during times of spiritual transition. Quite often prophetic destinies are aborted when we fail to stay connected and submitted to the men and women of God who have been given a spiritual mandate to take us to our next level of purpose.

"How are the mighty fallen in the midst of the battle! O Jonathan, thou wast slain in thine high places. I am distressed for thee, my brother Jonathan: very pleasant hast thou been unto me: thy love to me was wonderful, passing the love of women. How are the mighty fallen, and the weapons of war perished!"[8]

Notes on Chapter Six

1. Gen 9:12-15
2. Matt 15:22-28
3. Isa 14:12-15
4. Gen 12:10-15
5. Gen 27:23-27
6. 1 Sam 16:1-30
7. 1 Sam 18:3-4
8. 2 Sam 1:25-27

Chapter Seven

Too Heavy To Fly

I am always amazed by the amount of junk people accumulate over the years and end up stashing in their attics. You should see the look of disbelief on many people's faces when they discover the amount of junk they cannot take to their new home! Most people discover that most of the "stuff" that they thought they had to have, was nothing more than glorified junk.

In the United States of America, garage sales are increasingly becoming more and more popular as a medium of getting rid of the junk that has accumulated in people's garages and attics. One of the spiritual dangers that we must be aware of during periods of transition is the danger of carrying excess spiritual and emotional baggage into our future destiny.

#4. The Danger Of Carrying Excess Baggage Into Our Future Destiny:

Whether we are called to church or corporate world ministry, carrying excess spiritual and emotional baggage will soon take its toil and seriously tax our personal advancement. I hope and pray that the following case study will help clarify this important matter.

CASE STUDY: MISREADING THE CALL (JOHN ALEXANDER DOWIE'S ATTEMPT TO ENTER POLITICS)

After the legendary apostle and faith healer, John Alexander Dowie moved from Scotland to Australia, through a series of tragedies at his parish, God introduced this hungry soul to the ministry of divine healing. Even though much of church tradition denied the existence of the healing ministry, Dowie refused to believe that the day of miracles had past with the passing away of the apostles. Dowie's burning passion to experience the power of God launched him into one of the most powerful healing ministry since the days of early church.

Thousands began to come from all over Australia to receive a touch of God through the ministry of this powerful servant of God. Being the only man who was praying for the sick with dazzling results, Dowie's ministry exploded and his influence over Australia grew rapidly. It was during this time of great success that Dowie misread the administrations of his apostolic mantle and how it to use the vast influence of his office.

Church historian Roberts Liardon has this to say about this period in Dowie's life. "...Dowie's leadership was gaining a strong national influence. So seeing his potential and knowing his stand, the Temperance Society asked him to run for Parliament. At first, he opposed the idea. But he later changed his mind, thinking he could possibly influence more in the political arena and decided to enter the race.

But Dowie suffered a sound defeat in the elections. The local newspapers that had been so damaged by his ministry waged an all-out attack against him. The politicians and alcoholic beverage industry paid untold amounts of money to see him slandered and defeated. After the election, Dowie had wounded his church, and disgraced his ministry.

While campaigning for office, Dowie also neglected his commandment to preach divine healing. He simply steered away from his calling to pursue a personal goal, thinking he could reach a greater mass of people. And as a result, the rest of his time in Australia was spent in darkness and futility."

(God's Generals by Roberts Liardon, pg 29)

There are a variety of ways that we can accumulate spiritual and emotional baggage during periods of spiritual transition. In most cases, excess spiritual and emotional baggage comes in the form of good ideas which have no bearing on the original call of God upon our lives. My dear friend Tim Storey has a saying, *"God ideas always come to pass, while good ideas may or may never come to pass."* This means that we should never abandon *God*

ideas to pursue good ideas. We must never forget that
there might be a hidden agenda behind some of the good
ideas that come from our friends. We must be careful that
we do not allow our friends to misuse our God given platform to fulfill their own dreams, which have no bearing on
what God has called us to do.

> *"We must be careful that we do not allow
> our friends to misuse our God given platform
> to fulfill their own dreams."*

John Alexander's Dowie's friends, who pushed him
into the arena of politics, probably had their own personal
agenda as to why they wanted him to be in that position.
They did not have the national influence of Dowie, so they
used him to fulfill their personal desire for politics. Entering
the political arena brought unnecessary personal and spiritual baggage into Dowie's life which destroyed his ministry
in Australia. The political baggage only served to distract
him from his true calling. When we accumulate excess
spiritual and emotional baggage, we open doors which
facilitate the devil's attacks on our life, especially during
the vulnerable times of transition. Dowie's enemies who,
prior to his entry into politics, had been unable to attack
him personally, now found plenty of reasons to slander his
great ministry and smear his personal character. Such are
the spiritual dangers of periods of transition.

CASE STUDY:
THE COCA COLA STORY

*Several years ago Coca Cola, one of the most successful
companies in the twenty-first century came up with a new*

formula for their Coca Cola drink that almost cost Coca Cola its long history of success and threatened to destroy its market share in the global market.

The management of Coca Cola came up with new brand of Coca Cola that they called "The New Coke." This brand of Coke was designed to be of a sweeter taste than the old Coca Cola drink. Coca Cola was trying to bite into the Pepsi market, whose Pepsi drink has a little bit of a sweeter taste. When this new brand of Coke arrived in the stores, the sales of Coca Cola plummeted. The millions of Coca Cola drinkers were horrified by this sweeter tasting Coke that lacked the power, taste and feel of the older Coca Cola brand that they were used to.

Not only did Coca Cola fail to take a bite out of the Pepsi market, they were now in serious danger of losing their millions of Coca Cola drinkers who simply loved the old Coke. The management quickly pulled the plug on the "New Coke Brand" and reintroduced the old Coke brand under the new name, "Coke Classic." But not before they lost millions of dollars in this very expensive experiment. Their so called "New Coke Brand" was nothing less than excess weight, a distraction at best. Coca Cola is not the only company that has lost millions of dollars for products that were nothing more than good ideas that had no real bearing on the true calling of the Company.

Not even the legendary tour de France cyclist Neil Armstrong could have won any races if he had been carrying excess baggage on his bicycle. The excess baggage would have simply weighed him down; sapping the energy he desperately needed to win races. We, on the other hand, are running a race with eternal consequences, a race we cannot afford to lose. The race we have been called to run and win is just too important to mess with.

Besetting Sins and Spiritual Weights

"Wherefore seeing we also are compassed about with so great a cloud of witnesses, let us lay aside every weight, and the sin which doth so easily beset us, and let us run with patience the race that is set before us, Looking unto Jesus the author and finisher of our faith; who for the joy that was set before him endured the cross, despising the shame, and is set down at the right hand of the throne of God."[9]

The apostle Paul in his epistle to the Hebrews identified two forms of spiritual baggage that we must be aware of when walking through the valley of transition.

Besetting Sins

Besetting sins are habitual sins that are intricately inter-woven into the very fabric of our personality and have the power to derail us from pursuing our God given destiny. For example, Peter's besetting sin was his impulsiveness. He would always say things before he had the time to fully digest what he was saying. He made commitments that he couldn't possibly keep.

Coincidentally, this was my besetting sin. I am a very generous person by nature. I love to give and open doors for people. There is absolutely nothing wrong with being a generous person. My problem was that I did not allow the Holy Spirit to govern my spirit of generosity and unfor-tunately my generosity was being driven by a spirit of impulsiveness.

Like Peter, I found myself making impulsive decisions to help people that God was not leading me to help. I found myself making financial commitments to people who were in financial trouble and I felt sorry for, whom God had not commissioned me to bail out. As soon I had made the financial or emotional commitment, I found that the money or the resources weren't available for me to effectively help the people I had promised to help.

"I became a prisoner of my own impulsive behavior, and a victim of my own generosity."

Some of these impulsive commitments that I made caused a serious strain in my relationship with my wife. In some of these instances I had made these commitments before talking to my wife. Anybody who has been married for a while will tell you this inaccurate behavior spells trouble in a marriage. Worse still, the people that I had made the financial, emotional or social commitments to became very angry with me when I failed to come through. I became a prisoner of my own impulsive behavior, and a victim of my own generosity.

"And the Lord said, Simon, Simon, behold, Satan hath desired to have you, that he may sift you as wheat: But I have prayed for thee, that thy faith fail not: and when thou art converted, strengthen thy brethren. And he said unto him, Lord, I am ready to go with thee, both into prison, and to death. And he said, I tell thee, Peter, the cock shall not crow this day, before that thou shalt thrice deny that thou knowest me." [10]

I can identify with impulsive Peter. We could have been twin brothers had we lived in the same era. Peter was not a frivolous person, with no sense of integrity. He was a genuine apostle of Jesus Christ who struggled with a besetting sin of impulsiveness. Nevertheless, the Lord Jesus knew that *if Peter's besetting sin of impulsiveness was not purged from him, it would eventually destroy his apostolic calling by creating unnecessary spiritual baggage for him to deal with during periods of transition.*

The Lord Jesus allowed the devil to sift Peter so he could see for himself the spiritual dangers posed by his besetting sin of impulsiveness. Without thinking, Peter told the Lord Jesus that he was going to stick with Him all the way to the cross. The Lord Jesus told him that he would deny Him three times before the cock crowed once. Peter even argued his point with the Lord as if he were wiser than God.

In the aftermath of Peter's historic denial of the Lord, he struggled with the guilt he felt for what he had done. His impulsiveness had placed a tremendous strain on his conscience. He was living with the guilt of having to face the fact that he had just denied the Son of God not once, but three times. The spiritual baggage that Peter carried from this experience drove him back to the fishing career that he had before Jesus called him to become an apostle and the Lord Jesus had to "fish" him back to his prophetic calling. During periods of transition the Lord will divinely orchestrate circumstances which are designed to circumcise us from every besetting sin that has resulted in excess spiritual baggage for us to carry.

Some people's besetting sin is *their weakness for exaggeration or their short temperedness, like Moses for instance. Moses' short temperedness created excess spiritual baggage in his future destiny which eventually stopped him from entering the promise land.* God was forced to retire Moses earlier than planned. This is why God is committed to setting His people free from besetting sins so that they do not carry excess baggage into their future destiny. Jesus did not want Peter to carry spiritual baggage into his post Pentecost apostolic ministry.

Spiritual Weights

I will never forget an incident I had at the Hartford International airport in Hartford, Connecticut. I arrived at the airport late. Being short on time, I was in a hurry to get through the security checkpoints so I could board my flight. When I got to the ticket counter, the ticketing agent told me that one of my suitcases was over the official weight limit and I had to pay more money before I could proceed to board my plane.

I tried to persuade the ticketing agent to let me slip by with a warning, but he insisted that the fine had to be paid or he was not going to let me board my flight. I told him that the ticketing agents from my originating airport in Dallas had said nothing about my excess baggage and neither did they charge me anything. His reply to me was, *"Sir, just because you got away with it in Dallas, does not in anyway change the fact that company policy requires me to charge you for the amount of the excess baggage!"* I ended up paying him eighty dollars and I arrived at my boarding gate just in time to catch my flight back to Dallas.

While I was working on this book, the Lord brought this incidence to my remembrance. He told me that many of His people are carrying *excess spiritual baggage from their past into their future destinies* and they have been getting away with it until now. God told me that many of

His people are about to start paying heavy prices for the excess spiritual baggage that they have been carrying. *This excess spiritual luggage from the past can present legal openings to the devil which become breeding grounds for his attacks against our lives.*

Spiritual weights unlike besetting sins are not habitual sins, but they can become so if they are not handled properly. Spiritual weights are social or religious interests that Christians accumulate while going through life which have no bearing on their destiny. For instance there is nothing wrong with watching football. Watching football is one of America's number one family pass times. Family and friends get together to watch their favorite NFL teams play. But when a person who has a higher calling in God begins to spend countless hours watching football on television, and has little time to pray and read their Bible, there is a serious problem.

"All things are lawful for me, but all things are not expedient: all things are lawful for me, but all things edify not."[11]

Can you imagine seeing Jesus spend countless hours watching television or waiting in line for hours to get into a baseball game, instead of working His way to the cross? Dying on the cross to pay for the sins of the whole world was His primary reason for coming to the earth. Anything that took away from the valuable time that Jesus needed to fulfill His primary assignment on earth would be regarded as a spiritual weight. There are thousands of believers who have accumulated *excess spiritual baggage* during periods of spiritual transition. These extra weights are stealing the time they need to fulfill their spiritual assignments. These spiritual weights also serve the purpose of slowing our spiritual pace toward our God given destiny.

The Martha Complex

"Now it came to pass, as they went, that he entered into a certain village: and a certain woman named Martha received him into her house. And she had a sister called Mary, which also sat at Jesus' feet, and heard his word. But Martha was cumbered about much serving, and came to him, and said, Lord, dost thou not care that my sister hath left me to serve alone? bid her therefore that she help me. And Jesus answered and said unto her, Martha, Martha, thou art careful and troubled about many things: But one thing is needful: and Mary hath chosen that good part, which shall not be taken away from her."[12]

When we lack the discipline and discernment to prioritize Divine presence over human performance, we are refusing to release our earthly "lot" to gain God's best. We make the same mistake Martha made and become what the King James Bible calls "cumbered." Sometimes we can get into sensory overload and we miss those moments of divine visitation or impartation. We get so busy that we forget to choose and pursue the best thing.

The original Greek word translated as "cumbered" means "to drag all around." Sometimes you're dragging around so much excess baggage; you can't feel it when He taps you on the shoulder. Both the New King James Version and the New International Version add another dimension when they say Martha was "distracted." The Scottish pastor and author, A. Moody Stuart, put it this way:

193

Martha...may be taken as doing many things in the service of Jesus Christ, for the purpose of pleasing and honoring Him. The case is a sadly common one; of doing much for Christ, yet caring less for Christ himself, his teaching, presence, and fellowship. Absent from Jesus she was working for Jesus, and she grudged to be left by her sister unaided in her work. She imagined that Christ had great need of her services, and that it would please him best to provide many things to honor him. But she mistook the character and calling of him who came not to be ministered unto but to minister, and to give his life a ransom for many. Jesus sought not hers, but her; he came not to receive but to give; he needed not Martha, but Martha was in urgent need of him.

(Chasing God Serving Man, by Tommy Tenney, page 56)

Like Martha of old, so many of God's people suffer from what I call the *"Martha Complex."* They fail to realize that before God can truly promote them, He will first attempt to teach them the importance of treasuring His presence above the activities of ministry. Martha was more concerned about the **"Kitchen of ministry than sitting at the feet of Jesus to receive the impartation of His presence!"** There is absolutely nothing wrong with working hard to save souls and ministering to the saints. However, if these ministry activities take precedence over the pursuit of His sweet presence these spiritual activities become spiritual weights. Had Martha known that she only had a three-year transitional period in which she could host the physical presence of Jesus of Nazareth, she would have suspended much of her religious activities to host the manifest presence of God.

And He Took Lot with Him

"Now the LORD had said unto Abram, Get thee out of thy country, and from thy kindred, and from thy father's house, unto a land that I will shew thee: And I will make of thee a great nation, and I will bless thee, and make thy name great; and thou shalt be a blessing: And I will bless them that bless thee, and curse him that curseth thee: and in thee shall all families of the earth be blessed. So Abram departed, as the LORD had spoken unto him; and Lot went with him: and Abram was seventy and five years old when he departed out of Haran."[13]

When God called Abraham, He made it explicitly clear that He was calling **ONLY** him and his household to go to the land of Canaan. Nevertheless, when Abraham left, he felt compelled to take Lot, the son of his late brother, with him. The Bible tells us that Abraham was *sent* but *Lot simply tagged along*. One of the spiritual dangers of periods of transition is the danger of carrying *the wrong people* into our future destiny. The wrong people are those whom God has not appointed and qualified to be part of our future.

In many instances the real reason that we carry unnecessary people into our future is because we feel sorry for them. Some of us are simply too terrified to walk into our destiny by ourselves so we take friends with us to keep us company. There is nothing wrong with carrying people into the new spiritual dimension of destiny that God is calling us into, if those people are also sensing the same call of God upon their lives. In most cases we carry people into our future destiny who have no business being there! It's very easy to recognize men and women who have become

excess spiritual baggage in our lives. They do not carry the same grace that is upon our lives and are usually more flesh driven than purpose driven.

> *"One of the spiritual dangers of periods of transition is the danger of carrying the wrong people into our future destiny."*

It is quite clear that Abraham took Lot with him simply because he felt guilty leaving an orphaned child with his aging father. Nevertheless, this was obviously not God's will for Abraham and it soon became quiet evident. After a couple of years of tagging along, a serious problem rose between Abraham and Lot which severely tested their already strained alliance. This is why God wants us to surrender our emotions at the altar of total obedience to His will during periods of spiritual transition.

The land that Abraham and Lot were sharing became too small to support both them and their livestock. This led to serious fights between Abraham's and Lot's herdsmen. Lot was proving to be too much excess weight on Abraham's shoulders and the time had come to cut him loose. When he finally left, Abraham and Sarah may have asked themselves why they had taken him with them in the first place.

During periods of transition we must be very careful not to carry every relationship from our past into our future destiny. God never intended for some of the relationships in our lives to last forever. If we force certain past relationships or associations to cross into our future destiny when God has not ordained them to be there, they will soon become toxic to us and sap our spiritual strength.

*"And the LORD said unto Abram, after that Lot was sepa-
rated from him, Lift up now thine eyes, and look from the
place where thou art northward, and southward, and east-
ward, and westward: For all the land which thou seest,
to thee will I give it, and to thy seed for ever. And I will
make thy seed as the dust of the earth: so that if a man can
number the dust of the earth, then shall thy seed also be
numbered. Arise, walk through the land in the length of it
and in the breadth of it; for I will give it unto thee."*[14]

When Abraham finally let go of Lot, something very
spectacular happened. The Bible says that immediately
after Lot's departure, the Lord spoke to Abraham about
his spiritual inheritance. It was then that Abraham realized
Lot's presence in his life had been blocking the voice of
God. This is one of the serious dangers of transition that we
cannot afford to ignore. ***If we carry the wrong people into
our future destiny, their presence in our lives will begin
to shut down the voice of God, hiding from us our spiritual inheritance.*** God began to measure the boundaries of
Abraham's spiritual inheritance and showed Abraham the
land of Palestine which was going to be given to him and
his natural descendants. God also allowed Abraham to see
his spiritual descendants, those who would walk by faith
through the corridors of time.

Promises That Bind

*"Then the Spirit of the LORD came upon Jephthah, and
he passed over Gilead, and Manasseh, and passed over
Mizpeh of Gilead, and from Mizpeh of Gilead he passed
over unto the children of Ammon. And Jephthah vowed a
vow unto the LORD, and said, If thou shalt without fail*

deliver the children of Ammon into mine hands, Then it shall be, that whatsoever cometh forth of the doors of my house to meet me, when I return in peace from the children of Ammon, shall surely be the LORD's, and I will offer it up for a burnt offering."[15]

During periods of spiritual transition, we must be aware of the dangers of making hasty promises to people and vows to God, which we might have no power to fulfill. I call these, "promises that bind." **Most hasty promises or vows are made during times of great personal crisis or spiritual warfare.**

During these times it is quite human to feel like we need to negotiate with God in order to get some quick and miraculous relief. In our times of pain, we sometimes feel that negotiating with God will help shorten our time of testing because we have lost our ability to see our prophetic future. Like Jephthah, we make hasty promises to God and the people around us which can become a noose around our necks. Hasty vows to God and to other people during periods of transition can quickly translate into excess spiritual baggage in our future destiny.

"And Jephthah came to Mizpeh unto his house, and, behold, his daughter came out to meet him with timbrels and with dances: and she was his only child; beside her he had neither son nor daughter. And it came to pass, when he saw her, that he rent his clothes, and said, Alas, my daughter! thou hast brought me very low, and thou art one of them that trouble me: for I have opened my mouth unto the LORD, and I cannot go back. And she said unto him, My father, if thou hast opened thy mouth unto the LORD, do to me according to that which hath proceeded out of thy

mouth; forasmuch as the LORD hath taken vengeance for thee of thine enemies, even of the children of Ammon. And she said unto her father, Let this thing be done for me: let me alone two months, that I may go up and down upon the mountains, and bewail my virginity, I and my fellows."[16]

Offload or Sink

"And we being exceedingly tossed with a tempest, the next day they lightened the ship; And the third day we cast out with our own hands the tackling of the ship."[17]

Experienced sailors who have sailed through many seas will be the first ones to tell you that one of the first things sailors do when a ship is sinking is shed the excess weight. Everything that is unneeded is quickly tossed into the raging sea. The sailors know they have one of two choices – dump the excess weight or sink to the bottom of the sea.

For most of us, God is clearly instructing us to get rid of the extra weight. We need to go on a rigorous spiritual diet in order to bring our spiritual weight down to its proper measure. In the natural, if we put on too many pounds, we can open ourselves up to serious breathing problems and become susceptible to heart attacks, which threaten our life span. Hospital records are filled with death reports of thousands of people who died much too early from health problems or diseases which were induced by having too much excess fat in their bodies.

The accumulated body fat began to clog up the arteries that circulate blood to the heart, thus causing a heart attack. When I was pastoring a church in Chicago, one of my worship leaders died of a heart attack in her sleep.

She was a beautiful, but extremely over weight, sister who had failed to bring her weight under subjection. It was a sobering tragedy. This illustration is also true in the spirit realm. Excess spiritual body fat will eventually clog up our spiritual arteries which may eventually bring spiritual death upon us. We cannot afford to carry excess spiritual baggage during periods of spiritual transition as we journey into our destiny.

Notes on Chapter Seven

1. Gen 9:12-15
2. Matt 15:22-28
3. Isa 14:12-15
4. Gen 12:10-15
5. Gen 27:23-27
6. 1 Sam 16:1-30
7. 1 Sam 18:3-4
8. 2 Sam 1:25-27
9. Heb 12:1-2
10. Luke 22:31-34
11. 1 Cor 10:23
12. Luke 10:38-42
13. Gen 12:1-4
14. Gen 13:14-17
15. Judges 11:29-31
16. Judg 11:34-37
17. Acts 27:18-1

Chapter Eight

When Fools Are In Power

Amerian Leadership Expert, Dr. John C. Maxwell, in his famed book *"Developing the Leader within You"* says, *"Everything rises and falls on leadership."* There is nothing more terrifying than fools holding the reigns of power. One of the spiritual dangers during periods of transition is the danger of having wise and mature leadership replaced by emotionally hyped and immature leadership!

"The words of wise men are heard in quiet more than the cry of him that ruleth among fools."[1]

Having been born and reared in Africa, I really appreciate the role that leadership plays in the rise or fall of a nation. The continent of Africa has some of the richest and largest deposits of natural resources among the continents of the world and yet Africa has some of the poorest and financially mismanaged countries in the world. The lingering curse of Africa is the inaccurate transfer of power from one government to another! Transitioning from one government to another has always been the glaring weakness of so many African nations. ***The issue of inaccurate***

succession during periods of political transition has hurt many African nations, leaving many of their citizens disfranchised and their economies in a serious state of disrepair.

Inaccurate succession during periods of spiritual transition is even more dangerous for churches and ministries because our business is first and foremost, spiritual. Inaccurate succession during periods of transition is even more disastrous for multibillion dollar business organizations, whose future stake in the global market depends upon continued excellent and visionary leadership. The following case study may help to illustrate this important fact.

CASE STUDY:
THE RISE AND FALL OF TELEDYNE INC
(THE HENRY SINGLETON STORY)

Singleton grew up on a Texas ranch, with the childhood dream of becoming a great businessman in the model of the rugged individualist. Armed with a Ph.D from MIT, he founded Teledyne. The name Teledyne derives from Greek and means "force applied at a distance" – an apt name, as the central force holding the far-flung empire together was Henry Singleton himself.

Through acquisitions, Singleton built the company from a small enterprise to number 293 on the fortune 500 list in six years. Within ten years, he'd completed more than 100 acquisitions, eventually creating a far-flung enterprise with 130 profit centers in everything from exotic metals to insurance. Amazingly, the whole system worked, with Singleton himself acting as the glue that connected all the moving parts together. At one point, he said, "I define my job as having the freedom to do what seems to be in the best interest of the company at any time". A 1978 Forbes feature story maintained, "Singleton will win no awards for humility, but who can avoid standing in awe of his impressive record?"

Singleton continued to run the company well into his seventies, with no serious thought given to succession. After all, why worry about succession when the very point of the whole thing is to serve as a platform to leverage the talents of your remarkable genius? "if there is a single weakness in this otherwise brilliant picture," the article continued, "it is this: Teledyne is not so much a system as it is the reflection of one's man's singular discipline".

What a weakness it turned out to be. Once Singleton stepped away from day to day management in the mid-1980s, the far-flung empire began to crumble. From the end of 1986 until its merger with Allegheny in 1995, Teledyne's cumulative stock returns imploded, falling 66 percent behind the general stock market. Singleton achieved his childhood dream of becoming a great businessman, but failed utterly at the task of building a great [lasting] company. {End of quote. Good to Great by Jim Collins, pg 47)

The world we live in is full of *"Henry Singletons"*-men who are dazzling success gurus so intoxicated by their personal achievements that they have failed to adequately prepare their families and organizations for their personal exit. While they are still in the drivers seat, the future of their families and organizations may look quite promising until times of transition in leadership proves them otherwise. There are many great pastors leading some of the largest churches in the world, who operate like *"spiritual Henry Singletons." **They have a one generational*** *ministry that is doomed or programmed to crumble after their demise.* This mentality is an experiment in foolishness, and only serves to fuel an old adage, *"it's a terrible day when fools hold the reigns of power."*

#5. The Danger Of Inaccurate Succession or
The Danger Of Success Without A Successor

Good and Bad Success

"For the turning away of the simple shall slay them, and the prosperity of fools shall destroy them."[2]

I lost a very dear friend a while back, after he lost his fight with cancer. He was the pastor of a great and thriving church of about seven hundred people. When he died, he was survived by a beautiful wife and two children. His only son, who should have succeeded his father, was regarded by many in the congregation as nothing more than a *"glorified spiritual Casanova."*

When his father was alive, this young man was busy fooling around with some of the sisters in the church and many of the people in the church knew about his flirtatious ways. They tolerated him because he was the pastor's son, plus nobody thought that my dear friend would suddenly die of cancer within a couple of months. Needless to say, he left behind a serious leadership vacuum.

While my friend was working tenuously to build a great church, he failed to prepare his son to succeed him during the period of transition in leadership. When that time came, things were quite messy. The church was hijacked by associate pastors who also had visions and spiritual agendas of their own. Relationships within the church soon became highly strained and strife was spreading like a malignant cancer throughout the once thriving church.

> ***"The church was hijacked by associate Pastors who also had visions and spiritual agendas of their own."***

One of the associate pastors left and took some people with him. It was obvious to me that my dear friend had died on the wrong side of the law of transition, leaving behind no adequate successor and thus leaving his ministry at a dead end. *God wants His anointed ministers to have the power to minister beyond their days here on earth through their spiritual successors. God never intended for spiritual leaders to have a "one generational ministry" which does not last beyond their lifetime here on earth.* I once heard a man of God say, *"Success without a successor is a failure,"* and I couldn't agree more.

"This book of the law shall not depart out of thy mouth; but thou shalt meditate therein day and night, that thou mayest observe to do according to all that is written therein: for then thou shalt make thy way prosperous, and then thou shalt have good success."[3]

God showed Joshua the divine formula for attaining *"good success,"* indicating that there is such a thing as *"bad success!"* I really believe that pastors are making a serious error in judgment when they focus so much on succeeding that they neglect taking the time to "father" sons and daughters in the ministry. Every church needs

205

spiritual sons and daughters who can grab hold of the spiritual passion and mandate of their leader. *At the end of his earthly ministry, the great prophet Elijah's spiritual legacy and ministry was carried on by his spiritual son named Elisha.*

Elisha took Elijah's spiritual legacy and imparted it to the second and third generation of Israelites, some of whom had never met the prophet Elijah in person. What would have happened to Elijah's great spiritual legacy if he had just taken off to heaven in the chariot of fire without transferring his life and anointing to the young and upcoming prophetic apprentice, Elisha? I believe the wicked woman and false prophetess Jezebel would have remained in power, wreaking spiritual havoc in Israel longer than she did.

Through Elisha's ministry, the prophet Elijah was able to overthrow a *"ruling spirit"* that he had fought with for most of his life. What the prophet Elijah could not accomplish through direct confrontation with the spirit of Jezebel, he accomplished through proper succession during the period of spiritual transition in leadership. *This is the secret of some of the greatest corporations in the world, who have longevity. They spend a lot of money and time on staff training so that their corporations do not suffer or lose their profitability once there has been a transition in management.* Corporations that were not as prudent have suffered great and sometimes irreparable damage. Some corporations lost a great percentage of their market share during these periods of transition in management. In most cases, many of these failing corporations were taken over by more aggressive and prudent corporations. Their founders failed to plan for a successful transition in management.

"Now Absalom in his lifetime had taken and reared up for himself a pillar, which is in the king's dale: for he said, I have no son to keep my name in remembrance: and he called the pillar after his own name: and it is called unto this day, Absalom's place."[4]

When Absalom the son of King David died, the only thing he left behind that people could remember him by was **a pillar of stone that he had erected and named after himself.** How tragic and depressing this must have been! In his blind obsession to seize the reigns of political power, Absalom had no time to sire a son. His political ambition to sit on the throne of Israel blinded him to the importance of raising a natural or spiritual son who could continue his spiritual legacy. As a result, he was as quickly forgotten as a whisper on a stormy night. The only things that some men and women of God will be remembered by after their death, are the books and teaching tapes that they will leave behind. This is because true success can never be measured in dollars and cents but only in the changed lives of the men and women who came in contact with their life and ministry.

Eli: The High Priest Who Died With a Broken Heart

The spiritual dangers of inaccurate succession or the lack of a successor is fully revealed to us through the life of Eli. Eli was the high priest of Israel at the temple in Shiloh when Hannah, the mother of the Prophet Samuel, arrived for prayer. Hannah was a beautiful young woman who was married to an honorable and devout man by the name of Elkanah.

She was barren and desperate for a child. She came to the temple in Shiloh and in a time of intense personal prayer she poured her soul out to God and pledged to give Him the first child who came out of her womb. Eli saw her stammering lips and thought that she was drunk and was about to chase her away when she told him why she was there. Eli prayed for her and told her to go home. When she got home, God remembered her and she gave birth to Samuel, who was later moved to the temple in Shiloh to live under Eli's care and tutorage.

"And Eli said unto her, How long wilt thou be drunken? put away thy wine from thee. And Hannah answered and said, No, my lord, I am a woman of a sorrowful spirit: I have drunk neither wine nor strong drink, but have poured out my soul before the LORD. Count not thine handmaid for a daughter of Belial: for out of the abundance of my complaint and grief have I spoken hitherto. Then Eli answered and said, Go in peace: and the God of Israel grant thee thy petition that thou hast asked of him."[5]

According to the Bible, Eli was a sincere man of God from the house of Aaron, who truly loved God. He took care of the temple at Shiloh to the best of his ability, but he had a serious problem in his own house. He had two sons serving with him in the priesthood who were sons of the devil. They did not live like men of the cloth. Even though Eli was a great high priest, he proved to be a great failure as a father.

His two sons Hophni and Phinehas, were bringing the work of God in serious disrepute. They were stealing the best parts of the sacrificial offerings that were prepared for the Lord. They even went as far as sleeping with women in the temple of the Lord, while masquerading as priests of God. God was so angry with them that He spoke to the young boy, Samuel and told him to take a very sobering prophecy of impending judgment to Eli. God told Eli that he was cutting his entire lineage from the priesthood because he had failed to discipline and train his sons for succession during this period of spiritual transition.

When the Philistines rose to fight against Israel, God lured the two sons of Eli into the battlefield. The two sons of Eli, in blatant defiance of God's holiness, put their hands to the Ark of the Covenant. They lifted it and carried it to the frontlines of the battlefield assuming that its very presence would make the Philistines flee for their lives. It was a gross miscalculation on their part. The presence of the Ark of the Covenant at the battlefront only served to strengthen the resolve of the Philistines who fought back with the tenacity of a wounded buffalo.

Israel was soundly defeated, Eli's two sons of were killed instantly, and the Ark of the Covenant was captured by the Philistines. A man who escaped from the battlefront raced back to the temple at Shiloh and told Eli the news that his sons were dead. When Eli heard that the treasured Ark of the Covenant was now in the hands of the Philistines, he fell and broke his neck, dying instantly. It was the classic case of a great and promising priesthood that had come to a tragic and abrupt end because of inaccurate succession during the period of transition. Eli's inability to discipline and train his sons for succession in the priestly service had placed a sentence of death upon his life and priesthood legacy.

"And the messenger answered and said, Israel is fled before the Philistines, and there hath been also a great slaughter among the people, and thy two sons also, Hophni and Phinehas, are dead, and the ark of God is taken. And it came to pass, when he made mention of the ark of God, that he fell from off the seat backward by the side of the gate, and his neck brake, and he died: for he was an old man, and heavy. And he had judged Israel forty years."[6]

The Sons of Samuel

Without a doubt, Samuel was one of the most powerful prophets of the Old Testament era. He was raised in the house of God at Shiloh from the time that his mother weaned him as a child. At the tender age of twelve years, God spoke to him in an audible voice to carry a prophecy of judgment against the house of Eli, because of the abominable behavior of his two sons. This was Samuel's first prophecy. You would think that it must have left a lasting impression upon his young mind about how serious God is about the issue of succession. Samuel grew into such a spiritual stature that his governmental anointing was able to effectively provide adequate spiritual covering for the nation of Israel. The Philistines could not cross the borders of Israel all the days of Samuel's life. His prophetic anointing was so strong it was keeping the powers of the enemy at bay.

"And as Samuel was offering up the burnt offering, the Philistines drew near to battle against Israel: but the LORD thundered with a great thunder on that day upon the Philistines, and discomfited them; and they were smitten before Israel. So the Philistines were subdued, and they came no more into the coast of Israel: and the

hand of the LORD was against the Philistines all the days of Samuel. And the cities which the Philistines had taken from Israel were restored to Israel, from Ekron even unto Gath; and the coasts thereof did Israel deliver out of the hands of the Philistines. And there was peace between Israel and the Amorites. And Samuel judged Israel all the days of his life."[7]

Samuel's ministry was very successful, but like his predecessor Eli, he was not successful in fathering his own sons for spiritual succession. Even though Samuel had deep personal integrity and was a zealous lover of God, his sons failed to follow in his footsteps. The rebellious behavior of Samuel's sons did not pose a serious problem for the nation of Israel while Samuel was younger. But the older Samuel got, their undesirable behavior started unsettling many of the elders of Israel who were afraid that Samuel might die and leave them to be forced to serve under the immature and corrupt spiritual leadership of his two sons.

The elders of Israel knew that Samuel's season as the presiding judge over Israel was coming to an end. They also knew that Samuel in all his greatness had failed to prepare his sons to successfully succeed him at the end of his life journey. To protect their own interests, the elders of Israel went to Samuel and told him that they wanted to have a king who could rule over them.

They told Samuel that his sons were not walking in his ways. Samuel was devastated by the request of the elders of Israel. He was grieved because by asking for a king to rule over them, Israel was in fact rejecting God as their true King. God had always been the sovereign ruler of the nation of Israel through the yielded life of a godly man or woman.

Unfortunately, Samuel's sons were neither prophetic nor yielded to God and their ungodly behavior created a serious spiritual leadership vacuum during this period of spiritual transition. The spiritual lesson contained in this story for all leaders is simply this, *if spiritual leaders fail to raise up anointed successors during the tenure of their ministry, the flock will be forced to abandon the ways of the Spirit and seek natural alternatives to protect themselves from the new leaders.*

"And it came to pass, when Samuel was old, that he made his sons judges over Israel. Now the name of his firstborn was Joel; and the name of his second, Abiah: they were judges in Beersheba. And his sons walked not in his ways, but turned aside after lucre, and took bribes, and perverted judgment. Then all the elders of Israel gathered themselves together, and came to Samuel unto Ramah,

And said unto him, Behold, thou art old, and thy sons walk not in thy ways: now make us a king to judge us like all the nations."[8]

When Fools Sit On the Throne

King Solomon was one of the wisest and richest men who ever lived. He was a man of scrutiny who interrogated everything and did not take anything at face value. Solomon, being a man of great wealth and power, was particularly interested in the character of the successor who would carry on his legacy. Solomon knew about the spiritual danger of inaccurate succession during times of transition.

"Yea, I hated all my labour which I had taken under the sun: because I should leave it unto the man that shall be

after me. And who knoweth whether he shall be a wise man or a fool? yet shall he have rule over all my labour wherein I have laboured, and wherein I have shewed myself wise under the sun. This is also vanity. For there is a man whose labour is in wisdom, and in knowledge, and in equity; yet to a man that hath not laboured therein shall he leave it for his portion. This also is vanity and a great evil."[9]

King Solomon knew that everything rises and falls on leadership. He must have been visited by many foolish kings and nobles from other nations who proved to him that it's possible for fools to sit on the throne of power. King Solomon had the wisdom to prepare a successor who could take the reigns of power when his end was in sight.

King Solomon understood the following things about succession:

1. *Solomon understood that we are all going to die and all that we have accumulated in terms of money and assets will be passed to someone else.*
2. *Solomon understood that nobody knows for certain whether their successor will reign with wisdom.*
3. *Solomon understood that the only way to ensure that the successor is filled with the spirit of wisdom is to prepare and train them yourself.*
4. *Solomon understood the successor's character must contain three main ingredients- wisdom, knowledge and integrity, in order to ensure a continuing legacy.*

Where Are The Fathers?

There is a serious need for spiritual parenting in this generation. The absence of fathers on a spiritual and natural level has grown to cataclysmic proportions. Many of today's children are being raised in single parent homes with the mothers struggling to fill both rolls of parenting. Many men who are called to be father figures in the home are "AWOL" (a military term meaning absent without official leave). This generation of fatherless children filtering into our churches is not looking for great preachers; they have a desperate need for *"spiritual fathers"* who can lead them into their spiritual inheritance and prepare them for spiritual leadership positions.

"Behold, I will send you Elijah the prophet before the coming of the great and dreadful day of the LORD: And he shall turn the heart of the fathers to the children, and the heart of the children to their fathers, lest I come and smite the earth with a curse."[10]

Malachi, the last prophet of the Old Testament era declares that in the last days, God will begin to release the Elijah anointing and mandate upon mature ministries. God is going to position these mature ministries to become fathering ministries for this generation of sons. These men and women of God are going to take it upon themselves to spiritually parent the second generation.

The Elijah anointing will cause the hearts of fathers and/or mothers, to turn toward their spiritual children in the same way that the heart of the prophet Elijah was turned toward the young Elisha. I really believe that in this transitional period before the second coming of Christ, the Holy Spirit is going to raise many fathering ministries so God can put to an end to the *"curse of success without a successor."*

"For though ye have ten thousand instructors in Christ, yet have ye not many fathers: for in Christ Jesus I have begotten you through the gospel." [11]

How to Raise Spiritual Sons Who Can Handle Success

God wants mature ministries to raise sons and daughters who can handle success, because their spiritual life is more important to them than success. The following are some of my personal suggestions on how spiritual leaders can raise spiritual sons and daughters who can handle success and spiritual succession.

1. *Spiritual sons and daughters must be taught how to labor in wisdom, knowledge and integrity.*
2. *Their spirits must be trained to become bigger than success, so that success does not become their undoing. This can be achieved by increasing their spiritual capacity to contain more of God by teaching them to live a life of prayer and worship.*
3. *They must be taught the importance of living in the fear of the Lord.*
4. *They must be taught the power of living in the "spirit of prayer."*
5. *They must be taught how to subdue their fleshly appetites with seasons of fasting.*
6. *They must be taught to respect the law of transition and live by it.*
7. *They must be taught the importance of meditating on the word of God day and night.*
8. *They must be taught how to live by faith through a lifestyle of total obedience to God.*

9. *They must be taught how to become better stewards of what God has entrusted to them (especially finances).*
10. *They must be taught the importance of "soul restoration" so that they can avoid the pitfalls of a contaminated soul. Healing from unresolved soul conditions must be aggressively pursed.*

This is not by any means an exhaustive list on the subject of spiritual fathering, but it provides us with a rough working draft. We will do well to skillfully train our spiritual sons and daughters to carry the spiritual legacy of our ministry to future generations that we will leave behind.

Notes on Chapter Eight

1. Eccl 9:17
2. Prov 1:32
3. Josh 1:8
4. 2 Sam 18:18
5. 1 Sam 1:14-17
6. 1 Sam 4:17-18
7. 1 Sam 7:10-15
8. 1 Sam 8:1-5
9. Eccl 2:18-21
10. Mal 4:5-6
11. 1 Cor 4:15

Chapter Nine

Can You Still Hear His Voice

T here is nothing more important than having the undiluted presence of the Holy Spirit in our spiritual arsenal when navigating the valley of transition. Nothing of any real spiritual value can ever be accomplished for the kingdom of God which is not birthed and inspired by the Holy Spirit.

Jesus so treasured the person and work of the Holy Spirit that He was in a hurry to step out of the way so the Holy Spirit could take His place in the life and ministry of His apostles. As powerful as the ministry of Jesus was, His physical body limited the reach of His ministry. He couldn't be in all places at the same time and was limited to the regions of Palestine. But after the day of Pentecost, the ministry of Jesus became a global ministry with infinite reach through the person and power of the Holy Spirit!

#6. The Danger Of Becoming Insensitive To
The Voice Of The Holy Spirit.

The Promise & Person of the Holy Spirit

"Howbeit when he, the Spirit of truth, is come, he will guide you into all truth: for he shall not speak of himself; but whatsoever he shall hear, that shall he speak: and he will shew you things to come. He shall glorify me: for he shall receive of mine, and shall shew it unto you. All things that the Father hath are mine: therefore said I, that he shall take of mine, and shall shew it unto you."[1]

Have you ever been in a place where the people in the room acted like you did not exist? It's a very humiliating and demeaning experience. I have never in my lifetime met a person who enjoys being ignored by others. If we were just pieces of furniture or animals of instinct, being ignored by others would not affect us. Emotional sensitivity to how other people treat us can only be ascribed to entities that have both presence and personality.

I must admit that I was quite surprised when I received the revelation of the Holy Spirit's being and realized that He is not an inanimate spiritual force operating in the universe. He is a real person with personality and presence! This revelation forced me into a spiritual revolution. Unsettling thoughts and questions began to bombard my mind like relentless torpedoes. *"If the Holy Spirit is a person, then I can no longer relate to Him as some inanimate spiritual force. If the Holy Spirit is a person with both personality and presence, then I cannot live and act like*

218

He has no feelings. I cannot ignore His voice and presence in my life without grieving Him."

I was astounded by how much my attitude changed after this spiritual revelation. A special reverence for the Holy Spirit came upon me, mixed with an unsettling sense of excitement. *"If the Holy Spirit is a person with personality and presence, then He has the capacity to feel compassion towards me when I am in trouble. If He feels compassion then He would not hesitate to use His power to deliver me?"* The realization that the Holy Spirit was a very real person completely changed my life and empowered me to fully embrace my prophetic destiny with confidence.

> **"The realization that the Holy Spirit was a very real person completely changed my life."**

Jesus never called the Holy Spirit an *"it"* or a *"something"* like some Christians do. Jesus ascribed to the Holy Spirit a real sense of personality and presence by calling him a person (He). Unfortunately there are so many believers who still act and talk like the Holy Spirit is anything but a person. It's no wonder so many believers find it difficult to navigate the valley of transition because they go through spiritual and social transition in their own power, as though the Holy Spirit does not exist. The *"super spiritual"* people try to make a mental acknowledgement of the power and person of the Holy Spirit but rarely do they consult Him or allow Him to speak. *This inaccurate behavior toward the person of the Holy Spirit has resulted in disastrous consequences for some Christians during periods of spiritual transition.*

After the Lord Jesus Christ rose from the dead, He spent forty days prior to His ascension into heaven, talking to the disciples about things pertaining to the Kingdom of God. Central to the Kingdom message was the importance of receiving the person and power of the Holy Spirit. Jesus was emphatically clear that the apostles were not to attempt to fulfill the Great Commission without waiting on the "Promise of the Father."

Jesus told His apostles that once they received the Holy Spirit, their entire lives and ministry would change drastically. Their ministries were going to be accompanied by many miracles, signs and wonders just like Jesus.

"For John truly baptized with water; but ye shall be baptized with the Holy Ghost not many days hence. But ye shall receive power, after that the Holy Ghost is come upon you: and ye shall be witnesses unto me both in Jerusalem, and in all Judaea, and in Samaria, and unto the uttermost part of the earth. And when he had spoken these things, while they beheld, he was taken up; and a cloud received him out of their sight."[2]

They say that the last words of a dying man are the most important ones because they are chosen very carefully. Jesus knew that His time to leave His disciples had come, and the last words He spoke to them were centered on the importance of receiving the person and power of the Holy Spirit. If anybody understood the importance of the Holy Spirit, it was the Lord Jesus Christ because there were no records of miraculous signs and wonders in His life before the Holy Ghost came upon Him.

From the time that the Holy Spirit descended upon Him, the door to the supernatural suddenly swung wide open. Jesus went from living in obscurity to becoming the center of attraction for masses of hurting people in search of a miracle. *Unfortunately, one of the most tragic dangers during periods of transition is the danger of becoming insensitive to the voice and leading of the Holy Spirit, causing us as to take matters into our own hands.*

CASE STUDY:
THE FINAL DAYS OF THE MINISTRY OF WILLIAM BRANHAM

In 1909 a baby boy was born to poor Baptist parents in the hills of Kentucky. They named their little boy William Marion Branham. His childhood was sauced with some of the most amazing encounters with the presence of the Lord. While pastoring a small Baptist church, an angel of the Lord walked into his room with a message from God. The angel told him that he was to carry a very special gift of healing to his generation. Within months from this angelic visitation young Branham began to pray for the sick with amazing results. Soon there was no Coliseum big enough to contain the crowds that were coming to the Branham meetings.

God also gave him the prophetic ability to read the secrets of men's heart, with such detail that people felt like they were standing in the presence of God. F.F Bosworth who worked with Branham confessed that he and never met a man who was as sensitive to the Holy Spirit like Branham.

I wish I could tell you that brother Branham's ministry ended as an astounding success. Branham's ministry came to a close in a cloud of deception and confusion. Branham diverted from praying for the sick to teach heresies, because he wanted to compete with the teaching ministries of those God was raising at the time with strong gifts of teaching.

This is what church historian Roberts Liardon has to say about the end of Branham's ministry. "...Branham felt that there would come a day in his ministry were the "spoken Word" from his mouth would change physical bodies into glorified bodies for the Rapture. This tremendous power would be unleashed because Branham's words would restore God's original name of JHVH. Previously, the name had never been pronounced correctly, however "Branham's mouth was specially formed to say it." (God's Generals by Roberts Liardon, pg 340)

"The truth of the matter is that we can be very successful and still be very misguided."

Unfortunately, the ministry of the great William Branham ended, shrouded in public shame and personal deception. The man who had been called one of the most sensitive men to the voice of the Holy Spirit, had missed the Holy Spirit by a wide margin. How could this be? How could a man who knew the Holy Spirit so well, die believing such foolishness? Such are the spiritual dangers during periods of spiritual transition.

It's interesting to note that the most likely time to miss the voice of the Holy Spirit is during seasons of great personal and ministerial success. There is a tendency to believe that spiritual or business success is synonymous with divine approval. The truth of the matter is that we can be very successful and still be very misguided. This is why it's critical for us to maintain an attitude of humility, especially during seasons of great successes and personal triumphs.

The Assignment of the Holy Spirit

In order to really appreciate the assignment of the Holy Spirit, we must first consider the nature and work of the Holy Spirit. The assignment of the Holy Spirit is best viewed through understanding His work and also His nature. We will now examine what the Scriptures have to say about the blessed Holy Spirit.

1. ***He is the Spirit of Creation.*** He is the one who created man, angels, heaven and earth and all that is in it.

Job 33:4
The Spirit of God hath made me, and the breath of the Almighty hath given me life.

2. ***He is the Spirit of wisdom.*** He is the one who gives wisdom to every person when they ask God for it. He is the one we are to call upon when we need wisdom to navigate our valley of transition. He is the one who gave King Solomon amazing wisdom, which also made him the richest man who has ever lived.

Job 32:6-8
And Elihu the son of Barachel the Buzite answered and said, I am young, and ye are very old; wherefore I was afraid, and durst not shew you mine opinion. I said, Days should speak, and multitude of years should teach wisdom. But there is a spirit in man: and the inspiration of the Almighty giveth them understanding.

3. ***He is the Spirit of righteousness.*** He is the one who births the passion for righteousness inside the spirits

of God's people. He craves to live in an atmosphere of righteousness. He detests the atmosphere of sin.

John 16:7-8
Nevertheless I tell you the truth; It is expedient for you that I go away: for if I go not away, the Comforter will not come unto you; but if I depart, I will send him unto you. And when he is come, he will reprove the world of sin, and of righteousness, and of judgment:

4. **He is the Spirit of Joy.** The Bible tells us that the joy of the Lord is our strength. The Holy Spirit is the communicator and administrator of joy which is full of glory.

Acts 13:52
And the disciples were filled with joy, and with the Holy Ghost.

5. **He is the Spirit of peace.** He is the one who brings peace in troubled waters. He is the One who calmed the raging storms of the sea when Jesus rebuked them. He supplies the supernatural peace that is beyond the comprehension of the finite mind.

Rom 14:17
For the kingdom of God is not meat and drink; but righteousness, and peace, and joy in the Holy Ghost.

6. **He is the Spirit of revelation.** He is the one responsible for uncovering hidden and mysterious truths in the word of God. He is the one who is responsible for revealing satanic assignments against our lives and teaches us how to cancel them.

II Ki 6:11-12

Therefore the heart of the king of Syria was sore troubled for this thing; and he called his servants, and said unto them, Will ye not shew me which of us is for the king of Israel? And one of his servants said, None, my lord, O king: but Elisha, the prophet that is in Israel, telleth the king of Israel the words that thou speakest in thy bedchamber.

7. **He is the One who reveals the secrets and hidden motives of the human heart.** He particularly hates liars who are bent on deceiving His apostolic servants and hindering the advancement of the Kingdom of God.

Acts 5:3-5

But Peter said, Ananias, why hath Satan filled thine heart to lie to the Holy Ghost, and to keep back part of the price of the land? Whiles it remained, was it not thine own? and after it was sold, was it not in thine own power? why hast thou conceived this thing in thine heart? thou hast not lied unto men, but unto God. And Ananias hearing these words fell down, and gave up the ghost: and great fear came on all them that heard these things.

8. **He is the Spirit of Resurrection.** He is the One who raised our Lord Jesus Christ from the dead. He is the one who raised the widow's son when Elijah prayed for him and He will one day raise our mortal bodies and carry us into the presence of Almighty God. He hates the smell and presence of death.

Rom 8:11

But if the Spirit of him that raised up Jesus from the dead dwell in you, he that raised up Christ from the dead shall also quicken your mortal bodies by his Spirit that dwelleth in you.

9. **He is the breath of God.** God's breath is "Spirit" filled. When God breathed into Adam's nostrils, the spirit of man was created by the Holy Spirit.

Gen 2:7
And the LORD God formed man of the dust of the ground, and breathed into his nostrils the breath of life; and man became a living soul.

10. **He is a prophetic Spirit.** He is the author of all prophecies and prophetic operations. He is the one who anoints prophets to function in their respective offices.

Joel 2:28
And it shall come to pass afterward, that I will pour out my spirit upon all flesh; and your sons and your daughters shall prophesy, your old men shall dream dreams, your young men shall see visions:

11. **He is the author of dreams and visions.** Dr. David Yongi Cho, pastor of the largest church in the world, writes in his book *"The Fourth Dimension," "Visions and dreams are the language of the Holy Spirit."* In the last days, visions and dreams will become very common as the Church moves toward the finish line. Many in the body of Christ will enter into the fullness of the Spirit.

Joel 2:28

And it shall come to pass afterward, that I will pour out my spirit upon all flesh; and your sons and your daughters shall prophesy, your old men shall dream dreams, your young men shall see visions:

12. **He is a teaching Spirit.** He is the greatest teacher on earth. He has taken former murders, rapists, liars, and thieves and taught them how to live their lives according to God's purpose and become great men and women of God.

John 16:12-13

I have yet many things to say unto you, but ye cannot bear them now. Howbeit when he, the Spirit of truth, is come, he will guide you into all truth: for he shall not speak of himself; but whatsoever he shall hear, that shall he speak: and he will shew you things to come.

13. **He is the spirit of intercession.** He knows how to pray, when to pray, and who to pray for. He is the greatest intercessor because He knows the mind of God at all times and can thus lead us into God's perfect will.

Rom 8:26-27

Likewise the Spirit also helpeth our infirmities: for we know not what we should pray for as we ought: but the Spirit itself maketh intercession for us with groanings which cannot be uttered. And he that searcheth the hearts knoweth what is the mind of the Spirit, because he maketh intercession for the saints according to the will of God.

14. ***He is heaven's "Navigational Specialist."*** When
sailors set out to sea, they know that it's very easy
to get lost. The vast ocean surface is interfaced with
many potential dangers. These seasoned sailors make
sure that they have enough food, water and other
essentials to last them through the duration of their
journey. They make sure that they have navigational
charts in place and that their compass is functioning
properly before they set sail. Unfortunately, as meticulous as their preparations may be, their navigational
ability is limited by their lack of prophetic insight into
the future. If anything happens which catches them
off guard, they find themselves in real trouble. If they
encounter an unexpected hurricane at sea, they are
completely at its mercy. Tragically, thousands of men
and women through the corridors of history, have
entrusted their entire lives in the hands of men with
limited navigational ability. On the other hand, the
Holy Spirit has ***never*** shipwrecked! It's a tragedy that
only a select few really trust the navigational ability
of the Holy Spirit.

Acts 16:6-10
*Now when they had gone throughout Phrygia and the
region of Galatia, and were forbidden of the Holy Ghost
to preach the word in Asia, After they were come to Mysia,
they assayed to go into Bithynia: but the Spirit suffered
them not. And they passing by Mysia came down to Troas.
And a vision appeared to Paul in the night; There stood a
man of Macedonia, and prayed him, saying, Come over
into Macedonia, and help us. And after he had seen the
vision, immediately we endeavored to go into Macedonia,*

assuredly gathering that the Lord had called us for to preach the gospel unto them.

Imagine being invited to board a ship whose captain can navigate you all the way to your destination with a hundred percent accuracy and guarantee that there will be no casualties. How many people do you think would run over each other to board such a ship? Everybody, I dare say! The Captain of this ship called life is the Holy Spirit. He knows exactly where God has called you to go, because He has already been there. He knows the problems and pitfalls that you will face on your journey toward your destiny and He knows how to prevent the casualties.

The Holy Spirit knows every person that Satan will assign to our lives in order to destroy or derail us from our destiny. He knows every person whom God has assigned to bless us on our spiritual journey. He knows where and when we can invest our money for the best and highest return. In the event that we make a huge mistake or collide with a spiritual storm, He has the power to calm the storm and turn our lemons into lemonade. What a navigator! I know of billionaires who would pay millions to have a navigator like the Holy Spirit on their staff!

The Holy Spirit knows the spiritual terrain of any valley of transition that we will ever go through and how to navigate it. Nevertheless, if we allow ourselves to become wrapped up in other things during our period of spiritual transition and become insensitive to His voice, we will suffer the consequences.

It's not within the scope of this book to write an exhaustive exegesis on the Holy Spirit and what He is assigned to do in the life of the believer. It suffices to say that one of the most invaluable friends and mentors we can have, while navigating the valley of transition, is the Holy Spirit. Without the leading of the Holy Spirit, we will inevitably end up on the wrong side of the law of transition and most likely will suffer shipwreck!

A Disease Called Marthaitis!

"When I was in College, I helped to build houses to earn extra money. I had calluses on certain parts of my hands from swinging the hammer because the two came into constant contact day after day. The same "calluses effect" takes place in your conscience when it comes into constant contact with extreme emotions, violence, or sensuality. Spiritual and emotional "calluses" develop at whatever point you are exposed to these extreme sensory barrages. God did not design the human body, soul, or spirit to take such sensory overload.

Constant exposure and contact – whether to the holy or to the unholy- produces callousness in the human heart. Even sacred things can become common! Ask Uzzah! The mother of an infant can grow "deaf" to the less urgent cries of her child (even though everyone else around her may be pulling their hair out). In the same way someone who works in an environment of constant profanity and ungodliness becomes nearly oblivious to their destructive effects on the human spirit. "Marthas" in the Body of Christ tend to grow callous toward or overly familiar with the manifest presence of Divinity when they focus exclusively on the needs of humanity day after day.

(Chasing God Serving Man by Tommy Tenney, pg 58)

One of the major reasons many people of faith become insensitive to the voice of the Holy Spirit during periods of spiritual and social transition is because they suffer from a spiritual disease that I call *"Marthaitis."* While her sister Mary was busy entertaining and hosting the presence of God, Martha was *"encumbered"* with the activities of ministry. She was lost in the activities of *"ministry,"* while her sister was listening to the *"minister."*

Martha was upset with Jesus for not instructing Mary to join her in her laborious tasks. Jesus rebuked her for not placing priority on hosting His presence. It's very easy for us to get lost in the constant activities of ministry and become dull of hearing in the process. The constant inter-action with the activities of ministry can make our hearts become *"calloused"* to the point where we no longer hear the voice of the Holy Spirit. When this happens, we will start making wrong choices and possibly lose our way during times of spiritual transition.

Fire, Lightening & Thunder

"And he said, Go forth, and stand upon the mount before the LORD. And, behold, the LORD passed by, and a great and strong wind rent the mountains, and brake in pieces the rocks before the LORD; but the LORD was not in the wind: and after the wind an earthquake; but the LORD was not in the earthquake: And after the earthquake a fire; but the LORD was not in the fire: and after the fire a still small voice. And it was so, when Elijah heard it, that he wrapped his face in his mantle, and went out, and stood in the entering in of the cave. And, behold, there came a voice unto him, and said, What doest thou here, Elijah?"[3]

The passage above is one of the most powerful biblical examples of the importance of listening to the voice of the Holy Spirit during periods of spiritual transition. Elijah had just finished conducting one of the most historical revivals in the history of the nation of Israel. He had just called fire out of heaven and killed over four hundred prophets of Jezebel. Nevertheless, Elijah knew that he was nearing the end of his ministry and he went to the mountain of God to seek God's counsel during this very critical period of transition in his life. When Elijah got to the mountain of God, God tested him to see if he was still sensitive to the voice of the Holy Spirit.

Elijah was confronted with three spectacular manifestations of God's supernatural power. First, there was a supernatural gush of wind, which was followed by a thunderous earthquake. Then there was a supernatural flashing of fire which could have dazzled anybody. Most preachers I know would have been dazzled by these spiritual manifestations. Most of us would have used them to prove the presence of the Holy Spirit in our ministry. Elijah on the other hand was not moved by these spectacular manifestations because he discerned that the Lord was not in any of them.

Suddenly Elijah was moving; *he had heard a whisper, a still small voice and knew that it was the Lord.* God showed him how he was to end his ministry and how to prepare for his spiritual succession. If Elijah had not been sensitive to the voice of the Holy Spirit, he would have left the planet without providing a successor to carry on his great ministry.

As a result of his sensitivity to the voice of the Holy Spirit, Elijah was able to anoint and commission Elisha as a prophet to take his place. Elisha was responsible for anointing Jehu and Hazel, who collectively destroyed the territorial spirit of Jezebel, which had caused the Israelites to worship Baal and forget the living God. Insensitivity to the voice of the Holy Spirit during periods of spiritual transition can hinder the success of the next generation and destroy our spiritual legacy.

Pioneers and the Holy Spirit

Periods of transition require pioneers who are not afraid to push the envelope and go where no man has ever gone before. Pioneers are men and women who have a "rare spiritual DNA" which gives them a spiritual predisposition for doing the extraordinary. Pioneers love adventure and also love to operate outside the box. The future, to a great degree, is the *"Brain Child of Pioneers." Pioneers are champions of transition, but they can also find themselves on the lethal side of transition if they are not sensitive to the voice of the Holy Spirit.*

"As apostolic pioneers in the open field they do not have role models or examples to pattern themselves after. As pioneers, they are often ahead of everybody else and they need to know whether they are going in the right direction. Pioneers who are breaking into new horizons lack mentors, in whom they can confide, bounce off their decisions and confirm their directions. They seldom have any opportunity of turning to someone for help in these uncharted waters. This sense of loneliness and uncertainty can cast unnecessary doubts upon their faith and thus slow down their forward thrust. As apostolic pioneers, they must develop a place of sensitivity in the Holy Spirit and command a place of intimacy with the Lord.

This is not just a privilege but the secret of success for pioneers in the open battlefield. The Holy Spirit must be given that place of total trust and obedience. The Lord Jesus Himself was led by the Holy Spirit into God's perfect will and plans. Pioneers need to be able to pick up the spiritual stirrings of the Holy Spirit and move on with strong convictions about their destiny. Pioneers need to be dependent upon the guidance of the Holy Spirit as they are in the front lines of the battle.

Captains of ships and scuba divers fathom the depth of the oceans using sonar equipment. They rely upon the readings registered upon the equipment. These findings help divers survive in an area where they have never been or know very little about. The sonar equipment also warns the divers of the cliffs and other dangerous portions of the seabed The Holy Spirit knows the depths of each man's heart and He can communicate His knowledge to the pioneer who can act in response to His leading. This will help the pioneer pull down the strongholds and establish the God given vision".

(Apostolic Strategies Affecting Nations,
by Dr Jonathan David, pg 46)

I cannot over emphasize the importance of being sensitive to the voice and leading of the Holy Spirit during periods of spiritual transition. Insensitivity to the voice and leading of the Holy Spirit during periods of spiritual and social transition can prove disastrous and derail us from pursuing our God given destiny. King David misread the leading of the Holy Spirit when he numbered the people of Israel which resulted in a serious *"divine genocide of the masses!"* God was incensed by David's prideful act. David's sin had opened a door to the powers of darkness.

"And David's heart smote him after that he had numbered the people. And David said unto the LORD, I have sinned greatly in that I have done: and now, I beseech thee, O

LORD, take away the iniquity of thy servant; for I have done very foolishly. For when David was up in the morning, the word of the LORD came unto the prophet Gad, David's seer, saying, Go and say unto David, Thus saith the LORD, I offer thee three things; choose thee one of them, that I may do it unto thee. So Gad came to David, and told him, and said unto him, Shall seven years of famine come unto thee in thy land? or wilt thou flee three months before thine enemies, while they pursue thee? or that there be three days' pestilence in thy land? now advise, and see what answer I shall return to him that sent me. So the LORD sent a pestilence upon Israel from the morning even to the time appointed: and there died of the people from Dan even to Beersheba seventy thousand men. And when the angel stretched out his hand upon Jerusalem to destroy it, the LORD repented him of the evil, and said to the angel that destroyed the people, It is enough: stay now thine hand. And the angel of the LORD was by the threshing place of Araunah the Jebusite."[4]

David's insensitivity to the voice and leading of the Holy Spirit during this period of spiritual transition resulted in the deaths of over seventy thousand people. Insensitivity to the voice of the Holy Spirit during periods of transition can affect and impact the lives of others negatively. We must strive to command a place of intimacy with the Holy Spirit. **The Holy Spirit must become our greatest ally in times of transition.** We cannot fail if we hold on to Him and follow His lead into our prophetic destiny.

Notes on Chapter Nine

1. John 16:13-15
2. Acts 1:5-9
3. IKing 19:11-13
4. 2 Sam 24:10-16

Chapter Ten

Somebody Holla!

Nothing is as gullible and so easily manipulated as human emotions. Correctional facilities are now the homes of many people who committed murder after listening to heavy metal music tainted with lyrics of killing, death and every abomination imaginable. Nothing has the power to stir the souls and emotions of the human spirit like the sound of music. Music is the quickest way to manipulate the soul and activate man's emotional faculties. The lyrics of a song determine the type and intensity of emotions that the listener will experience. When I was a man of the world, I partied and frequented nightclubs. It was not uncommon to see men and women, who were total strangers, end up in bed together because they were moved into fornication by the wooing lyrics of songs about romance.

After the numbing effects of the booze and emotional high of the song have waned down, the two lovers quickly discover that they have nothing in common. Some awaken the "morning after" not even remembering what led to the overnight rendezvous. In worst case scenarios, the women end up with unwanted pregnancies and find themselves emotionally bound to men who want nothing to do with them, nor the child that was conceived in the heat of the moment. I rarely listen to songs written in foreign languages, no matter how captivating the beat of the song is. I cannot allow my emotions to carry my soul to a spiritual destination that God never ordained for me.

Even the most spiritually mature among us is not immune to falling prey to the spiritual dangers of living a life based on emotion. We must understand that moments of spiritual inspiration must never be allowed to overshadow unshakeable divine principles as set forth in God's word as our case study will show.

CASE STUDY:
THE GOSPEL OF INCLUSION-
THE CARLTON PEARSON STORY

In the Seventies God raised a powerful young black man by the name of Carlton Pearson, who had the privilege of working alongside legendary gospel generals like the late Kathryn Khulman and Dr. Oral Roberts. This young African American man quickly rose to stardom in many Christian circles. As a talented musician, his songs were sung by thousands of people. His Tulsa based church, Higher Dimensions Family Worship Center, became a melting pot of all races and grew into thousands of members.

Every year, Carlton Pearson hosted one of the most popular Charismatic conferences in the world called "Azusa" which attracted thousands of people, including a parade of high caliber gospel preachers and recording artists. This popular conference brought millions of dollars annually to the City of Tulsa. Hundreds of pastors brought their churches under the spiritual oversight of this rising star, Bishop Carlton Pearson. Carlton Pearson's ministry continued to flourish and attained international fame and things looked like they would only get better.

Then the unthinkable happened as the flourishing ministry was set on course for one of the most contro-versial and divisive spiritual declines of any 21ˢᵗ century ministry. Bishop Carlton Pearson began to teach a bizarre, off the chart doctrine that angered and appalled many Bible believing Christians. His new doctrine was titled "The Gospel of Inclusion," which essentially taught that everybody on the planet is already saved and that they do not need to accept Jesus as their personal Lord and Savior to secure a place in His heavenly Kingdom. Carlton's new message went as far as saying that there is no literal hell that unregenerate souls go to after death. Great men of God like Dr. Oral Roberts and others begged him to refrain from teaching this heretical teaching, which violated many infallible scriptures in the Holy Bible. He refused to listen to them. As a consequence, he lost his entire ministry and thousands of his flock began to flee to other churches.

The Carlton Pearson story, in my opinion, is one of the saddest stories about the demise of a good ministry. During periods of spiritual transition, we must not deceive ourselves into thinking that every inspired thought we have is the voice of God. We must measure our inspirations against the unchanging principles of God's eternal word. If our spiritual or emotional inspiration does not hold up to the standards of God's word, we must see them as false; regardless of how "right" they may feel. The Scriptures declare, *"Let every man be a liar and God be true!"*

Business men and women have suffered serious financial losses from running with new business ideas without weighing the pros and cons of the possible outcomes. *Inspiration without principle during periods of transition is very dangerous, especially in business arenas.* How many well meaning business people have lost vast amounts of money because they made a major investment without conducting a proper feasibility study? Some are devastated when they discover what *seemed* to be an excellent idea, has resulted in catastrophic financial loss. It is my prayer that this book will serve as a divine compass to lead people back onto the road to success. The old adage *"all that glitters is not gold,"* is especially true during periods of spiritual and social transition.

CASE STUDY:
THE COLMAN MOCKLER, GILLETTE STORY

Colman Mockler was the Chief Executive Officer of Gillette from 1975 to 1991. He led Gillette through one of the most difficult times the company has ever faced. One writer has this to say about Mockler and Gillette during this very tumultuous time.

"...During Mockler's tenure, Gillette faced three attacks that threatened to destroy the company's opportunity for greatness. Two attacks came as hostile takeover bids from Revlon, led by Ronald Perelman, a cigar-chomping raider with a reputation for breaking apart companies to pay down junk bonds and finance hostile raids. The third attack came from Coniston Partners, an investment group that bought 5.9 percent of Gillette stock and initiated a proxy battle to seize control of the board, hoping to sell the

company to the highest bidder and pocket a quick gain on their shares.

Had Gillette been flipped to Perelman at the price he offered, shareowners would have reaped an instantaneous 44 percent gain on their stock. ...Colman Mockler did not capitulate, choosing instead to fight for the future greatness of Gillette, even though he himself would have pocketed a substantial sum on his own shares. ...In the end, Mockler and the board were proved right [for not selling Gillette for quick profit] stunningly so. If a share flipper had accepted the 44 percent price offered by Ronald Perelman on October 31, 1986, and then invested the full amount in the general market for ten years, through the end of 1996, he would have come out three times worse off than a shareholder who had stayed with Mockler and Gillette. Indeed, the company, its customers, and the shareholders would have been ill served had Mockler capitulated to the raiders, pocketed his millions, and retired to a life of leisure.

(Good to Great by Jim Collins, pg 23-24)

Nothing on this planet can inspire and motivate people like the chance to *"get rich quick."* The promise of quick profits inspired a disciple named Judas to betray the Son of the Living God. I watched a reality show on ESPN which was created by legendary actor Sylvester Stallone and six time world boxing champion Sugar Ray Leonard. The reality show is called *"The Contender."* Each season, sixteen young boys from the boxing world are brought to Los Angeles for a chance to win a million dollars. I have never seen boxers hit each other with so much passion and determination as on this reality TV show. I walked away from the program thinking, *"Money truly inspires all types of emotions and human behaviors."*

More often than not, men and women will violate the unchanging principles of God's word for the chance to make a quick profit. This is especially true when there is a transition in our personal economy. These are the times when we need the *"Colman Mocklers"* of this world to lead us through troubled waters without compromising the sacred principles of God's word.

One of the critical dangers of transition is the ever-present danger of living a life of inspiration while violating spiritual and moral principles. We will now examine this danger of transition more fully.

---

7. The Danger Of Living A Life Of Inspiration Without Principle.

There is a Divine Blueprint for Everything

If God were to apply for a regular job here on earth, what career would He choose that would best describe who He really is? Would He be a movie star? Would he be a Politician? ***Wait a minute! God did come to the earth for a short while and worked a regular job. He worked with his father Joseph as a Carpenter!***

"Is not this the carpenter, the son of Mary, the brother of James, and Joses, and of Juda, and Simon? and are not his sisters here with us? And they were offended at him."[2]

"The carpenter stretcheth out his rule; he marketh it out with a line; he fitteth it with planes, and he marketh it out with the compass, and maketh it after the figure of a man, according to the beauty of a man; that it may remain in the house."[3]

Having been born in Africa, I did not fully appreciate the spiritual ramifications of Mark 6:3. In Africa, carpenters are men who make wooden tables, stools, beds and so forth. My attitude was, "So Jesus and his father Joseph made a bunch of tables, so what?" Upon further investigation, it suddenly dawned on me that the carpenter's Son was not an ordinary manufacturer of wooden tables and chairs; He was an architect! He designed the blueprints for buildings!

I can imagine Jesus bent over analyzing the architectural drawings on a table. If they were constructing a building, He had to determine how much sand and cement would be needed for the construction. He determined the height, width and depth of the building and the type of foundation on which it would sit. Perhaps He determined how many rooms the building was going to have and the square footage. He probably calculated just how much money and manpower was going to be needed to finish the construction. He was a man who understood the importance of building everything from architectural blueprints.

Unfortunately, most of God's people are not good imitators of Christ. Some people of faith have very little respect for divine design and spiritual order. Many have been led to believe that spiritual inspiration equals divine order. Nothing can be further from the truth. This is one of the spiritual dangers we are likely to face during periods of spiritual, moral and social transition.

"For which of you, intending to build a tower, sitteth not down first, and counteth the cost, whether he have sufficient to finish it? Lest haply, after he hath laid the foundation, and is not able to finish it, all that behold it begin to

mock him, Saying, This man began to build, and was not able to finish."[4]

In the above passage of Scripture, Jesus warned His disciples to be aware of the dangers of living a life of inspiration while violating God's principles. Obviously, the builder who began to build the house, must have felt inspired when he started building it, but failed to finish what he had started.

When couples get ready to buy a new house, they sometimes take a *"dream drive"* around some very expensive and ritzy neighborhoods looking at million dollar homes. Unfortunately, many of these *"dream drives"* quickly become financial nightmares. Drunk with the inspiration of owning a huge home in a flashy neighborhood, many over zealous couples rush to the bank and secure loans that they can't possibly afford.

The excitement of living in a lavish home begins to wane down, as the month-by-month financial responsibility of maintaining such a high priced lifestyle becomes a stark reality. The adrenaline of inspiration evaporates like water on a hot sunny day. The over zealous couple who felt inspired when they bought their expensive dream home, suddenly finds themselves living in a nightmare on the wrong side of the law of transition.

What happened to their dream? How did their dream home quickly become a living nightmare? The answer is simple yet rarely understood. They mistook their feelings of inspiration for divine order. During periods of transition, we must be careful not to equate our feelings of inspiration with the leading of God. There is nothing wrong with feeling inspired. ***Inspiration is the fuel which drives the "God given dream machine" inside the soul*** *of every man. Nevertheless, fuel in a leaking gas tank will not take us very far.* The real purpose of inspiration is to motivate us and excite our passion until we are certain that we are in God's will. On the other hand, the purpose of divine principles is to give us the power to fulfill our purpose within the boundaries of God's unchanging word. Inspiration gives us the passion to act on the divine principles that we need to adhere to until our dreams and aspirations become reality.

> *"During periods of transition, we must be careful not to equate our feelings of inspiration with the leading of God."*

Each year hundreds of men and women accept the call to full time ministry. These zealous saints quickly enroll into a Bible school with hopes of changing the world. In their young minds, nothing could ever go wrong. After all, God is the one who has called them to reach the world. These young inexperienced zealots live under the assumption that the devil has more sense than to mess with them. They are convinced that the whole world has been waiting anxiously for their arrival! The only problem with their conclusions is that their spiritual survey failed to include the stories of men of faith like, Joseph and King David, who had genuine calls of God upon their lives but went through distressing times before God fulfilled the promises that He gave to them.

Statistics show that many young Bible school ministry graduates drop out of full time ministry within the first five years. Most of them feel emotionally crushed and spiritually disillusioned by the harshness of hands on ministry and how much it differs from the vision they had from the comfort of their dormitories. Many believers make the mistake of thinking that the energy of spiritual inspiration they felt when they discovered the call of God upon their life was sufficient to push them to the finish line. This is a very dangerous spiritual assumption. It's like jumping out of a plane and realizing your parachute was left behind. There are many emotional and spiritual obstacles along the road to our destiny which will require much more than our spiritual sense of excitement to overcome.

During periods of emotional and spiritual transition, many believers fail to seek God's divine blueprint for their life and establish governing principles from God's word which can guide them into their spiritual destiny. God has a specific plan of execution for every spiritual project. *When we combine God's unchanging principles with the fuel of God given spiritual inspiration, we have a powerful winning combination.*

Revelation Must Bring Movement

"By faith Noah, being warned of God of things not seen as yet, moved with fear, prepared an ark to the saving of his house; by the which he condemned the world, and became heir of the righteousness which is by faith. By faith Abraham, when he was called to go out into a place which he should after receive for an inheritance, obeyed; and he went out, not knowing whither he went."[5]

One indication that we are living a life of spiritual and emotional inspiration without respecting God's principles is that we eagerly receive knowledge from God's word, but rarely act on it. We accept our pastor's sermons as a fresh revelation from the Lord and support the message with our *"Amens"* and *"Preach it brother!"* exhortations. Unfortunately, when the service ends and we rush out the door to "slay the dragons," we quickly forget to **apply** that knowledge to the daily challenges. This is the equivalent of being armed with a loaded arsenal, yet forgetting to pull the trigger as the enemy approaches for the attack.

Times of spiritual transition require that we behave like Noah of old. When the revelation of God's impending judgment against an ungodly generation reached the ears of Noah, he moved into swift action. He immediately began building the largest ship in the history of the ancient world. God not only gave Noah the inspiration to build the Ark, but also the blueprints to build the massive ship which would withstand the barrage of the coming flood.

What would have happened if Noah had simply rushed to build the ark without waiting on God to give him the blueprints? Just imagine the spiritual and physical ramifications Noah would have encountered had he chosen to act on inspiration alone. Had Noah been so spiritually impulsive, he would have aborted the call of God upon his life and the world as we know it would never have existed. His ability to combine emotional inspiration with divine principles during this period of spiritual transition saved the human race and the animal kingdom.

Spiritual Emotional Roller Coaster Rides

"Having a form of godliness, but denying the power thereof: from such turn away. For of this sort are they which creep into houses, and lead captive silly women laden with sins, led away with divers lusts, Ever learning, and never able to come to the knowledge of the truth."[6]

It's time for God's people to come off of the spiritual emotional roller coaster rides! They are preachers and teachers of the Word who have mastered the art of emotional manipulation. They know how to set the stage for highly emotional services. From the selection of music, down to what they will say and how they will say it, they have learned how to get the desired reaction from their congregation.

Many have become conditioned to this routine of emotion packed services and find themselves feeling "unspiritual" if they fail to achieve the "euphoric" emotional high that is expected. Like cocaine addicts, some of these precious saints float from one highly emotional service to the next, in search of more and more inspiration. Their "perception" of the service is based on what they "feel" rather than the message they hear. While there's nothing wrong with enjoying a service and allowing the atmosphere of praise and worship to lift our spirit and emotions, we must be careful not to use our emotions as a "spiritual thermometer." We need a healthy balance of both inspiration and God's word to properly navigate the valley of transition. The power of true godliness is found in building our lives around the unchangeable principles of God.

I once held a healing crusade in a church in Chicago. While I was praying for the sick, I came across a woman who had been diagnosed with full-blown AIDS. As the power of God was going through her body, she started weeping uncontrollably. A sad story unfolded as she told me about attending a revival meeting where the preacher had told her that if she sowed a $1000 seed into his ministry, God was going to heal her immediately. In the emotional inspiration of the moment, she sowed her $1000 seed but never got healed. She found herself caught on a roller coaster of emotional hype running to and fro in search for a true spiritual breakthrough. That night God healed her instantly.

"They are preachers and teachers of the Word who have mastered the art of emotional manipulation."

This woman continued shedding tears of joy as she savored her glorious healing. I am not against people giving sacrificially to the Lord. Nevertheless, I am very much against the emotional manipulation of God's people without giving them governing principles from God's word upon which they can stand for their complete deliverance. The spirit of greed that has gained control of some ministers of the gospel has brought shame upon the body of Christ

I have been at conferences where people were challenged by preachers to claim every conceivable blessing from God they could think of. They were told that God was going to give them whatever they wanted, even though some of them were living in habitual sin. Some preachers and teachers tell people that God is going to bless them in a great way, but they fail to tell them that God can bestow His richest blessings only upon those who are actively obeying His holy principles.

I was told about a story of a married pastor who attended a prophetic conference and ended up divorcing his wife for a total stranger he met there. At one point during the meeting, the moderator instructed the people to turn and pray with the person directly behind them. When this pastor turned around, his gaze fell upon a beautiful Caucasian woman. When their eyes met, they said they knew instantly that they were meant to be together, never giving a thought to the fact that both of them were already married to someone else. When the conference was over, they both divorced their spouses and married each other. They passionately defended their illicit affair by saying that God had brought them together through divine circumstances. I have no doubt they were both emotionally inspired when they looked into each other's eyes, but they violated God's unchanging principles which govern marriage relationships! When you look at this story, you begin to see the danger of making decisions based on feelings of spiritual and emotional inspiration without applying God's principles. This is yet another critical danger of periods of transition.

Judas Iscariot: Ministry without The Cross

"Men and brethren, this Scripture had to be fulfilled, which the Holy Spirit spoke before by the mouth of David concerning Judas, who became a guide to those who arrested Jesus; "for he was numbered with us and obtained a part in this ministry." (Now this man purchased a field with the wages of iniquity; and falling headlong, he burst open in the middle and all his entrails gushed out. And it became known to all those dwelling in Jerusalem; so that field is called in their own language, Akel Dama, that is, Field of Blood.)" For it is written in the book of Psalms: 'Let his dwelling place be desolate, and let no one live in it'; and, 'Let another take his office."[7]

The life of Judas Iscariot is a classic example of the danger of living a life built on emotional inspiration which is not governed by God's principles. Judas was called to be an apostle through a face-to-face encounter with Christ. He quickly rose to the position of chief financial treasurer for the ministry of Jesus.

Judas was among the seventy disciples who were sent by the Lord Jesus to cast out devils. When the seventy returned they returned in great Jubilation, when they discovered that demons were subject to them through Jesus' name. When the Lord Jesus raised Lazarus (the brother of Martha and Mary) from the dead, Judas Iscariot was standing next to him. Unfortunately, Judas misused this time of prophetic training and apostolic impartation. Judas was too busy stealing money from the ministry to get involved with the true purpose of his calling. He was also strategizing with the Pharisees and Sadducees on how to betray the Lord Jesus for thirty pieces of silver! Whatever emotional inspiration Judas may have felt when he decided to betray Jesus disappeared quickly. The emotional high of having made a few bucks from his act of betrayal quickly lost its appeal when the spiritual ramifications set in. Judas' emotional high suddenly turned into depression and thoughts of suicide. He hanged himself in the same field that he had bought with the blood money.

When we live a life built on emotional inspiration without obeying God's principles, we negate the finished work of the cross. God designed the cross of Christ as a divine instrument of carnal death. The cross of Christ is where the lust of the flesh and the things that damage our character are crucified in order for us to arrive at our prophetic destiny. No amount of spiritual "highs" will carry us as close to our prophetic destiny as we can get by following God's divine principles. We must be careful to not end up like Judas, who allowed the euphoria of controlling money (greed) to destroy his true destiny.

> *"Judas was too busy stealing money*
> *from the ministry to get involved with*
> *the true purpose of his calling."*

God wants us to be spiritually and emotionally inspired but He also wants us to do what is right based on the principles set forth in His word. He wants us to build our lives according to His divine blueprint and not place our trust on moments of emotional hype.

The House Church Fallacy

"Now I say to you that you are Peter (which means 'rock'), and upon this rock I will build my church, and all the powers of hell will not conquer it."[8]

There is a growing *"house church"* movement in this country. The house church movement is mushrooming among born again Christians who are fed up with the "traditional church." Many of the people involved in this movement are those who have been hurt or abused by authority figures within mainstream churches, while some become involved because they do not want to submit to spiritual authority. This movement makes it easy for God's people to avoid being held accountable for things such as "bringing their tithes and offerings into the storehouse" (church) as required by Scripture. The house church movement is rapidly becoming an asylum for believers who, for whatever reason, have failed to transition into God's Kingdom order. Many sincere believers do not realize that their honest rebellion to the traditional church structure is a rebellion against God's divine structure.

The prevailing philosophy of the house church movement is *fellowship among the saints without the restraints of spiritual authority.* Most propagators of the house church movement are terrified of being accountable to delegated authority because they still carry pain from wounds and abuse that occurred while attending a traditional church. I am in no way defending the abuse of spiritual authority that has transpired under the traditional structure of church. But we can never correct a wrong by rebelling against God's method. Since the birth of the church on the day of Pentecost, the Spirit of God rallied the new believers around a church structure which was governed by His delegated authority. As we read the book of Acts, we come face to face with the apostles and elders as the spiritual leaders of the church. Whenever there was a dispute between the saints or the need to correct false doctrine, these matters were settled by the governing council of apostles and elders.

"While Paul and Barnabas were at Antioch of Syria, some men from Judea arrived and began to teach the believers: "Unless you are circumcised as required by the law of Moses, you cannot be saved." Paul and Barnabas disagreed with them, arguing vehemently. Finally, the church decided to send Paul and Barnabas to Jerusalem, accompanied by some local believers, to talk to the apostles and elders about this question. "[9]

In the house church movement, the government of apostles and elders is quickly replaced with the fellowship of the brethren. In a typical house church the structure is very simple. Believers get together in someone's home where one or more persons are chosen to share from the word. There is a season of prayer and they sometimes observe the Lord's Supper (Communion). Most house churches do not, as a rule, collect tithes except on certain occasions when they feel led to support some worthy project. *The absence of spiritual government means that there is no way to discipline saints within the fellowship who are blatantly disobeying the word of God.* These house churches are creating a spiritual climate and culture which is contrary to God's word and principles, because the Kingdom of God is built upon the concept of spiritual authority.

> *"The house church movement in the book of Acts was intricately connected to the spiritual oversight of the apostles and elders."*

Most adherents to the house church philosophy refrain from calling anyone by a spiritual title because these titles are inherently connected to church government. They seem to forget that spiritual titles such as apostle, prophet, evangelist, pastor or bishop originated from the mind of God. These titles help to describe who a person is, their rank, and what their responsibilities are within the structure of God's government. Granted, there are people in the traditional church who have abused these titles and the authority given to them, but that does not nullify the fact that they originated from the mind of God. The present version of the house church movement claims that it finds its origins from within the roots of Scripture. Nothing can be further from the truth. *The house church movement in the book of Acts was intricately connected to the spiritual oversight of the apostles and elders.* The house churches of the book of Acts were not independent house fellowships with no discernable ties to apostolic oversight. Most of the present day house church fellowships are completely autonomous with no obvious ties to a governing council of spiritual leaders.

Notes on Chapter Ten

1. John 4:19-21, 2. Mark 6:3, 3. Isa 44:13,
    4. Luke 14:28-30
5. Heb 11:7-8, 6. 2 Tim 3:5-7, 7. Acts 1:16-20
8. Matthew 16:18 NLT, 9. Acts 15:1-2 NLT

Chapter Eleven

The Place Where Two Roads Meet

❦

The story is told of a fox that was chasing two rabbits. For a short while the two rabbits were running on the same trail. The fox pursued them ferociously, his mouth dripping with saliva. The hungry fox could see himself having a great meal that day. *"I am so lucky!"* he thought. The fox was almost catching up to the fleeing rabbits, when the dusty trail suddenly split off into two different directions. The starving fox knew he had a serious choice to make. In order for him to have a meal that fateful day, all he had to do was surrender his claim on one of the rabbits and settle for half as much food than he originally planned.

Out of his greed, the fox decided that he was going to continue chasing both rabbits by attempting to travel both trails at once. Not long after this fateful decision, the greedy fox was torn in half and died instantly. The rabbits stopped and looked at the dead fox, lying in a puddle of blood between the two dusty trails. One of the rabbits said to the other rabbit, *"If that fox hadn't been so stupid, one of us would be dead!"* The greedy fox died that day when he failed to make the right decision at the place where two roads meet.

Unfortunately, the tragic story of the death of the greedy fox repeats itself every day in the arenas of human endeavor. The corridors of history are filled with stories of men and women who faced a decisive moment during a time of spiritual and social transition, but failed to make the right decision. *"One of the spiritual dangers we are most likely to face during periods of transition is the danger of becoming stuck at the place where two roads meet!"*

8. The Danger Of Becoming Stuck At The Place Were Two Roads Meet.

The Comfort Zone Syndrome

One of the greatest human pursuits is the pursuit of financial success. Many young African boys and girls brave the hot African sun, walking barefoot for many miles, to school for an education. The pleasures of the present are willingly sacrificed for the hope of a better and prosperous future. The pursuit of personal success is the reason why the pilgrims left the shores of Europe in search of the New World.

The pursuit of a pleasurable life is the reason why *"pioneers rise to the occasion and break through into new frontiers."* The pursuit of personal comfort paradoxically is the also the reason why many pioneers, eventually become settlers. The pioneers reach a stage in their life where they become comfortable with their present level of success. They achieve a certain level of comfort and become weary of always being the ones who have to fight for a new day. *How ironic that the very thing that once motivated them to break out from the rest of the pack, is now the reason they have decided to settle at their present level of comfort.* One of the main reasons thousands get stuck at the place were two roads meet, during periods of spiritual and social transition is because for most people the *"pull of their comfort zones is as equal or greater than the pull of their future destiny in God!"* This is why God sends revival. *True Spirit inspired revival has a way of messing with our comfort zones, by shattering our present structures and comfort zones.*

The destruction of *"spiritual comfort zones"* that keep God's people bound at the place where two roads meet during periods of transition, is also why God allows seasons of persecution to arise against His church. Jesus told the apostles and all His disciples to go into the whole world and preach the Gospel of the Kingdom. Instead of going to the ends of the earth, most of the disciples were content to *"bask in the apostolic fire that was flowing through the church in Jerusalem, instead of obeying the great commission!"* The Lord allowed the devil to stir up persecution of the church at Jerusalem. The demonic persecution quickly scattered the disciples across different regions of Asia and those who were running away from the persecution began preaching the gospel to every region they came to (Acts 11:19-20).

"Rise up, ye women that are at ease; hear my voice, ye careless daughters; give ear unto my speech. Many days and years shall ye be troubled, ye careless women: for the vintage shall fail, the gathering shall not come. Tremble, ye women that are at ease; be troubled, ye careless ones: strip you, and make you bare, and gird sackcloth upon

your loins. They shall lament for the teats, for the pleasant fields, for the fruitful vine. Upon the land of my people shall come up thorns and briers; yea, upon all the houses of joy in the joyous city:"[1]

This passage of Scripture gives us some refreshing insights as to why God is determined to set us free from every comfort zone that keeps us from pursuing our prophetic destiny. Here are some of the things we will encounter if we stay in our comfort zone after receiving divine marching orders to press toward our destiny.

Spiritual carelessness: When we stay in our spiritual or natural comfort zones after we have received marching orders from God to go to the next level of our destiny, a spirit of carelessness will come upon us. The word careless carries the meaning *"to cast off restraint or to be undisciplined."* This happens because we lose our prophetic vision for the future God has for us. Whenever we are spiritually careless we open doors for the devil to attack us.

We Will Lose Our Peace and Prosperity: The second thing that happens when we stay too long in our spiritual comfort zone is that we will begin to gradually lose our peace and prosperity. Peace and prosperity are only guaranteed to us at the place of divine assignment. *"For as long as Elijah was at the place of divine assignment, God made provision both peace and prosperity for His obedient servant. Even the raven (one of the most self centered birds in nature) brought him bread and meat."* (1 Kings 17:4-7)

We Will Lose The Fear Of The Lord: Another consequence of staying in our spiritual comfort zones is that we will become too familiar with the presence of God and the things of God and lose the fear of the Lord.

Our Land Shall Become Cursed: In the final analysis, if we stay in our spiritual and natural comfort zones beyond the call of destiny, the curse of lack and poverty will eventually come upon our lives. Please remember that when Adam and Eve disobeyed God, the curse came upon the land and hindered their prosperity. The spiritual lesson behind the story of Adam and Eve is simply this, *"Every time we refuse to obey God, we are opening a spiritual door for a curse to come upon our life!"* Money, jobs and houses do not fall from heaven they come as a result of God commanding a blessing upon our land (immediate environment). How can we prosper with a curse on our lives?

The Double Minded Man

"But let him ask in faith, nothing wavering. For he that wavereth is like a wave of the sea driven with the wind and tossed. For let not that man think that he shall receive any thing of the Lord. A double minded man is unstable in all his ways."[2]

Imagine the horror of trying to broker a multimillion-dollar deal with a chief executive officer who has a split personality. At any given moment, you are never really sure which personality you are dealing with. In one instance it may seem like the man really wants to do business with you; but in the very next moment he acts like doing business with you isn't such a good idea after all. He is a man with two minds. His two personalities switch between each other so rapidly that you are never really sure with whom you are dealing.

This is the prophetic picture the Bible gives us of the double-minded man. ***Double mindedness is a serious***

***disease of the soul, which plagues so many of God's
people. It's the reason many people of faith become stuck
at the place were two roads meet, during periods of spiritual and social transition***. Most people can't make up their
minds, whether to stay in their comfort zone or follow the
call of God to the finish line. On one hand, they like the
idea of being used by God but on the other hand, they are
satisfied with their worldly comforts and pleasures.

The Bible tells us that the *"double minded person"*
is *"unstable in all his ways."* This is serious business.
Double mindedness does not stay in one area of our lives;
it quickly spreads like a malignant cancer to other areas
our life. Double mindedness makes us become untrust-
worthy. When God and the people around us cannot trust
us, our spiritual ministry is over. When the angels of God
came to rescue Lot and his family before the destruction of
the cities of Sodom and Gomorrah, they told him that he
had no time to collect his material possessions. The fire of
God would soon be falling on the city and the angels gave
Lot and his family a stern warning not to look back while
they were running to safety.

Before they reached their destination, Lot's wife looked
back and instantly became a pillar of salt. This was her
fork in the road where she had to choose between the road
of her past and the road to her future place of safety. She
made the wrong decision and became the evidence of the
spiritual dangers of double mindedness during periods of
transition. During periods of spiritual and social transition
we are going to have to win the battle of the mind. The
devil will try to force us into a position of double mindedness. He will try to entice us with the pleasures of the
moment, at the expense of moving forward into our spiritual destiny. We cannot give in to the temptations of the

enemy. We must choose the road toward our prophetic destiny in God, even when the road is filled with difficult challenges. The decision to move toward the finish line of our spiritual purpose is always the best decision, no matter how many road blocks or detours we might face.

Loose that Donkey!
Called To a Higher Purpose

When mother donkey gave birth to *"Little donkey,"* she did not know the special call of God which was upon the life of *"Little donkey."* *"Little donkey"* grew into a beautiful donkey. One day a man came and gave a purse full of silver to its owner; *"Little donkey"* had just been sold. The new owner tied *"Little donkey"* to a rope and pulled it to his home. He was a very happy buyer. He had bought her for a good price. She was a beautiful and strong donkey. He knew that she would give him many years of good service. Better still; no man had ever sat on her.

Like the mother donkey, the new owner did not know that *"Little donkey"* had a great call of God upon her life. The new owner had the bill of sale in his hands, proving that he was the sole owner of *"Little donkey."* What he did not know is that God Almighty had a special call on her life, which transcended the earthly claims of her new owner. When the new owner arrived at his house, he tied *"Little Donkey"* **at the place where two roads meet.**

"And when they came nigh to Jerusalem, unto Bethphage and Bethany, at the mount of Olives, he sendeth forth two of his disciples, And saith unto them, Go your way into the village over against you: and as soon as ye be entered into it, ye shall find a colt tied, whereon never man sat; loose him, and bring him. And if any man say unto you,

Why do ye this? say ye that the Lord hath need of him; and straightway he will send him hither. And they went their way, and found the colt tied by the door without in a place where two ways met; and they loose him."³

As soon as *"Little Donkey's"* new owner tied her to a pole near his house at the place, Jesus knew that it was time for His long awaited triumphal entry into Jerusalem. ***Eternity and time were getting ready to collide on the back of the*** *"Little Donkey."* ***Jesus told his disciples to go into the city and look for a donkey which was tied at the place where two roads come together.***
The disciples were slightly troubled and puzzled by what the Lord Jesus was suggesting. How does one just walk up to somebody's house and take their donkey without asking for the owner's permission. Was Jesus suggesting that they go on a *"Donkey Heist?"* Adventurous Peter must have liked this particular mission. What they failed to understand is that *"from God's point of view, the claims of spiritual destiny are far more important than the claims of a career, job or natural talent."* Jesus told them that if the current owner of the donkey asked them why they were taking *"Little Donkey,"* they were to tell him, *"The Master has need of her!"*
When *"Little Donkey"* was loosed from the place were two roads came together, she found herself walking on the spiritual road that led to her destiny. *"Little Donkey"* was brought before the Lord Jesus Christ and as their eyes met, *"Little Donkey"* instantly knew that she was born to carry Him on her back. No man had ever ridden her, but now she knew why. She was called to carry His glorious presence into Jerusalem for one last time.

"Little Donkey" knelt humbly before Him so He could ride on her back. Together, they initiated their prophetic journey toward the city of Jerusalem. The King of kings and Holy One of Israel was coming and He was riding on the back of *"Little Donkey."* Little did she know that she was the subject of an ancient Messianic prophecy! Old Testament prophets looked through the annals of time and caught a glimpse of this glorious triumphal entry.

Suddenly *"Little Donkey"* was surrounded by hundreds of children, men and women who were singing, *"Hosanna! Hosanna! Blessed is He who comes in the name of the Lord!"* Women and children were waving palm branches as *"Little Donkey"* carried her divine cargo. Some people were spreading their garments before *"Little Donkey"* and within moments there was a carpet of garments everywhere she stepped. "Little Donkey" was enjoying every second of the journey. She had been born for one memorable moment of divine visitation! In that moment of time, she realized she was walking in her prophetic destiny, carrying **DESTINY** on her back!

I'm sure when she grew old and was no longer able to carry any size load; she sat around the camp fire with other donkeys and told them about her unforgettable day of divine destiny. She probably taught her descendants a very important lesson about not being stubborn because one day, they might find themselves "tied to a pole where two roads meet;" the day she stepped out of her time of transition, into her destiny!

Brethren we must never forget that one of the greatest dangers we face during periods of transition is the danger of becoming stuck at the place were two roads meet. *We can become stuck at the place where the call of God upon our lives collides with our highly successful earthly careers.*

265

We may know that there is a serious call of God upon our lives, but our earthly careers or political aspirations may be standing in the way.

We can become stuck when our loyalty to our family and friends collides with our loyalty to God and His call upon our lives. This is why Jesus said, *"If a man or woman loves his father, mother, spouse and children more than Me, he or she is not fit for the Kingdom of God."* During periods of spiritual and social transition, our loyalties will be seriously tested. Depending on the choices we make, we can become stuck at the place were two roads meet or we can move forward into our spiritual inheritance.

"Then Elijah talked to them. How long are you going to waver between two opinions?" he asked the people. If the Lord is God, follow him! But if Baal is God, then follow him!"[4]

> ***"We can become stuck at the place where the call of God upon our lives collides with our highly successful earthly careers."***

The Curse of King Solomon

One of the most notable spiritual tragedies in the Bible is the spiritual decline of King Solomon. King Solomon became the wisest and richest person who has ever lived, through a very powerful encounter with God. He composed hundreds of songs. He wrote thousands of proverbs and poems. His wisdom was sought after by the most prestigious people of his time. The Queen of Sheba, with a train of gold and spices, traveled hundreds of miles from her kingdom in Ethiopia to hear the wisdom of Solomon.

Unfortunately the great King Solomon had a serious moral weakness which set him up for a major fall. King Solomon loved *"many foreign women."* The Bible calls them *"strange women"* because their spiritual practices of worshipping demons and man made idols were not part of the covenant of Israel.

"But king Solomon loved many strange women, together with the daughter of Pharaoh, women of the Moabites, Ammonites, Edomites, Zidonians, and Hittites; Of the nations concerning which the LORD said unto the children of Israel, Ye shall not go in to them, neither shall they come in unto you: for surely they will turn away your heart after their gods: Solomon clave unto these in love. And he had seven hundred wives, princesses, and three hundred concubines: and his wives turned away his heart. For it came to pass, when Solomon was old, that his wives turned away his heart after other gods: and his heart was not perfect with the LORD his God, as was the heart of David his father."[5]

Even though King Solomon was one of the wisest men who has ever lived, he found himself stuck at the place were two roads meet, because of his lust for strange women. During this period of spiritual transition, Solomon's emotional attachment to these *"forbidden women,"* destroyed his ability to effectively move into his God given destiny and corrupted his supernatural wisdom. The wisest and richest person who has ever lived was caught between his higher calling to the Kingdom of God and his love for these foreign women. Such are the spiritual dangers of periods of transition.

You Cannot Serve Two Masters

"No man can serve two masters: for either he will hate the one, and love the other; or else he will hold to the one, and despise the other. Ye cannot serve God and mammon. Therefore I say unto you, Take no thought for your life, what ye shall eat, or what ye shall drink; nor yet for your body, what ye shall put on. Is not the life more than meat, and the body than raiment?"[6]

Nothing is more deadly than an *"unhealthy attachment to money,"* during periods of spiritual and social transition. God wants us to be financially blessed for the extension of His glorious Kingdom here on earth. Nevertheless, if we fall in love with *money,* we are opening a door to the demon spirit called *"mammon"* which will harden our heart, causing us to switch our spiritual allegiances.

Once the switch has been made from spiritual loyalty to God, to the service of mammon, we will become stuck at the place were two meet. We will find ourselves stuck between the high calling of God in Christ Jesus and the deceitfulness of riches. This is exactly what happened to Judas Iscariot. He was called to be one of the founding apostles of the Lamb, but he failed to move into the fullness of his apostolic calling because of a serious lust for money.

I really believe that Judas Iscariot loved God, but he loved the *gold* a little bit more. There was a constant tug of war within his spirit between his faith in God and his lust for money. His love for money slowly pulled him away from God. ***The sad fact is that Judas Iscariot never broke free from the hold that greed had on his soul, so he committed suicide at the place where two roads meet.*** During periods of spiritual transition, God will attempt to set us free from the love of money, which can hinder our forward advancement in His Kingdom.

Life on the Other Side of The Cross

"And you, being dead in your sins and the uncircumcision of your flesh, hath he quickened together with him, having forgiven you all trespasses; Blotting out the handwriting of ordinances that was against us, which was contrary to us, and took it out of the way, nailing it to his cross; And having spoiled principalities and powers, he made a shew of them openly, triumphing over them in it."[7]

The death and resurrection of Jesus disrupted centuries of approaching God for divine salvation through the sacrifices of animals. This was the most critical spiritual transition in history; when God shifted the plan of salvation from the sacrificing of animals onto a Man who was beaten and crucified for the sins of the world. This one event changed the cross from an instrument of death and punishment to an instrument of divine salvation and deliverance for the troubled soul. Every troubled soul who looks to the cross and believes on Him who died on it, finds spiritual relief from the oppression of the enemy.

The cross is the divine instrument God uses to kill fleshly desires in our lives. This is why the apostle Paul calls the cross *"the power of God unto divine salvation."* God will orchestrate seasons of transition to draw us into a deeper work of the cross. Many people think that the Lord Jesus Christ died on the cross so we don't have to die. To the contrary, Jesus died on the cross to make our death to self possible. On the cross Jesus died in obedience to His Father's will. We need to embrace the power of the cross.

The power of the cross of Christ will set us free from any sinful and demonic entanglements which can cause us become stuck at the place where two roads meet.

Notes on Chapter Eleven

1. Isaiah 32:9-13, 2. James 1:6-8
3. Mark 11:1-4, 4. I King 18:21
5. I King 11:1-4, 6. Matt 6:24-25
7. Col 2:13-15

Chapter Twelve

Success Without Humility

Regardless of what part of the world we live in or the particular race we identify ourselves with, we all share a common fear- the fear of failure. This fear is universal and transcends all races. You see it on the petrified face of a grade school student who has just received a bad report card from school and in the tear drenched face of a boxer who has just lost his heavy weight title to a new contender. You see it in the grief smitten face of a young woman whose husband has just left her for another woman. She can hardly believe that her dreams of living happily ever after have been shattered so quickly. She shies away from her friends and family to avoid the embarrassment of telling them that her marriage has failed. Such is our universal fear of failure.

Our inherent fear of failure masks and clouds a very important truth that the Lord wants us to learn very quickly during our earthly pilgrimage- *"Failure in some cases is good for the soul!"* Learning this very important truth about failure will deliver us from the beast within. In certain incidents, failure is good for us because our sinful Adamic nature houses a ferocious beast called pride.

Our sinful nature does not know how to handle unbroken success. *I strongly believe that in certain incidents, failure is God's mercy, preventing the beast of pride within us from running unchecked.* This is not to say that we are to plan on failure, but it does mean that failure is not the end of the story.

Another important spiritual danger during periods of transition is the *"danger of achieving success without humility."* God wants His people to succeed and prosper, but never at the expense of maintaining a humble attitude and spirit before God and man.

---

9 The Danger Of Success Without Humility.

The Gospel of Good Success

"This book of the law shall not depart out of thy mouth; but thou shalt meditate therein day and night, that thou mayest observe to do according to all that is written therein: for then thou shalt make thy way prosperous, and then thou shalt have good success. "[1]

God is a God of success. This is a very important truth to know about the person of God. If God has called us to church or corporate ministry, we can be most assured that His plan for our lives includes success. God loves to see His children succeed in the same way we, as parents, want our own children to succeed. This is why God has written the formula of success in His holy word.

*"In certain incidents, failure is good
for us because our sinful Adamic nature
houses a ferocious beast called pride."*

The book of Joshua opens up with a very sad statement... *"Now after the death of Moses the servant of the Lord,"* indicating the fact that the people of Israel were in mourning over the loss of their great leader, Moses. The man whom God had used to deliver them from the bondage of slavery at the hands of the Egyptians was now dead.

This was the same Moses who had helped them to cross the Red Sea as on dry land, who had caused water to come out of a rock when they were thirsty and the one whose face they had seen shine like that of an angel when he received the Ten Commandments on tablets of stone. They would never see his face or hear his voice again. The pain of their unbearable loss left a somberness in the air that hung over them like a wet blanket.

I am sure they must have been asking themselves questions like, *"Who is going to lead us to the promise land? Who is going to perform the miracles that Moses performed?"* Such were the questions on everybody's mind. It was in this atmosphere of sorrow, fear and regret that the voice of God came to Joshua. God told Joshua that he was to be Moses' successor.

The Lord knew that Joshua was being called to fill some very big shoes. Moses was a very powerful and extraordinary man. Who could possibly take his place? As God spoke to Joshua, he showed him the divine formula for good success. God told him that He desired to give him *good success* because, as we shall soon discover, there is such a thing as *"bad success."*

God gave explicit instructions to Joshua on how to achieve good success. He told him that he was to be courageous and meditate on God's word day and night. God was guaranteeing him success through obeying and applying the Scriptures to his daily life. God wants His people to govern the affairs of their lives according to His word as they prepare for success. He wants His people to be bigger than success. *In order for us to manage success, our spirits must become bigger than success.*

The Curse of Unbroken Success

"And he spake a parable unto them, saying, The ground of a certain rich man brought forth plentifully: And he said, This will I do: I will pull down my barns, and build greater; and there will I bestow all my fruits and my goods. And I will say to my soul, Soul, thou hast much goods laid up for many years; take thine ease, eat, drink, [and] be merry. But God said unto him, [Thou] fool, this night thy soul shall be required of thee: then whose shall those things be, which thou hast provided!"²

The story of the foolish rich man underscores why God wants His people to be bigger than success in order for them to handle success. As I mentioned earlier in this chapter, millions of people on our planet are afraid of failing. *Nevertheless, what most people fail to realize is that it is far more difficult to manage success than to manage failure. Failure is discouraging and in most cases humbling, but success can be very intoxicating and pride inflating.* Handling success requires far more character and humility than managing failure.

Let's consider the parable of the foolish rich man. Jesus tells us that this man came into a period of unprecedented success. Everything he touched turned into gold. God blessed this man's fields in such a way that he had a historical harvest of untold proportions. When he sat down to take stock of just how much God had blessed him with, he became filled with pride. Instead of giving the credit to God, he began to worship himself and his own abilities. Not once did this rich man consider and appreciate the involvement of God in his staggering success.

The Bible tells us explicitly that *"the earth is the Lords and the fullness thereof."* This means that the ground (soil) that the rich man was boasting over and giving himself credit for actually belonged to God. The seeds he used to plant his fields belonged to God, as well as the rain that watered those fields.

What about his soul? Who was responsible for keeping this man alive? Without a doubt, the rich man's soul also belonged to God. Nevertheless when the rich man did his final calculations, God was a non-factor in his success. As far as this rich man was concerned, his personal wits and business acumen were the only reasons he was so successful. God looked into the heart of this rich man and was grieved to discover that he had left no room for a relationship with his heavenly Father. While the rich man was rehearsing how he was going to spend all his money, God took his soul. He died and left behind everything that he had worked so hard to acquire.

During periods of transition, one of the spiritual dangers that we must be mindful of is the danger of achieving great success without humility. ***When we have long periods of unbroken success, our success may become a curse to us.*** If we are not careful, we will begin to feel like we have a monopoly on success. Success is a gift from God which He bestows upon us for obeying His principles. This is why God, in is His infinite wisdom, allows moments of failure to brush our shores from time to time.

> *"Nevertheless, what most people fail to realize is that it is far more difficult to manage success than to manage failure."*

The Armor Bearer Principle

"And it came to pass, when Moses held up his hand, that Israel prevailed: and when he let down his hand, Amalek prevailed. But Moses' hands [were] heavy; and they took a stone, and put [it] under him, and he sat thereon; and Aaron and Hur stayed up his hands, the one on the one side, and the other on the other side; and his hands were steady until the going down of the sun. "[3]

We must never forget that success is not a destination; it's a journey. We can never say that we have "arrived" in our success journey because we always have the capacity to do better. We must quickly come to terms with the fact that, *"the success journey is not a casual stroll, it's a marathon. You will not win it on your own."* Nobody has ever succeeded alone because success is always a team effort.

Not even the great Moses (the prince of Egypt) could fulfill his prophetic destiny without the participation of His brother Aaron. From the time Moses had an encounter with God at the burning bush, God made it very clear that he would need the support of his brother. Moses had a stuttering problem which hindered his speech so God assigned Aaron to be his spokesman. Aaron was also Moses' armor bearer. The armor bearer principle is, *"the quest for success cannot be achieved without the efforts of others."*

Even Hollywood has enough sense to know that you cannot make a blockbuster movie using a great movie star without an equally good cast of supporting actors. This is why every year at the Academy Awards they present Oscars to the best supporting actors and actresses. In order to ensure continued success in our churches or business organizations, we must never forget to passionately celebrate the efforts of others who have invested in our success.

In the 2005/2006 NBA season, the Miami Heat emerged as the new world basket ball champions. This was their first NBA championship since the franchise was started in 1987. At their championship parade in the city of Miami, two hundred thousand fans filled the streets to savor this victory with their beloved team. After seventeen years of *"nearly hitting the mark"* and then being eliminated during the NBA playoffs, the anxious fans were more than ready for a heartfelt celebration.

Like any success story, there were some important and intrinsic factors that went into the stew of the Miami Heat's championship season. The stew began to simmer when the Miami Heat, through the visionary leadership of basket ball hall of fame coach, Pat Riley, acquired a young and shy looking black star, by the name of Dwayne Wade. At the time they acquired him, they were unaware of just how good an athlete the young man really was.

The stew began to steam when Coach Riley acquired the player affectionately known in the basket ball world as the *"Diesel."* This giant of a man was none other than the legendary basket ball player, Shaquile Oneal. In his first speech to the thousands of Miami Heat fans, who had gathered to catch a glimpse of him, Shaq promised to bring an NBA championship to the city of Miami. Shaquile Oneal then did something that shocked many of his critics and showed the basketball world just how big he was on the inside.

He told the basketball world that he had not come to the Miami Heat to be the center of attention; he was coming to work alongside the young upcoming basketball star Dwayne Wade. *"I have come to make Dwayne Wade the best basket ball player that I know he can be and to show the world just how good this young man really is,"* Shaq promised. Coach Riley then added one of the best supporting casts of veteran players to this stew of success. He acquired the seasoned NBA veterans Gary Payton, Antoine Walker and NBA all defensive player, Alonzo Mourning.

In the ensuing two NBA seasons Dwayne Wade's talent for basketball exploded and the world began to say, *"Could this be the next Michael Jordan?"* Coach Riley's stew of success finally led to their first ever NBA championship at the home court of the indomitable and highly talented Dallas Mavericks. In the fourth quarter, when it seemed like the Dallas Mavericks were going to deny the Miami Heat their first NBA championship, Dwayne Wade exploded for one of the most amazing NBA fourth quarter performances. During the last eight minutes of the fourth quarter, young Dwayne Wade single handedly carried the championship hopes of his entire team and forced a stunning Dallas Mavericks loss. When the timer went off to announce the end of the fourth quarter, an exhausted Dwayne Wade threw the basketball into the air while screaming with tears of joy.

> *"Failure is discouraging and in most
> cases humbling, but success can be very
> intoxicating and pride inflating."*

When NBA commissioner David Stern presented the award for NBA finals MVP, the young star was quick to humbly acknowledge that he could not have done what he had done throughout the whole NBA season if it were not for the confidence that Shaquille Oneal, Coach Riley and the rest of the team had placed in him. Dwayne was quick to acknowledge that the stew of success had far more ingredients in it than just his dazzling basket ball talent.

When Shaquile Oneal was asked to comment on young Dwayne Wade's greatness, Shaq told the reporter that he was very impressed with Dwayne Wade's ability to manage the aura of success with a deep sense of heartfelt humility. All the Miami Heat players, including Coach Riley made comments about how they were dazzled by Dwayne's ability to mingle his incredible talent with an unfeigned sense of humility. This was quite a contrast to the behavior another basketball legend by the name of Kobe Bryant had displayed while playing for the Los Angeles Lakers during the Shaquile O'Neal era. Kobe's arrogance and defiance of authority led to the initial dismissal of basket ball hall of fame Coach Phil Jackson. In his book released after his dismissal from the Lakers, Phil Jackson admitted that Kobe Bryant was one of the most difficult players that he had ever coached. On a redemptive note, Coach Jackson was asked to return to the Lakers and young Kobe Bryant promised to do his best to work with his coach.

One of the most legendary CEO's of the twenty first century was a man by the name of Lee Iacocca, who took over the Chrysler Corporation when it was at the brink of eminent collapse. The Lee Iacocca story is the classic case of the dangers of success without humility during times of transition. This is what one writer had to say about Lee Iacocca's tenure as the head of the Chrysler Corporation.

CASE STUDY:
THE LEE IACOCCA/ CHRYSLER STORY

"...Lee Iacocca, for example, saved Chrysler from the brink of catastrophe, performing one of the most celebrated (and deservedly so) turnarounds in American business history. Chrysler rose to a height of 2.9 times the market at a point about halfway through his tenure. Then, however, he diverted his attention to making himself one of the most celebrated CEOs in American business history. Investors Business Daily and the Wall Street Journal chronicled how Iacocca appeared regularly on talk shows like the Today Show and Larry King Live, personally starred in over eighty commercials, entertained the idea of running for president of the United States (quoted at one point, "Running Chrysler has been a bigger job than running the country...I could handle the national economy in six months), and widely promoted his autobiography. The book, Iacocca, sold seven million copies and elevated him to rock star status, leading him to be mobbed by thousands of cheering fans upon his arrival in Japan. Iacocca's personal stock soared, but in the second half of his tenure, Chrysler stock fell 31 percent behind the general market.

Sadly, Iacocca had trouble leaving center stage and letting go of the perks of executive kingship. He postponed his retirement so many times that insiders began to joke that Iacocca stood for "I Am Chairman of Chrysler Corporation Always." And when he did finally retire, he

*demanded that the board continue to provide a private jet
and stock options. Later, he joined forces with noted takeover artist Kirk Kerkorian to launch a hostile takeover bid
for Chrysler." (Good to Great by Jim Collins, pg 29-30)*

The church and business worlds are full of *"Lee
Iacoccas."* These are the men and women who are simply
incredible and possess a certain genius for fueling the train
of success, but lack the power to finish well. This is because
most of them have never developed the personal character that is bigger than success. Even though legendary
CEO Lee Iacocca was instrumental in bringing about one
of the most powerful business turnarounds in business
history for the Chrysler Corporation, he was also personally involved in its ultimate decline. The man who started
out as Chrysler's deliverer, failed to conquer his personal
demons that drove him to crave the center stage at all
costs. Intoxicated by fame, stardom and the accompanying
media blitz, Iacocca forgot the hidden intangibles that go
into the stew of success. He forgot that uncommon success
is always a result of team effort. As is always the case,
great success without humility always ends up in a scan-
dalous disaster. Such are the spiritual and social dangers of
periods of transition.

The King Nebuchadnezzar Memoirs

*"That they shall drive thee from men, and thy dwelling
shall be with the beasts of the field, and they shall make
thee to eat grass as oxen, and they shall wet thee with the
dew of heaven, and seven times shall pass over thee, till
thou know that the most High ruleth in the kingdom of
men, and giveth it to whomsoever he will."*[4]

Without a doubt, Nebuchadnezzar, the king of ancient Babylon, was one of the most powerful and successful of all the kings of the Old Testament era. His great military might and his vast wealth were the talk of the ancient world. It was during the glorious reign of this Babylonian King that most of Israel went into captivity.

Among those who were taken into captivity were four very brilliant Hebrew boys Daniel, Mishach, Shadrach and Abednego of whom the most excellent was Daniel. Daniel had the prophetic ability to interpret visions and dreams. He quickly rose to prominence and became the chief of the magicians and personal adviser to the Babylonian king. One night King Nebuchadnezzar had a very disturbing dream and when he woke from his sleep, he demanded that they bring Daniel and all the magicians in his kingdom before him. When King Nebuchadnezzar finished telling his dream to Daniel, Daniel's face became very pale. He was so saddened by the prophetic meaning of the dream that he hesitated telling it to the anxious king. King Nebuchadnezzar charged Daniel to hold nothing back.

Daniel proceeded to tell King Nebuchadnezzar the full meaning and future implications of the dream. He told the stunned Babylonian king that God was going to take his sanity away from him. He was going to be driven into the wilderness where he would live like an animal for seven years, feeding on grass until he learned the power of humility towards the only true and living God.

Immediately after this, the Babylonian King was touring his glorious empire and was so astounded by his own success that he began to worship himself and all his political accomplishments. While he was basking in his personal success, a decree was issued from heaven and he lost his sanity. He was driven into the wilderness for seven years and lived like a wild animal, eating grass and dirt (I don't know about you, but I do not want God to go this far to teach me the power of humility). After seven years had expired, the Lord returned the sanity of the Babylonian King and restored him to the throne of His Kingdom.

After his miraculous restoration, King Nebuchadnezzar realized just how foolish and vain he had been in worshipping his own success. He had reveled in his own success without giving God the praise that was due Him. He suddenly realized that everything he owned came from the hand of God. He realized that God was able to strip him of everything he owned at any moment. He became a very humble king indeed. He came to know firsthand the spiritual danger of having success without humility during periods of spiritual transition.

Public Success, Private Pain

"And the king was much moved, and went up to the chamber over the gate, and wept: and as he went, thus he said, O my son Absalom, my son, my son Absalom! would God I had died for thee, O Absalom, my son, my son!"[5]

When Adam and Eve sinned against God and introduced sin in the human genome; there was a profound spiritual and demonic mutation in the human DNA. This mutation reconfigured man's DNA from one which propelled him to pursue God to one which generates lust for his own selfish desires. Man's mutated DNA had set him on the pathway of death.

To place man's altered DNA in check; God in His sovereignty allows *"pain"* to be the divine method for restraining man's selfish desires. This is why very few people change without pain. In order to restrain the inherent evil in man and his propensity towards self worship, God permits moments of failure to visit even the most spiritual of us. *An introspective look at the heroes of the Bible will quickly expose a very common trend. These great men and women of God were not given divine immunity from failure and personal tragedy.* No matter how anointed and how close some of them were to God, their lives were never insulated from experiencing moments of personal tragedy and failure which are common to all.

Consider the story of David, the beloved King of Israel, who announced his arrival on the public scene by killing Goliath the Philistine giant. Within days of his stunning victory over Goliath, women were composing the most daring songs about the new kid on the block. King David went on to become a legendary warrior who expanded the natural borders of the nation of Israel through a series of military conquests. Standing in the midst of his garden of success, like uninvited tares in a wheat field, was painful family troubles which constantly brought this great king to tears. He was temporarily ousted from his throne by his own son, Absalom. In the ensuing battle between David's men and Absalom's army, Absalom was killed. When King David received the news, he cried bitterly over the loss of his son.

"God in His sovereignty allows "pain" to be the divine method for restraining man's selfish desires."

King David was known as a man after God's own heart. Why did God allow such tragic situations to occur in David's life? The reason is obvious. These contrary situations kept David on his knees and helped him to live in humility as he realized just how hopeless and fragile he was without God's help. The Bible tells us of Namaan, (2 Kings 5) the great Syrian general, whose resume of victories and military accolades dazzled even royal families, but yet he was a leper. *Public success combined with private pain; what a paradox!* The underlying spiritual truth behind this paradox is simple but powerful. God knows that if He does not allow moments of failure to interrupt our success journey, our personal pride may go unchecked and destroy us during periods of spiritual and social transition.

Seeds of Wisdom on Managing Success

As we come to the close of this chapter, I will endeavor to give you some seeds of wisdom on managing success and failure.

1. We must realize that the success journey is not a private stroll it's a public marathon that calls for the contribution of others.
2. We must realize that one of the spiritual dangers of transition is the danger of having great success without walking in humility.
3. We must realize that we serve a God of success, who is the principle engineer behind all great successes.
4. We must realize that failure is God's mercy, restraining the devil of pride and self worship from corrupting us and taking credit for the success that God has given us.
5. We must realize that the stew of success is a mixture of our God given creative genius plus the contributions and talents of others.

6. We must realize that in order for God to trust us with great success, we must allow our personal character to become bigger than success.
7. We must realize that success is a journey and not a destination, leaving us with the capability of doing better.
8. We must realize that failure is an event and not a destination. It only becomes a destination when we choose to stay at the place of our failure.
9. We must realize that failure is God's way of telling us what does not work, so we can focus our energy on what really works.
10. We must realize that the Bible says that the prosperity of fools is their destruction. We must make up our mind to passionately pursue the wisdom of God.

Notes on Chapter Twelve

1. (Joshua 1:8), 2. (Luke 12:16,18-20)
3. Ex 17:11-12, 4. Daniel 4:25
5. 2 Samuel 18:33

Chapter Thirteen

Toxic Relationships

S aul, the son of Kish, met the Prophet Samuel and became a king. King David met Bathsheba and his life was never the same. David's encounter with Bathsheba unleashed a spirit of adultery, deception and murder and brought the judgment of God upon his house which continued to the end of his life. David's encounter with Bathsheba also resulted in the birth of Solomon. Solomon succeeded David as the next King of Israel, and became the richest and the wisest person who has ever lived. King Solomon built God a glorious temple. King Solomon fell in love with foreign women who worshipped other demon gods and messed up his life. His love for these idol worshipping women forced his kingdom into a serious downward spiral.

King Ahab married a Sidonian woman by the name of Jezebel, and became the most wicked of all the kings of Israel. Judas Iscariot met some Pharisees who wanted to kill Jesus and his life was tragically altered from the pathway of destiny. Samson, the mighty warrior with super human strength, met Delilah and lost his power, his eyes and his freedom. Young Timothy met the apostle Paul and went on to become an apostle.

The point I want to make is, ***there is nothing more powerful and more lethal than the relationships we develop with people!"*** Mike Murdock says, *"Relationships are like water currents. They will either drive you toward your dreams and goals or they will drive you away from them."* And I say that relationships with people are like elevators; they will either take you up (heaven) or down (hell). ***One of the dangers during periods of spiritual transition is the danger of getting entangled by stagnant and undefined relationships.*** In this final chapter on the dangers of transition, we will fully analyze why relationships become toxic and why they must be severed during periods of transition before they destroy our prophetic destiny.

---

10. The Danger Of being Entangled by Stagnant & Undefined Relationships.

We Were Created For Relationship

"Thou art worthy, O Lord, to receive glory and honor and power: for thou hast created all things, and for thy pleasure they are and were created."[1]

The popular saying, *"No man is an island,"* is true indeed! Even island nations, surrounded by vast oceans cannot survive by themselves. In today's borderless world of cyber space, the Commonwealth of Nations has been reduced into one tiny global village. No one nation can exist by itself. Relationships between people or nations can exist on many levels as we will see when we study relationships. Every human being has two basic needs, the *inherent need to love and be loved, and the need to belong.*

The need to love and be loved: We were all created by love. The Bible says that God is love and God is the one who created us. It is therefore not surprising that man's greatest need is to love and be loved. You don't have to look further than the fascination of Hollywood with romantic love story movies. They have discovered the deepest need of the human race and are profiting from it. This basic need to love and be loved is what drives every human being and gives us hope for the future. Have you ever listened to starry eyed teenagers talk about their dreams of a future mate? Anticipation of this future love encounter gives them a hope for the future and consumes their thoughts and actions.

"There is nothing more powerful
and more lethal than the relationships
we develop with people!"

The need to love and be loved is so strong that it will drive innocent girls into the hands of strange men to secure even a dismal feeling of being loved and needed. During times of spiritual transition, the devil will try to manipulate our inherent need to love and be loved to force us to make alliances with men and women who will detour us from the pathway of destiny. There is absolutely nothing wrong with having relationships with people, but we must allow the Holy Spirit to govern and initiate these relationships.

289

The need to belong: The second basic need of all mankind is the need to belong. No one is born in a vacuum. We are not called to be an island unto ourselves. The very fabric of our personality is interwoven with the basic need to belong to a community of people with a common destiny. This sense of belonging adds to our self worth and also fills us with the confidence to face the future and all that it entails.

The need to belong is the primary motivation behind a young man joining a notorious street gang and going through a violent beating ceremony in order to be initiated into the gang. What some sociologists do not understand is that most young people do not join gangs for the purpose of committing crime and breaking the law; most do it to satisfy the deep seated emotional need to belong to something. Most people will go to great lengths in order to feel needed and wanted. It is my prayer that these simple but powerful relationship principles will help you know how to govern and define every undefined and stagnant relationship in your life. ***Navigating the valley of transition requires tremendous wisdom, especially in interpersonal relationships.***

Relationships Are Like Elevators

All human relationships are like elevators, they will either take you up and toward your prophetic destiny, or down and away from what God has intended for your life. During periods of spiritual transition, while God is moving us into our Kingdom assignment, we need to make sure that every relationship in our life has been qualified by the Holy Spirit, especially relationships we maintain with the opposite sex. The corridors of history have shown us that some of the greatest kings, pastors and business men have been destroyed by toxic relationships with the opposite sex.

"Be not deceived: evil communications corrupt good manners."²

The truth of the matter is, when the wrong people enter our life, wrong things begin to happen. When someone enters an elevator, they know without a shadow of doubt that there are only two possible outcomes. The elevator will take them as low as the ground floor or it will take them as high as the top floor of the building.

I really believe that once we know our God given purpose, the wrong people who may try to attach themselves to us while we are walking through the valley of transition, will not easily derail us from our assignment. When we are in tune with the Holy Spirit's leading, we will easily see the *arrow sign pointing down* before our lives become entangled with theirs. One of the most powerful men who has ever lived was a man named Samson. Before his birth, his parents were visited by an angel of God. The angel told them that they were going to give birth to a child with extraordinary human strength who would deliver Israel from the hands of the Philistines. The angel also told them that the child would live in the power of a Nazarite vow. **The angel disclosed the secret of his supernatural strength would be his hair and told them that it was NEVER to be cut!**

"For, lo, thou shalt conceive, and bear a son; and no rasor shall come on his head: for the child shall be a Nazarite unto God from the womb: and he shall begin to deliver Israel out of the hand of the Philistines."³

There is nothing Satan fears more than the entrance of a champion or a deliverer into a generation. The birth of Samson changed and shifted the balance of spiritual power in the heavenly realms. His birth toppled the demonic over Israel that had subjected them to servitude to the Philistines. Unfortunately, Samson had a serious character flaw that proved disastrous during the tenure of his ministry.

Samson had a special lust for Philistine women. When he told his father about it, his father rebuked him for allowing his emotional feelings to interfere with his prophetic calling. His father knew that Samson was anointed by God to destroy the Philistines, not sleep with them! *During periods of spiritual transition, God will use the voice of our natural fathers, who walk in the faith, to expose spiritual weaknesses in our lives which have the power to destroy our destiny in God.* We can only ignore the counsel of the forefathers at our own peril. May God give us the grace to heed the mature voices that He has assigned to mentor us and protect us from associating with the wrong people.

"Navigating the valley of transition requires tremendous wisdom, especially in interpersonal relationships."

Samson refused to heed the wise counsel of his father. Instead, he allowed his sexual desires to transcend the righteous demands of his prophetic calling. It wasn't long before the devil launched his deadliest attack against Samson. The devil assigned *a woman of cunning nature by the name of Delilah* to Samson's life. She was very beautiful and Samson loved her desperately, even though her heart was made of stone. The great Samson had just established a dangerous soul tie with a cold and calculating Philistine woman. Once Delilah had lured the mighty Samson into a passionate romantic affair, she formed an alliance with some very powerful and wicked Philistine lords who wanted to see the destruction of Samson. They promised Delilah a generous bounty if she could uncover the secret of Samson's supernatural strength.

Delilah emerged from her meeting with the Philistine Lords, with a demonic determination to entice Samson until he revealed the secret of his superhuman strength. The first few times that she pressed for the secret to his superhuman strength, Samson lied to her and she called the Philistines lords to come and bind him with chains but Samson overpowered them easily. You might be thinking at this point, *"Did Samson not realize that his romantic relationship with Delilah was quickly heading towards disaster like a runaway train?"* The truth of the matter is that Samson was in such a state of spiritual decline, he could not hear the restraining voice of the Holy Spirit.

After many days of constant and relentless nagging from Delilah, Samson finally told her the greatest and most sacred secret of his life. While he was sleeping, she cut his long hair (which represented his Nazarite vow of eternal consecration to God). The Spirit of God immediately left Samson while he was asleep in Delilah's lap, totally unaware of the grave consequences that awaited him.

"And it came to pass afterward, that he loved a woman in the valley of Sorek, whose name was Delilah. And the lords of the Philistines came up unto her, and said unto her, Entice him, and see wherein his great strength lieth, and by what means we may prevail against him, that we

may bind him to afflict him: and we will give thee every one of us eleven hundred pieces of silver. And Delilah said to Samson, Tell me, I pray thee, wherein thy great strength lieth, and wherewith thou mightest be bound to afflict thee. And it came to pass, when she pressed him daily with her words, and urged him, so that his soul was vexed unto death; That he told her all his heart, and said unto her, There hath not come a rasor upon mine head; for I have been a Nazarite unto God from my mother's womb: if I be shaven, then my strength will go from me, and I shall become weak, and be like any other man. And when Delilah saw that he had told her all his heart, she sent and called for the lords of the Philistines, saying, Come up this once, for he hath shewed me all his heart. Then the lords of the Philistines came up unto her, and brought money in their hand. And she made him sleep upon her knees; and she called for a man, and she caused him to shave off the seven locks of his head; and she began to afflict him, and his strength went from him. And she said, The Philistines be upon thee, Samson. And he awoke out of his sleep, and said, I will go out as at other times before, and shake myself. And he wist not that the LORD was departed from him. But the Philistines took him, and put out his eyes, and brought him down to Gaza, and bound him with fetters of brass; and he did grind in the prison house."⁴

When the Philistines pounced on Samson, he tried to fend them off. ***To Samson's dismay, he realized the Spirit of God had left him.*** When the Philistine lords saw that he was powerless, they quickly gouged out his eyes and led him like a common slave to the land of the Philistines.

Tears of blood rolled out of Samson's eye sockets as they led him in chains to his new residence. His new home was a stinking Philistine prison dedicated to demon gods, where he was forced to work at pushing a grinding mill. Samson's relationship with Delilah had lowered his elevator to the basement floor. ***Samson's wrong associations during this period of spiritual transition had thrust him from the path of his prophetic destiny and cost him his anointing.***

Toxic Relationships

When relationships become stalled in the *"stagnant and undefined"* stage, they become toxic. I was raised in Africa so I am very familiar with the difference between a *river* and a *swamp*. The body of water in a river is constantly flowing, while the water in a swamp is in a continuous state of stagnancy.

"But the miry places thereof and the marishes thereof shall not be healed; they shall be given to salt."[5]

The water in the river remains fresh because it's in a state of continuous motion. This constant motion of the strong underwater currents provides a cleansing system which rids the river of debris. Swamps on the other hand, are simply huge puddles of water with no where to go. This is why the water in a swamp is also called *"dead water."* In the beginning stages, the waters in a swamp are relatively fresh but then become stale within a few days. After collecting dust, germs and dead debris, the body of water finally becomes toxic and soon becomes the breeding ground for mosquitoes, worms and snakes. For all practical purposes, the water in a swamp is poisonous and therefore undrinkable.

"There is nothing Satan fears more than the entrance of a champion or a deliverer into a generation."

When the Pharisees saw the Lord Jesus casting out demons, they accused Him of doing it through the power of Beelzebub. The name Beelzebub simply means *"Lord of the flies."* Beelzebub was the name that the Hebraic Jews gave to Satan.

"Then was brought unto him one possessed with a devil, blind, and dumb: and he healed him, insomuch that the blind and dumb both spake and saw. And all the people were amazed, and said, Is not this the son of David? But when the Pharisees heard it, they said, This fellow doth not cast out devils, but by Beelzebub the prince of the devils. And Jesus knew their thoughts, and said unto them, Every kingdom divided against itself is brought to desolation; and every city or house divided against itself shall not stand: And if Satan cast out Satan, he is divided against himself; how shall then his kingdom stand?"[6]

We must not allow any relationship to remain on the same level of spiritual impartation or communication. If you are in a relationship with someone and your main topic of conversation is about what happened in the past, that relationship has stagnated. If this relationship continues to remain in the same spiritual state, it will soon become stagnant and spiritually toxic. While we are going through the valley of transition, the devil will try to assign us these *"swampy relationships"* in order to inject demonic poison into the blood stream of our prophetic destiny. *These unholy and unsanctioned spiritual alliances will quickly become expressways for relentless demonic attacks against our lives.* These toxic relationships will quickly sap us of our spiritual strength and vision if we do not sever them during these periods of spiritual transition.

King Solomon and the foreign women: The sexual relationships between King Solomon and the foreign women from idol worshipping Gentile nations were toxic. These women were born and raised in spiritual cultures where worshipping demon spirits and man made idols was common practice. Their souls were spiritually contaminated. Having sexual intercourse with these strange women was like drinking water from a stagnant pond! The horrific consequences of the filth that entered his life through these women caused him to lose his respect, dignity and his right standing with God.

When we are going through the valley of transition, we must be very careful to examine every spiritual relationship that we have with people. *Some of these relationships may have been a blessing to us at one point in our spiritual journey. But if their season of divine purpose has expired, we must be willing to let them go.*

When we go into a grocery store to buy a carton of milk, we will notice that it has an expiration date on it. The reason prudent manufacturers place expiration dates on perishable goods is because they do not want to be held liable for poisoning the public. Spiritual relationships operate on the same premise.

Every relationship that God brings into our lives has an expiration date on it. When the appointed time of purpose for the relationship expires, we must be willing to move on. If we refuse to let go, the relationship will immediately become toxic. We cannot stay in any relationship beyond the transitional period that God has set.

"But king Solomon loved many strange women, together with the daughter of Pharaoh, women of the Moabites, Ammonites, Edomites, Zidonians, and Hittites; Of the nations concerning which the LORD said unto the children of Israel, Ye shall not go in to them, neither shall they come in unto you: for surely they will turn away your heart after their gods: Solomon clave unto these in love."[7]

One of the saddest Bible stories which clearly illustrates the spiritual dangers of being stuck in toxic relationships during periods of spiritual transition is the story of King Saul and Jonathan. The relationship between Jonathan and his demented father, King Saul, is worth scrutinizing. Jonathan was the first born son and immediate heir to the throne of Israel. His father had been appointed to the throne of Israel by the prophet Samuel. Unfortunately the spiritual contamination of King Saul's soul was constantly frustrating Jonathan's efforts to obey the Holy Spirit's voice, making it necessary for God to relinquish His hold on Saul's life. God told the prophet Samuel that He had rejected Saul and his lineage from being kings over the nation of Israel and had chosen David (whom He called a man after His own heart) to take the throne.

God supernaturally brought David into favor with King Saul, who hired him to work as his armor bearer. When Jonathan overheard David speaking to his father, his soul became interwoven with that of David. From that moment on, God knit their hearts together because they were both called to the same destiny. Unfortunately, *Jonathan's soul tie with his father was too strong. Even though he knew that God Himself had rejected and abandoned his father, Jonathan failed to follow suit.*

The Bible says that we are to be imitators of God. This means that when God rejects something or someone, we must follow His leading. Jonathan failed to allow the demands of his prophetic destiny to subdue the natural demands of his relationship with his father. Since God had rejected King Saul, any spiritual alliance with him was spiritually toxic and futile. There was a sentence of death upon King Saul's life and whosoever came into an alliance with him, received the same sentence. This is exactly what happened to Jonathan during this transitional period. He died prematurely in the field of battle on the very same day that King Saul killed himself. Unholy spiritual alliances are very real dangers we will most likely face during seasons of transition.

"And David said unto him, From whence comest thou? And he said unto him, Out of the camp of Israel am I escaped. And David said unto him, How went the matter? I pray thee, tell me. And he answered, That the people are fled from the battle, and many of the people also are fallen and dead; and Saul and Jonathan his son are dead also. And David said unto the young man that told him, How knowest thou that Saul and Jonathan his son be dead."[9]

The value of any spiritual relationship is in its contribution to our assignment in the Kingdom of God. If a relationship is not helping us become more like Christ and propelling us into our destiny, such a relationship is toxic and unnecessary.

The Spiritual Dynamics of Healthy Relationships

Periods of transition require great wisdom and discernment as we navigate through the network of relationships that comes into our lives as we journey toward our destiny. It's of critical importance that we become skilled at recognizing healthy relationships which God is orchestrating into our lives. We must not be concerned about connecting with the wrong people if we are allowing the Holy Spirit to guide us. I have come to this conclusion; *"Resisting spiritual darkness is not as important as embracing the light!"* When a candle is lit in a room filled with total darkness, even the smallest flame gives sufficient light to navigate the room with ease. If we embrace the light of God's word, the darkness will be dispelled. If we become skilled at recognizing healthy relationships, the wrong people will be expelled from our lives.

> *"The value of any spiritual relationship*
> *is in its contribution to our assignment*
> *in the Kingdom of God."*

The following is a glossary of spiritual dynamics that we are to look for in a healthy spiritual relationship.

1. Any healthy spiritual relationship is established on the premise of a *"win-win"* arrangement. Beware of people who want to advance at your expense.

2. In a healthy spiritual relationship, the parties involved can freely express their personal opinions and feelings without the fear of repercussions. If you are afraid of expressing your true

feelings to those you are in relationship with, you are in a dangerous situation.

3. In a healthy spiritual relationship, your companions will manifest an intoxicating passion to see you fulfill your dreams and goals. If you are in a relationship with people who show no excitement at the attainment of your dreams and goals, you need to cut them off.

4. A healthy spiritual relationship is one that makes you feel like they are a safe harbor for your deepest personal secrets. If you are in a relationship with some one with whom you can not trust, you need to reexamine the level of access those people have in your life.

5. In a healthy spiritual relationship, God is the central factor. When a relationship is not built around God and His principles, it will eventually lose its meaning and shipwreck your spiritual destiny.

6. All healthy spiritual relationships must be purpose driven. The relationships must carry an unmistakable sense of purpose and spiritual destiny.

Relationship Principles

1. *Every relationship that **God** brings into our lives is divinely engineered for a purpose.*

2. *Every relationship in our life must be purpose driven.*

3. *Every relationship has a divine expiration date on it.*

4. *Every relationship that outlives its season of divine purpose will soon become toxic.*

5. *God assigns the appropriate measure of grace for every relationship that He births into our lives.*

6. *God is not obligated to bless any relationship that He has not qualified and authorized.*

7. *Whenever God wants to bless us, He will birth a new relationship in our life.*

8. *Whenever Satan wants to destroy us, he will birth a new relationship in our life.*

9. *Relationships are like elevators; they will lift us to the highest level of our dreams and goals or plummet us to the depths of hopelessness.*

10. *We were all created for relationship.*

11. *The greatest relationship that we can ever nurture is our relationship with God.*

12. *All relationships flourish in the atmosphere of love and nurturing and wither in an atmosphere of strife and animosity.*

13. *We are ever one relationship away from the miracle we need.*

14. *We are ever one relationship away from spiritual and emotional disaster.*

15. *Relationships that God has ordained will always expand our vision and fuel our faith.*

16. *Relationships that Satan has engineered will always cloud our vision and fuel our doubts.*

17. *Relationship is the master key that opens all the treasures of the human heart.*

18. *It's our responsibility to discern relationships that enlarge our vision and fuel our faith and pursue them.*

19. *It's our responsibility to discern relationships that shrink our vision and fuel our doubts, and cut them off.*

20.   *Relationship is the master key that opens all the spiritual treasures of the heart of God.*

Notes on Chapter Thirteen

1. Rev 4:10-11, 2. 1 Cor 15:33, 3. Judg 13:5
4. Judg 16:4-21, 5. Ezek 47:11, 6. Matt 12:22-26
7. I Kings 11:1-2, 8. 1 Sam 18:1-4, 9. 2 Sam 1:3-5

Chapter Fourteen

The Place Called Finish

❧

They say that the journey of a thousand miles begins with the first step, but it doesn't end until we have made the final step. When Olympic runners are called to run a race, they enter the race knowing that there is an end in sight. These athletes run with all the energy that they can master because they know the winner will receive a prestigious reward. The closer they get to the finish line, the more tenaciously they run.

When we are navigating periods of spiritual transition, we must never forget that we are also racing toward the finish line. The finish line represents the fulfillment of our destiny and all the redemptive purposes of God since the beginning of time. Transition in the Kingdom of God must never be viewed as an end in itself. It's the means to a glorious end, when the kingdoms of this world will shall become the kingdoms of God and of His Christ.

The Place Called Finish

"Jesus saith unto them My, meat is to do the will of him that sent me, and to finish his work."[1]

Everything of God is driving itself to the place in God called finish. The place called finish is the ultimate destination of all of God's prophetic purposes in heaven and on earth. According to Jesus' statement to His apostles, *"The will of God is never done here on earth until it is finished."* The world is full of people who are great at starting projects they never finish. It is better not to build a house, than to lay the foundation and then fail to finish building.

"I have fought a good fight, I have finished my course, I have kept the faith:"[2]

This leads to a very sobering conclusion, *"the **fulfillment** of God's will rarely happens on earth, because many people who pursue the will of God, never make it to the finish line!"* Many people fail to make it through the different seasons of transition they encounter along their pathway to destiny. Some people allow themselves to be beaten up in such a way that they abandon the pursuit of destiny. Many die and go to heaven having never arrived at the place called finish. Instead of dying *"empty"* many people die *"full"* of unfulfilled spiritual dreams and destinies.

When the word of the Lord goes forth, it enters the earth realm traveling at the speed of light. It continues to drive itself to the finish line that God has set for it. One of the most powerful things that we must never forget about the word of the Lord is that *"it is self propelled, and operates on the same spiritual technology as a guided missile."* When a guided missile is launched, it's preprogrammed to hit a specific target. The guided missile is programmed with the specific coordinates of the location of the target. Once it makes contact with the target, the missile detonates and its mission is complete. ***It has arrived at the place called "finish" and has fulfilled its destiny.***

Figuratively speaking, the word of the Lord operates on the same premise.

For example, if God tells us that He is calling us to become the next president of our nation, anything other than winning the presidency falls short of the predetermined will of God for our life. The word of the Lord will continue to work inside us, propelling us toward our goal, until we are pronounced the winner of the election. Many believers, who have stopped pursuing the call of God upon their lives, are so unhappy because their conscience is continually working to suppress the word of the Lord inside their spirit. Giving up does not nullify the word of God that has gone forth. This would also explain why the Bible says; *"Happy is the man who does the will of God."* If we strive to stay faithful to what God has spoken to our spirits, we will receive enabling grace to come into what God promised us.

> ***"Instead of dying "empty" many people die "full" of unfulfilled spiritual dreams and destinies."***

The place called *"finish"* is not just a time in the future, it's a place of fulfillment for God's Kingdom purposes. We arrive at the place called finish on an incremental basis as we continue to fulfill specific portions of God's plan for our life. Every time we touch the place called *"finish,"* God rewards us for doing His will. This is a very important principle to understand because it will keep us motivated during seasons of spiritual transition. We must become like the Lord Jesus and the apostle Paul who lived their lives in the light of the finish line. The ultimate finish line is when we cross into eternity having done the will of God for our lives. *We must adopt a finishing mentality to ensure that we do not abort our prophetic destiny during the period of transition.*

From Promise to Possession

During the Great Depression, the American economy crumbled. Millions of people went bankrupt, including many financial institutions. Most people lost everything they owned or pawned it away in order to survive. Banks couldn't honor checks so they gave their customers *promissory notes*. The promissory note was the bank's way of guaranteeing that once they had the money, they would honor the promissory note with actual cash. Unfortunately, a promissory note is only as good as the integrity and financial resources of the one who gave it. If the person who gave it has no sense of integrity and is financially destitute, the promissory note is not worth the paper it's written on.

"For as the rain cometh down, and the snow from heaven, and returneth not thither, but watereth the earth, and maketh it bring forth and bud, that it may give seed to the sower, and bread to the eater. So shall my word be that goeth forth out of my mouth: it shall not return unto me void, but it shall accomplish that which I please, and it shall prosper in the thing whereto I sent it."[3]

The Bible is full of divine promissory notes containing some of the greatest promises of God to His people. In the passage above, God makes it very clear that He has the spiritual integrity to stand behind His word. God has vowed that the word that proceeds from His mouth shall never return unto Him void. This alone should seriously motivate us to press toward the finish line.

God longs to take His dear children from promise to possession. *God does not want His people to go through life simply talking about His promises. He takes great pleasure in watching them enjoy the manifestation (possession) of what He has promised.*

Unfortunately thousands of Christians fail to cross from promise to possession during periods of spiritual transition because they allow the attacks of the enemy and the cares of this world to choke their faith in God's prophetic promise. They find themselves wallowing in the mud of spiritual doubt and unbelief.

"Let us therefore fear, lest, a promise being left us of entering into his rest, any of you should seem to come short of it. For unto us was the gospel preached, as well as unto them: but the word preached did not profit them, not being mixed with faith in them that heard it."[4]

The Finishing Mentality of Jesus

"For which of you, intending to build a tower, sitteth not down first, and counteth the cost, whether he have sufficient to finish it? Lest haply, after he hath laid the foundation, and is not able to finish it, all that behold it begin to mock him, Saying, This man began to build, and was not able to finish."[5]

A closer and introspective study of the life and ministry of the Lord Jesus Christ will quickly reveal the face of one of the most powerful finishing mentalities known to man. In the passage above Jesus is teaching his disciples the danger of starting an assignment without preparing enough resources to actually finish it. He told his disciples that if they did not invest in developing a *"finishing mentality"* they would end up joining the multitude of people who start projects but never finish them.

The devil will also release *"mocking spirits"* against us every time we say that we are going to do something and then fail to do it. This is why so many Christians are oppressed by feelings of guilt and condemnation over spiritual commitments they made but never finished. One of the things that God seeks to accomplish in His people during periods of spiritual transition is to transform our lives through the renewing of our minds. God wants us to embrace an unshakable finishing mentality. *The mind of Christ is a purpose driven and sanctified mind which houses an uncompromising finishing mentality.* This finishing mentality is completely biased towards finishing the revealed will of God, through the power of the Holy Spirit.

> *"We must adopt a finishing mentality to ensure that we do not abort our prophetic destiny during the period of transition."*

The life and ministry of Jesus was the greatest earthly demonstration of this powerful prevailing spiritual mentality. When Jesus woke up in the morning, He went through the rest of the day like a man on a mission. Everything He did was done on purpose, for a purpose. Jesus did not waste time because He knew that He only had about three and half years of transition time to finish the work that His Father had ordained for Him to finish.

The finishing mentality of Jesus was powerfully displayed when the Lord Jesus embarked on His prophetic journey toward His ultimate death on the cross. In the Garden of Gethsemane, Jesus faced His greatest mental battle as the weight of the world descended and the canopy of His Father's presence began to lift. Living outside the circle of His Father's manifest presence was a terrifying prospect. The dreadful reality of living without the comforting presence of His heavenly Father became so heavy on His mind that He started sweating blood.

"Saying, Father, if thou be willing, remove this cup from me: nevertheless not my will, but thine, be done. And there appeared an angel unto him from heaven, strengthening him. And being in an agony he prayed more earnestly: and his sweat was as it were great drops of blood falling down to the ground."[6]

I know that we have all been through stressful situations, but none of us has ever stressed to the point of sweating blood. Most of us would either commit suicide or quit before we reached that degree of stress. No one would have blamed Jesus had He decided to change His mind about going through with the horrendous ordeal of dying on the cross. But His finishing mentality would not allow Him to abort His prophetic assignment during this very painful transition. He rose from the Garden of Gethsemane with a greater resolve to finish His Father's will. This is the type of finishing mentality that we need supernaturally downloaded into our spirit and mind.

Even though He had been beaten beyond recognition, Jesus refused to let go of His earthly life until He made sure that He had fulfilled everything that God had planned for His life and ministry here on earth. While he was hanging on the cross, He cried that He was thirsty and they gave Him vinegar. He spewed it out of His mouth and then made the most powerful statement ever made by a dying man in the history of the world. He cried, *"It is finished!"* and then gave up the ghost.

What a finishing mentality! Jesus refused to allow death to take Him before His divine assignment was fulfilled and His mission finished. Jesus knew that death before the completion of a divine assignment is murder. Murder is the breaking of the law of God. Death at the completion of a divine assignment is simply the final transition into glory.

"When Jesus therefore had received the vinegar, he said, It is finished: and he bowed his head, and gave up the ghost."[7]

Spiritual Incentives for Finishers

"Jesus saith unto them, My meat is to do the will of him that sent me, and to finish his work. Say not ye, There are yet four months, and then cometh harvest? behold, I say unto you, Lift up your eyes, and look on the fields; for they are white already to harvest. And he that reapeth receiveth wages, and gathereth fruit unto life eternal: that both he that soweth and he that reapeth may rejoice together. And herein is that saying true, One soweth, and another reapeth. I sent you to reap that whereon ye bestowed no labour: other men laboured, and ye are entered into their labours."[8]

When we adopt this powerful apostolic finishing mentality of Jesus, He promises us spiritual benefits to enjoy.

First of all, *"God will quicken the day of harvest in our lives."* When God is convinced that we mean business with Him and that we are willing to carry His will to the finish line, He will shorten the time and distance between the promise and the manifestation of the harvest that He has prepared for us to enjoy. We will find ourselves stepping into unusual financial breakthroughs as God quickly finances what He has called us to do because we have chosen to live only for His will. God will make sure that we do not have to stand in line for the things we need. This is one of the benefits of adopting this finishing mentality of Jesus during our time of transition here on earth.

Second, *"God will give us the supernatural grace to win many souls of men and women into the Kingdom of God."* This is what the Bible calls *"fruit unto eternal life."* What a privilege it is to be placed in a position where we can influence millions of souls into the saving knowledge of our Lord Jesus Christ! There is nothing more valuable on earth than the salvation of a lost soul from the power of sin and death. The salvation of lost souls is the reason the Lord Jesus came and died a horrific death on the cross. Being given the supernatural power to lead millions of people to Christ is a spiritual benefit worth dying for.

Third, *"God will also give us the grace to enter into the spiritual labors of the forefathers."* This means that we will supernaturally inherit the anointing and spiritual administrations of men and women of faith from past generations. This may sound weird to some people, but this a very real biblical principle. For instance, Jesus Himself said that John the Baptist was the *"Elijah to come,"* that the prophets of the Old Testament had spoken of. Jesus said that John the Baptist came in the spirit and power of Elijah. This does not mean that John the Baptist was the physical reincarnation of the Elijah of the Old Testament. The Bible does not teach reincarnation. Reincarnation is a Hindu doctrine, which emanates from the very pits of hell. The Bible teaches *resurrection* and not *reincarnation*.

However, the Bible does teach *apostolic succession*. ***Apostolic succession is the supernatural transfer of the spiritual accomplishments of the forefathers, through the administration of the Holy Spirit to the next generation of sons.*** When Jesus referred to John the Baptist as the Elijah to come, Jesus was simply alluding to the fact that John the Baptist was operating in the same type of prophetic anointing and calling, that was upon Elijah of the Old Testament.

What would happen if God anointed three thousand women in the world today with the same type of call and anointing that was upon the late Kathryn Khulman? The entire world would be shaken by the healing power of the Holy Spirit! What would happen in the spiritual climate of our world if God were to raise one thousand men with the same type of call and anointing as the late apostle of faith, Smith Wigglesworth? This is what it means to enter into the spiritual labors of the forefathers. When we make the decision to live for God's will and make up our minds to finish the work that He has called us to finish, this powerful grace will also come upon our lives. How exciting!

"Jesus refused to allow death to take
Him before fulfilling His divine assignment
and finishing His mission on earth."

Fourth, *God will give us the power to enter into the double portion blessing*. Until the day that the Lord chose to take the great prophet Elijah to heaven on chariots of fire, Elisha stayed with him all the way to the finish line. During the prophetic journey from Gilgal to Jericho, Elisha was instructed four times by the prophet Elijah to return to his own house but he refused to turn back. Elisha knew that God was going to take his master and he decided he was not going to miss this powerful time of the God encounter. He was determined to walk with Elijah all the way to the finish line! Some of the sons of the prophets tried to discourage him from following Elijah because they also knew that God was going to take Elijah into heaven; but their best efforts fell on deaf ears.

When they finally got to the finish line, Elijah turned to Elisha and asked him what he wanted before he was taken up to heaven. Young Elisha told the seasoned prophet that he wanted a double portion of the same spiritual dynamics that were operating in Elijah's prophetic ministry. Elijah told Elisha that he had asked a hard thing, but, was able to visibly watch as he (Elijah) was taken to heaven; he would have what he desired. When Elijah was miraculously taken to heaven by the chariots of fire, Elisha saw the magnificent exodus, and the mantle of the prophet Elijah fell upon him. Almost immediately, Elisha began to operate in the same spiritual power that Elijah once walked in.

"He took up also the mantle of Elijah that fell from him, and went back and stood by the bank of Jordan; And he took the mantle of Elijah that fell from him, and smote the waters, and said, Where is the Lord God of Elijah? And when he also had smitten the waters they parted hither and thither: and Elisha went over."[10]

These are some of the spiritual benefits that God gives to finishers. The double portion blessing is reserved only for men and women who have a finishing mentality upon their lives.

The Grace to Finish

We can never accomplish anything of any real spiritual value without grace. Grace is the power of God working through the very fabric of our being, adding God's "super" to our "natural." During periods of spiritual transition, God will begin to form our character and fashion our ministry so that we can contain more of His life and grace. The dealings of God upon our lives, produces enabling grace inside our spirits. This is why so many Christians lack enabling grace because they do not allow God to form their character and fashion their ministry so that He can produce grace in them. When God is forming a finishing mentality in our spirit and mind He may allow difficult circumstances to challenge our staying power. God does not want us to be plastic soldiers who melt away when things get hot. God wants His children to become finishers.

"For as the sufferings of Christ abound in us, so our consolation also aboundeth by Christ. And whether we be afflicted, it is for your consolation and salvation, which is effectual in the enduring of the same sufferings which we also suffer: or whether we be comforted, it is for your consolation and salvation. And our hope of you is stedfast, knowing, that as ye are partakers of the sufferings, so shall ye be also of the consolation. For we would not, brethren, have you ignorant of our trouble which came to us in Asia, that we were pressed out of measure, above

strength, insomuch that we despaired even of life: But we had the sentence of death in ourselves that we should not trust in ourselves, but in God which raiseth the dead:"[10]

The above passage of scripture is a very difficult passage for many *word of faith teachers* to digest. Some faith teachers teach that people who have the God kind of faith are not supposed to go trials and afflictions. They teach that people who are going through serious trials do not have enough faith and aren't making positive confessions. In their minds, the greatest display of having abundant faith is the manifestation of peace and abundance in the material world.

Unfortunately this is a half truth, because one of the greatest displays of true faith in God is how we respond to God during times of personal crisis. The apostle Paul made it very clear that it was God who had called them to go to Asia and preach the gospel. Nevertheless, when they got to Asia they were attacked viciously by the powers of hell and encountered great spiritual resistance and adversity. The circumstances they found themselves in were so grave, the apostle Paul himself felt disillusioned. This was not some small spiritual conflict; this was a major spiritual war!

> *"Grace is the power of God working through the very fabric of our being, adding God's "super" to our "natural."*

If the apostle Paul was like many Christians I know, he would have concluded that he had missed the will of God. But that is not what Paul said; instead he tells us how God allowed them to come under intense persecution so that they could learn not to trust in themselves but in God who is control. Paul and his ministry team came out of Asia with more grace to endure persecution than when they first went in. *If we do not allow God to work deep enough inside our lives during periods of transition, we will fail to finish our spiritual course.* God desires to do a deep work inside us so we can have the grace to finish!

"Being confident of this very thing, that he which hath begun a good work in you will perform it until the day of Jesus Christ:"[11]

Builders in the Spirit with the Mind to Finish

"I have glorified thee on the earth: I have finished the work which thou gavest me to do."[12]

We have been called to follow in the footsteps of Jesus as His dear children. Jesus was a builder in the Spirit. Nevertheless Jesus did not build at random. He knew the end from the beginning and built toward it. During periods of spiritual transition, God will make an attempt to teach us how to live and build our lives in light of the finish line. When a construction company begins to build a multimillion-dollar hotel, they do not construct it by chance. They do not roll dice and then begin to build. They have a set of blueprints from the architects, which contain the architectural design of the hotel.

The architectural designs reveal how the finished hotel will look and all that is needed to finish it. The construction team sees the finished product and then begins the step by step process of making the dream become a reality. They know that for as long as they stick to the blueprints, they will build the multi-million dollar hotel. This is what it means to build with the finish in mind. Jesus also told us of the perils that will befall those of God's people who do not build their lives and ministry with the finish in mind. The end of their lives will be one of great sorrow and deep regret.

"Not every one that saith unto me, Lord, Lord, shall enter into the kingdom of heaven; but he that doeth the will of my Father which is in heaven. Many will say to me in that day, Lord, Lord, have we not prophesied in thy name? and in thy name have cast out devils? and in thy name done many wonderful works? And then will I profess unto them, I never knew you: depart from me, ye that work iniquity. Therefore whosoever heareth these sayings of mine, and doeth them, I will liken him unto a wise man, which built his house upon a rock: And the rain descended, and the floods came, and the winds blew, and beat upon that house; and it fell not: for it was founded upon a rock. And every one that heareth these sayings of mine, and doeth them not, shall be likened unto a foolish man, which built his house upon the sand: And the rain descended, and the floods came, and the winds blew, and beat upon that house; and it fell: and great was the fall of it." [13]

The Apostle Paul: The Mentality of a Finisher

Without a shadow of doubt, the apostle Paul would stand out as one of the most powerful apostles of Christ who has ever lived. The apostle Paul also displayed the same unwavering, purpose driven finishing mentality that was seen in the life and ministry of the Lord Jesus.

"And now, behold, I go bound in the spirit unto Jerusalem, not knowing the things that shall befall me there: Save that the Holy Ghost witnesseth in every city, saying that bonds and afflictions abide me. But none of these things move me, neither count I my life dear unto myself, so that I might finish my course with joy, and the ministry, which I have received of the Lord Jesus, to testify the gospel of the grace of God." [14]

The apostle Paul, following in the footsteps of the Lord Jesus Christ had also seen the place called finish and became intoxicated by it. I believe that once we see, by faith, the finish line, our lives will change radically. I remember watching the movie *"Gladiator."* The actor who played the role of Caesar in the movie made a very powerful statement when he said, *"When a man reaches the end of his life, he finds himself wondering whether there was a purpose to his life."* This is a sure statement, but what would happen if a man could see his end while he is still living? How would he live the rest of his life?

Paul the apostle had seen the glory that was awaiting him on the other side of his earthly life and he was radically changed. I truly believe that God wants to bless His people with the finishing mentality of Jesus through the power of the Holy Spirit, which will guarantee that God's will, will be done on earth.

When the apostle Paul reached the end of his apostolic journey, he embraced death with the joy of a man who has just caught his connecting flight after hours of waiting at the airport. For many Christians, death is a tragedy; but for Paul, death was the final transition before entering into his eternal reward. Paul announced his death to his spiritual son, Timothy, with great joy and encouraged him to follow suit.

"I have fought a good fight, I have finished my course, I have kept the faith:"[15]

HALLELUJAH!

Notes on Chapter Fourteen

1. John 4:34, 2. 2 Tim 4:7, 3. Isa 55:10-11, 4. Heb 4:1-2, 5. Luke 14:28-30
6. Luke 22:42-44, 7. John 19:30, 8. John 4:34-38, 9. (2 Kings 2:13-14)
10. 2 Cor 1:5-9, 11. Phil 1:6, 12. John 17:4, 13. Matt 7:21-27
14. Acts 20:22-24, 15. 2 Tim 4:7

Self/Group Assessment Questions
(Based on chapter one)

1. Please explain why God tests us during periods of spiritual transition.

2. Why did Jesus allow Satan to sift Peter when he denied the Lord three times?

3. Please write down three definitions of transition.

4. Please explain the meaning of this statement *"God wants to drive the bus."*

5. Please explain the meaning of this statement *"Transition is a governing law of God."*

Self/Group Assessment Questions
(Based on chapter two)

1. Describe what is meant by the terms, *"Incremental technology and Disruptive technology."*

2. How can you use your answer to question one to explain why orthodox Jews found it very difficult to accept the message of the cross?

3. Explain the difference between *"Pioneers and settlers."*

4. Explain the statement *"The future belongs to pioneers."*

5. Explain why the people of Noah's day refused to heed his prophetic message.

Self/Group Assessment Questions
(Based on chapter three)

1. Explain the statement *"Transition is the safest way to transfer spiritual authority."*

2. Explain the statement *"Transition is the period between the promise and the manifestation."*

3. How did Absalom violate the law of transition and how did he die?

4. Why does God allow for transition in human relationships?

5. Explain the statement *"Transition is the birth canal of every prophetic promise of God."*

Self/Group Assessment Questions
(Based on chapter four)

1. Explain what is meant by the statement *"The Inherent Nature of Purpose."*

2. Can the people you surround yourself with affect the fulfillment of your purpose?

3. What is a demonic alliance?

4. Explain why it's so important not to make an alliance with people who are programmed for defeat.

5. Explain why the prophetic word of the Lord is so important to fulfilling spiritual destiny.

Self/Group Assessment Questions
(Based on chapter five)

1. Describe the function of the spirit, soul and body of man.

2. Why is stress or long periods of anger harmful to your body?

3. Briefly describe the condition known as the *"Log Jam Condition of the Soul."*

4. Please describe how Terah's loss of his son Haran (Gen 11:28-32) affected his ability to follow God's call upon his life.

5. Please explain why the Lord accepted Abel's offering while rejecting Cain's offering."

6. Please explain how unhealed soul conditions can lead people into violence or murder.

Self/Group Assessment Questions
(Based on chapter six)

1. Explain the statement, *"God is a Covenant Keeping God."*

2. Explain the meaning of this statement *"Covenants are made by words or broken by words."*

3. Explain the meaning of this statement *"Transition time can be the most powerful or dangerous time in our life."*

4. Please explain why Jonathan became the victim of his past instead of becoming a pioneer of the future?

5. Please explain why breaking covenant is one of the spiritual dangers of transition?

Self/Group Assessment Questions
(Based upon chapter seven)

1. What is the difference between a besetting sin and a spiritual weight?

2. Why did the great man of God, Moses fail to enter the Promise Land?

3. Please explain the meaning of this statement *"Carrying excess spiritual baggage can open doors for demonic attacks against our life."*

4. Please explain the meaning of this statement, *"Anything which saps our energy from pursuing God's primary assignment for our lives is excess weight."*

5. Using the story of Mary and Martha please explain what a *"Martha Complex"* is.

Self/Group Assessment Questions
(Based upon chapter eight)

1. Please explain the meaning of this statement *"Everything rises or falls on leadership."*

2. Is there such a thing as bad and good success?

3. Please explain the meaning of this statement *"Success without a successor is a failure."*

4. How does proper spiritual succession ensure the survival of our spiritual legacy?

5. Please explain why Eli's priesthood was cut short by the Lord.

Self/Group Assessment Questions
(Based upon chapter nine)

1. Please explain the meaning of this statement, *"There is nothing more important than the Holy Spirit in navigating the valley of transition."*

2. Please explain the meaning of this statement *"The Holy Spirit is a not a force He is a person with both personality and presence."*

3. Please write down five assignments of the Holy Spirit here on earth.

4. Please explain the meaning of this statement *"The Holy Spirit is heavens navigational specialist."*

5. Using the story of Mary and Martha please explain the dangers of allowing "ministry activities to overwhelm the pursuit of His presence."

Self/Group Assessment Questions
(Based on chapter ten)

1. Please explain the meaning of this statement, *"Music is the quickest way to manipulate the soul of a man."*

2. Please explain why it's dangerous for us to completely rely on our emotions when making important decisions during times of transition.

3. Please explain the danger of living a life of inspiration without principle.

4. Please explain the meaning of this statement *"Inspiration is the fuel of the soul which drives the divine dream machine inside every man."*

5. Please explain the meaning of this statement *"Revelation must bring movement."*

Self/Group Assessment Questions
(Based upon chapter eleven)

1. Please explain the meaning of this statement, *"If you are a fox, you cannot eat two rabbits that are running on two separate trails."*

2. Please explain why it's so difficult for most people to break out of their *"comfort zones."*

3. Please explain how *"True Spirit inspired revival messes with our comfort zones."*

4. Please explain the concept of *"Double Mindedness"* and how its affects people during times of spiritual transition.

5. Please explain the meaning of this statement *"One of the spiritual dangers of transition is the danger of becoming stuck at the place were two roads come together."*

Self/Group Assessment Questions
(Based upon chapter thirteen)

1. Please explain the meaning of this statement, *"Relationships with people are like elevators."*

2. Please write down the two basic needs of every human being.

3. Please write down three relationship principles as outlined in chapter thirteen.

4. Please explain the concept of *"Toxic relationships"* and how they affect people during times of transition.

5. Please explain the meaning of this statement *"the devil fears the entrance of a champion or a deliverer into a generation."*

Self/Group Assessment Questions
(Based on chapter fourteen)

1. Please explain the meaning of this statement, *"Everything in the universe is moving towards a place called finish."*

2. How will adopting a finishing mentality help us not to abort our prophetic destiny?

3. Please write a short essay on the *"The Finishing Mentality of Jesus."*

4. Please explain the meaning of this statement *"the word of the Lord is a self propelled word, which operates on the same technology as a guided missile."*

5. Please explain the meaning of this statement *"the will of God is not done here on earth until it is finished."*

Resources

For information on
Tapes of the complete *The Power and Dangers of Transition Seminar,*
Other books by Dr. Francis Myles,
A Catalogue of sermons, books and dvd's by Dr. Francis Myles,
How to book Dr. Francis Myles for a *Mastering Transition Seminar* at your Church,
How to book Dr. Francis Myles for one of your Conferences,

Contact

Dr. Francis Myles
P.O Box 2527, McKinney, TX 75069
Call 469-952-1424/293-4664
Email: drmyles@hotmail.com
Website: www.breakthroughcity.com

For Information on

The Mastering Transition Life Group Mentoring Program,
(*a cutting edge DVD mentorship program designed to train people in small life groups learn effective ways of dealing with social and spiritual transition*).

Contact
MASTERING TRANSITION
P.O Box 2527
McKinney, TX 75069
Email: drmyles@hotmail.com
Website: www.masteringtransition.com

Printed in the United States
115470LV00003B/211-249/P